THE MAN WHO NEVER WAS
FREUDIAN TALES

Biological Politics: Feminist
and Anti-Feminist Perspectives

Sexual Contradictions: Psychology
Psychoanalysis and Feminism

Engels Revisited: New Feminist Essays
(Ed. with M. Evans and N. Redclift)

Viola Klein: The Feminine Character (Ed.)

Mothering Psychoanalysis: Helene Deutsch,
Karen Horney, Anna Freud, Melanie Klein

THE MAN WHO NEVER WAS

FREUDIAN TALES

JANET SAYERS

Chatto & Windus
LONDON

First published in Great Britain 1995

1 3 5 7 9 10 8 6 4 2

Copyright © Janet Sayers 1995

Janet Sayers has asserted her right under the Copyright,
Designs and Patents Act, 1988 to be identified as the author
of this work

Published in 1995 by
Chatto & Windus Limited
Random House, 20 Vauxhall Bridge Road,
London SW1V 2SA

Random House Australia (Pty) Limited
20 Alfred Street, Milsons Point, Sydney,
New South Wales 2061, Australia

Random House New Zealand Limited
18 Poland Road, Glenfield,
Auckland 10, New Zealand

Random House South Africa (Pty) Limited
PO Box 337, Bergvlei, South Africa

Random House UK Limited Reg. No. 954009

A CIP catalogue record for this book is available from the British Library

ISBN 0 7011 6232 5

Phototypeset by Intype, London
Printed and bound in Great Britain by
Mackays of Chatham PLC, Chatham, Kent

to the memory of
Michael Brake

It still strikes me myself as strange that the case histories I write should read like short stories and that, as one might say, they lack the serious stamp of science. I must console myself with the reflection that the nature of the subject is evidently responsible for this, rather than any preference of my own.

Sigmund Freud, 1895[1]

Contents

Acknowledgements   xi
Introduction: Imagined men   1

I Childhood fixations
1 Virgin Birth   15
2 Don Juan   28
3 Penis Envy   42
4 Oedipus   53
5 My Father myself   66

II Acting-out rebels
6 Pervert   81
7 Wimp   93
8 Tough guy   103
9 Tomboy   114
10 Conman   126

III Inward defences
11 Repressed Abuse   141
12 Depression   153
13 Death Denied   169
14 Mania   183
15 Schizoid   195

Conclusion: Therapy and politics   211
Notes   217
Index   233

Acknowledgements

My thanks most of all to those who gave so generously of themselves in telling me their stories and in agreeing to their anonymous inclusion in this book; to the social workers and probation officers who introduced us; to the University of Kent for funding and giving me study leave to conduct and write up the necessary interviews; to Denyse Menne for transcribing some of the resulting tapes; to relations, friends, colleagues, students, patients, teachers and psychoanalysts who have taught me so much bearing on this book's argument; to many and varied audiences for their helpful observations on first hearing it; and last, but by no means least, to the following for their comments – Jill Barry, Steven Brownjohn, Kate Corr, Mary Evans, Stephen Frosh, Audrey Lane, Barry Lucock, David Morgan, Nicholas and Daniel Sayers, Joan Schachter, Lynne Segal, Shirley Toulson, and especially Jenny Uglow. Whether or not they agree with the results, their support, advice and encouragement have been invaluable.

I am also grateful to the following for permission to reproduce extracts from copyright material: Carcanet Press Ltd for II. D. 'The Master', *Collected Poems*, 1980; Faber and Faber Ltd for W. H. Auden, 'In Memory of Sigmund Freud', *Collected Poems* 1976; J. Berryman, *Dream Songs*, no. 384, 1969; T. S. Eliot, 'The Burial of the Dead', *The Waste Land*, 1922, and Sylvia Plath, 'Daddy', *Ariel*, 1965: W. H. Heinemann for Sylvia Plath, 'Poem for a Birthday', *The Colossus*, 1960.

Introduction: Imagined Men

> As I was going up the stair
> I met a man who wasn't there.
> He wasn't there again today.
> Oh how I wish he'd go away.
> Anon.

Men still rule the world. Dreams and nightmares about them – as friend or stranger, hero or tyrant – often dominate our lives. We imagine men when they are not there. We aggrandise them. But wishing will not make these male figments of our imagination go away.

That is why Freud is so important. He made it his business to undo the harm done by the defences that perpetuate our unwarranted ideas about men, not least as age-old father figures. How else but by becoming aware of patriarchy's often unconscious inscription can we overthrow its law?

This was the question Juliet Mitchell in effect asked in her 1974 book, *Psychoanalysis and Feminism*. Over twenty years later, however, her call for revolution scarcely informs either therapy or politics. Instead their psychoanalytic variants now often focus on mothering, to the neglect of men and fatherhood. The following tales are an attempt to redress the balance. Based on first-hand case histories, they highlight the damage done to everyone – women and men alike – by our defensive fictions of masculinity.

My stories, including my reactions to their telling, are straightforward. But the psychoanalytic theory of the defences involved is far from obvious. Many find psychoanalysis strange, absurd, offensive even, given Freud's seemingly immoral preoccupation with infantile sexuality, and apparent disregard for science in attending to dreams and the unconscious.

1

Above all many abhor Freud's male-centredness.[1] Yet it is crucial to undoing patriarchy's persisting ills. I shall therefore start with this aspect of Freud's work before introducing the mother-based insights of his Kleinian followers, and the counter-intuitive seeming claim of French psychoanalysts, Jacques Lacan and Julia Kristeva, that we inflate and symbolise men as phallus.

Freud and fathers

'Hysterics suffer mainly from reminiscences':[2] we suffer from repressing the past. So saying, Freud and his colleague Josef Breuer began the first ever collection of psychoanalytic case histories, *Studies on Hysteria.*

It starts with Breuer's patient, Anna O., whose symptoms included repressing a daydream of a snake attacking her father, so the fantasy could not be expressed consciously but only unconsciously, through her body. She imagined that her arm was stiffened with paralysis just as it had been numb when she first had her serpentine idea about her father.[3] Another patient was Katharina, whose nervous breathlessness seemed to involve bodily reliving an otherwise unavailable memory of her father hyperventilating as he sexually abused her some years before.[4]

Freud too was beset by fantasies about men. In July 1895, just before his father died, he dreamt that a fellow-doctor was going to give an injection to one of his patients, Irma. Analysis of this fantasy, he declared, revealed 'the secret of dreams'.[5] He went on to apply his discovery in analysing another patient, Dora. He attributed her symptoms – including anorexic disgust at food and a nervous cough – to her having repressed and displaced into her throat an image of her father's friend's erect penis pressing against her thigh when he once tried to kiss her.[6]

Treatment depends on freeing such images from repression, and on recognising their transference to the analyst. Otherwise they risk disrupting therapy. In Dora's case, having unconsciously equated Freud with her father and his friend, she avenged herself on them by prematurely quitting treatment, after mentally giving Freud two weeks' notice as a maid might her master.[7] Similarly,

Freud's so-called Rat Man patient was so frightened Freud would beat him as his father had when he was a child that initially he could not 'free associate' and say whatever came into his mind.[8]

Eventually Freud concluded that fantasies about fathers lie at the heart of our psychology. In this he drew on his supervision of a man's treatment of his five-year-old son, Hans. Hans's symptoms included fear of going out lest a horse bite his finger. Many children are frightened of animals, but Freud traced this phobia in Hans to his having displaced on to horses the fear that his father would take away his penis just as his baby sister, Hanna, seemed to have lost hers.[9] Freud similarly attributed the sexual malaise of another patient, a Russian now referred to as 'the Wolf Man', to the unconscious fantasy that, were he to have sex with his father, it would be on condition of his having no penis like his mother.[10]

Freud argued that the wish to have sex with one parent or the other is universal. That is why, he claimed, plays like Sophocles' *Oedipus Rex* and Shakespeare's *Hamlet* are still so gripping.[11] Subsequently Freud combined this observation with his 1917 theory that in depression we defend against losing or becoming disillusioned in others by clinging on to them, and by internalising them as idealised self-censoring judges within us.[12]

In the first place, he said, as children we all defend against disappointment that the mother does not have a penis with 'super-ego' identification with the father.[13] We then construct and reconstruct all other disappointments and losses – including loss of the breast in weaning, and of faeces in potty-training – as though they too involved losing a penis.[14]

Many people at the time were appalled by the male-centredness of Freud's final version of his theory. They were also shocked by his patriarchalism. Even his supporters played it down. Just after Freud's death, in 1939, the poet W. H. Auden wrote:

> He wasn't clever at all: he merely told
> the unhappy Present to recite the Past
> like a poetry lesson till sooner
> or later it faltered at the line where

3

long ago the accusations had begun . . .
If some traces of the autocratic pose,
the paternal strictness he distrusted, still
   clung to his utterance and features,
it was a protective coloration.[15]

By then, however, psychoanalysts had begun to replace Freud's paternalism with psychoanalysis's present mother-centredness. This about-turn was pioneered by, among others, the Vienna-born psychoanalyst, Melanie Klein, who settled in London in 1926 and whose work became the most important influence on British psychoanalysis after Freud.

Klein, mothers and others

Melanie Klein regarded the mother as the primary object of all our subsequent loves and hates, and of the fantasies involved.[16] From the moment of birth, she claimed, the baby dreads falling to pieces. He[17] instantly seeks to split off and get rid of this anxiety into what is most immediately available, usually the mother.[18] She now becomes the site of his self-destruction – someone he imagines will destroy and persecute him. Klein accordingly termed this state of mind – which she also said returns in children and adults – 'the paranoid-schizoid position'.

This 'position' includes a contradictory image of others, in the first place of the mother, not only as thoroughly bad but also as containing all we most love and cherish, until, consumed with envy, we seek to wreck everything inside them. Klein illustrated this fantasy, of what she termed 'projective identification', by reference to Julien Green's novel *If I Were You*. In this book a man is so envious of others that he makes a pact with the devil to get into their bodies and take them over.[19]

Klein wrote little about the effect of being subject to such invasion. Her followers, however, have written extensively about its impact, at least on the analyst,[20] especially in working with schizophrenics, when the countertransference sense of being taken over by the patient is often particularly intense.[21] Wilfred Bion likened the analyst's resulting experience to that of the mother intruded on by her baby's feelings. Ideally, he wrote, the mother absorbs and processes her baby's projected impulses so that he can 'reinternalise' them in more digested and thinkable form.[22]

Klein herself was sceptical of this development of her theory.[23] She was less concerned with the mother's psychology than with that of the baby, as it recurs in both children and adults.[24] She argued that our fragmented, divided, persecuting, idealised and envied images of ourselves and others are succeeded by more integrated figures, as both loved and hated. This however gives rise to 'depressive position' anxiety: we fear that if we attack the hated aspects of those we love we will alienate, harm or lose them.

To the extent that we can nevertheless people our minds with good and loving images of others, we gain confidence that we have enough resources within ourselves to repair the damage done by hate. Or we deny it, and manically imagine ourselves to be so self-sufficient that we have no need to depend on or regret others' loss. Alternatively, we obsessively control them, or retreat into schizoid fragmentation and self-dispersal so as not to know what is going on.[25]

Klein argued that all these defences – first experienced in relation to the mother – are then transferred to the father, who is initially imagined, in fantasy, as 'inside' her. Klein and her followers thus subsumed the father within the mother: indeed Kleinians arguably treat the mother's breast and the father's penis as essentially inter-changeable objects within the unconscious.

The 'object relations theory', as it is called, that Klein initiated, became even more gender-blind as it was developed by what has come to be known as the Independent stream of British psycho-analysis. This school's first leading exponents included John Bowlby and Donald Winnicott. Their accounts of maternal attach-ment and 'good enough' mothering, respectively, are now arguably the major psychoanalytic influence on today's therapy and casework.

Bowlby attributed children's early development and its cas-ualties to mothering alone – to whether the baby is deprived of the mother's presence during his first two years of life.[26] Bowlby scarcely, if ever, mentioned fathers. Nor did Winnicott, except to assimilate fathering to mothering, with his assertion that the father's job is to mother the mother.[27]

Both analysts gave priority, as Klein did, to the mother's presence (whereas Freud attended to the fantasies generated by men's absence). Unlike Klein, however, Bowlby and Winnicott also gave priority to the physical care the mother gives her baby. Winnicott in effect argued that, by initially anticipating and meeting her baby's needs as soon as they arise, and then by gradually failing to do so, the mother is the sole origin of the baby's psychological birth as separate and individuated from her.[28]

Ideally, Winnicott implied, the toddler at first deals with his recognition of the gap between them by creating a 'transitional object' – a much-sucked and thumbed blanket or rag which he subjectively suffuses with his mother's presence to comfort him when he feels anxious about being separated from her.[29]

Given Winnicott's reverence for women's work as mothers, it is perhaps hardly surprising that many feminists find his version of psychoanalysis very appealing. Particularly influential has been the development of his work by the American feminist psychoanalysts Nancy Chodorow and Jessica Benjamin.

To Winnicott's thesis that babies initially experience themselves as being the same as the mother Chodorow adds that infants forge their gender identity as female or male through affirming or negating their initial sense of sameness with her.[30] This in turn accounts, Chodorow implies, for women's and men's subsequent problems of over- and under-emotional involvement and identification with others.

Jessica Benjamin has supplemented Chodorow's thesis with the observation that, in male-dominated society, women are often chronically lacking in self-esteem. The mother is therefore very likely to feel overcome by her baby's attacks on her, thereby depriving him of the experience through which Winnicott claimed babies learn that their mothers are outside their omnipotent control.[31] The result, claims Benjamin, is that men and women often re-enact with each other their early experience of dominance and submission in relation to the mother.[32]

Fathers are seldom mentioned in this and other Winnicott-based theories, which now inform much feminist and non-feminist therapy and casework. By contrast, social and literary theorists are very mindful of the psychological centrality of the father in so far as they draw on the work of the French psychoanalysts Jacques Lacan and Julia Kristeva.

Lacan, Kristeva, and the 'return' to Freud

Lacan's writing is notoriously difficult to understand.[33] Put bluntly, he claimed that we all mistake ourselves for what we are not. This begins with the toddler, still a medley of fleeting impressions, mistaking himself for his reflection in the mirror as whole and undivided.

He also mistakes himself for everything his mother desires until he discovers she is not everything, that she does not have a penis. This makes him feel that he too is lacking – that he does not have the status his father represents, that the best he can do is approximate his authority or, in the case of the girl, court her father's and other men's desire.

What is crucial here is neither the father nor his penis but his symbolic representation – as phallus. It is not men themselves who are important but their effects – their 'traces'. Lacan illustrated the point with Edgar Allan Poe's story, 'The Purloined Letter'.[34]

Poe's story is about a love letter stolen from a Queen's boudoir. Fearing blackmail, the Queen hires the Chief of Police to find it. He gets his men to look high and low, in every nook and cranny, for the letter. All to no avail. The letter is finally discovered by a detective, Dupin, pursuing the tracks indicated by its thief, who stole the letter by substituting a similar-looking envelope in its place. Doubtless, Dupin reasons, the thief pursued the same tack in hiding it. Indeed he had. Dupin discovers it, in another similar envelope, in full view, in the thief's apartment.

Freud, argued Lacan, adopted the same strategy in pursuing his patients' trails of substitutions, their free associations, in unpicking the condensation and displacement of meaning involved in concealing their wishes in their symptoms and dreams. Language (notably metaphor and metonomy) – both conscious and unconscious – also depends, Lacan insisted, on this selfsame fluidity of meaning.

Its fixation indicates pathology. *In extremis* this can involve the megalomaniac's delusion that he is superman – phallus incarnate. It is a delusion because nobody can either have or be this monument to manhood, it is a symbol, not flesh and blood. This does not, however, prevent the madman's fantasy. Nor does it stop others acting it out, or neurotics repressing this fantasy into the unconscious from which it may then emerge symbolically (as in Dora's case).

Imagining ourselves to be the phallus is also the stuff of comedy – of the editor of *Private Eye*'s quip, for instance, when the law championed the Yorkshire Ripper's wife against his magazine: 'If this is justice, I'm a banana.'

Humour however seldom lightens either Lacan's version of Freud or its post-structuralist successors, in which, as social and literary theorists have pointed out, *contra* Lacan, there is no singular 'phallic truth' that psychoanalysis can reveal.[35] Rather there are a host of different masculinities, each produced by a variety of distinct 'signifying practices'.

The social psychologist Lynne Segal is particularly illuminating when she writes of the overlapping political struggles – centred on class, race and sex – producing today's male stereotypes.[36] She traces, for example, the way the nineteenth-century notion of muscular Christianity was generated in the battle of the American and European ruling class to secure, promote and extend its rule by westward expansion and imperial conquest. She demonstrates how the resulting image of aggressive manhood was adopted by the working class at the beginning of this century, in campaigning to improve its lot.

Similarly, Segal tracks the related path by which blacks exaggerated and embraced their equation with the 'untamed phallus', as noble or beastly savage, in opposing colonialism, slavery and racism – 'isms' ironically often involving this same phallic image. Another distinct, but again associated, development has been the donning by lesbians and homosexuals of the exaggerated, but contradictory, spectre of masculinity implied by the figures of the butch dyke and cruising queen. They thereby challenge the use of these caricatures to scourge them in today's moral panic about AIDS; just as related stereotypes used to pillory homosexuals at the turn of the century, as part of the then eugenic pressure by the dominant class to keep its members heterosexual, to reproduce and ensure the continuity of their line.

Some academics treat deconstruction as an end in itself, finding the instability and multiplicity of masculinities it reveals intoxicating. They revel in it. A recent example is the American cultural theorist, Kaja Silverman's celebration of 'the erotics of men's ruination' as a motif in Henry James's *The Turn of the Screw*, Proust's *Remembrance of Things Past*, T. E. Lawrence's *Seven Pillars of Wisdom*, post-Second World War Hollywood movies about returning veterans and their women, and the films of Rainer Werner Fassbinder.[37]

Others, Segal included, point out that questioning and unravelling male myth is only the beginning, that we also have to challenge and change the social conditions making masculinity so oppressive to both sexes – in fact, as well as in fiction. Meanwhile many academics have turned their attention to exploring the stages before what Lacan termed 'the symbolic'.

Julia Kristeva has been extremely influential in this. She draws attention to the pre-symbolic, 'semiotic' texture of language – its sound, timbre, rhythms, repetitions[38] – beginning with the burbling made by the baby to attract his mother's attention from being diverted to what Kristeva refers to as 'the father of individual pre-history'.[39]

Without some such paternal idea opening up a gap between mother and baby, Kristeva claims, the baby risks succumbing to the horror of 'abjection' – to the dread of disappearing back into the mother.[40] Hence perhaps the soothing effect, claimed by the Spanish poet Lorca, of the Andalusian peasant's song in which the mother lulls her baby to sleep by dwelling on an enigmatic absent male other:

> Lullaby, lullaby
> Of that man who led
> His horse to the water
> And left him without drink.[41]

9

Certainly Kristeva applies her project of 'semanalysis' to the work of male artists and writers – Giotto, Bellini, Holbein, Gérard de Nerval, Dostoevsky, James Joyce, Proust, Mallarmé, Céline and others.

The London-based literary critic, Jacqueline Rose, has in turn applied Lacanian theory to the poetry of Sylvia Plath. She shows how, in 'Poem for a Birthday' and elsewhere, Plath lucidly recounts what Kristeva and other psychoanalysts often describe much more obscurely: the baby's illusion of being orally one with the mother – or, as Plath puts it,

> Mother, you are the one mouth
> I would be a tongue to. Mother of otherness
> Eat me.[42]

Rose draws attention to Plath's indication of the phallic precursor of speech in her diary entry: 'Words, words, to stop the deluge through the thumbhole in the dike.'[43]

Insisting that there is a 'vacancy, and excess, at the heart of symbolic, paternal law' (in that nobody can be or have the phallus symbolising men's rule),[44] Rose quotes Plath's poem 'Daddy' as testament to the persistence of the fantasy of filling the void with epic male figures, especially when our ideas about men cannot be grounded in reality – in facts about the actual father's life. In Plath's case many details about her German-born father Otto were obliterated by the war, by the obscenities of Nazism, and by the fact that Otto died when she was only eight. He accordingly remained monstrous:

> Marble-heavy, a bag full of God,
> Ghastly statue with one gray toe
> Big as a Frisco seal

A terrifying figure:

> I have always been scared of *you*
> With your Luftwaffe, your goobledygoo.
> And your neat moustache . . .
>
> A man in black with a Meinkampf look
> And a love of the rack and the screw.[45]

Today, over thirty years after Plath committed suicide shortly after writing 'Daddy', similar spectres of men as tyrants and heroes still haunt us – especially when fathers die. Hence the continuing attempts of writers and poets to exorcise their ghosts. Recent autobiographical examples include Germaine Greer's *Daddy, We Hardly Knew You*, Tony Harrison's *V*, Blake Morrison's *And When Did You Last See Your Father?* and Sharon Olds's 'I have idolized the mouth of the silent man'.[46]

Yet, apart from a few notable exceptions,[47] psychoanalysts as therapists say little about the everyday harm done by the defences perpetuating our fantasies about fathers and men generally. Hence my tales.

Freudian tales

I shall begin with some of the childhood fixations Freud described, including imagining ourselves a fatherless origin, Don Juan identification with the penis, chronic envy of men, and Oedipal preoccupation with man as patriarch. I shall then explain the damage done by acting out the male stereotypes of the pervert, wimp, tough guy, tomboy and conman. Finally I will describe the injuries inflicted by patriarchal fantasy through repression and depression, or through denial, mania, obsessive control and schizoid fragmentation.

At the risk of caricature, I shall focus on each of these defences in turn, although, of course, they often overlap. I shall also concentrate on their paternal rather than maternal aspects, since the latter have been amply covered elsewhere.[48]

Exalted ideas about men arguably exercise their most obvious and pernicious allure on those who have least power. My case studies therefore tend to come from this disadvantaged group: they are based on the life stories told me by women and men I have seen in psychotherapy, and by those to whom I have been introduced by my colleagues in social services and probation.

No one was included unless they explicitly agreed, and even then only provided I changed all identifying details. I recognise that this is no safeguard against a sense of voyeurism, nor against the sad fact that my mostly very short-lived involvement (consisting usually of three or four hour-long interviews) sometimes awakened hopes, only to be dashed, of longer-term engagement.

Not that I did not become engaged. Indeed, in seeking to expose the damage done by the defences I shall be explaining, I extend Kleinian insights about mothering and the countertransference, and openly admit the feelings aroused in me by my patients' and interviewees' male-based defences.

In the tradition of Freud and his followers, I shall supplement my stories with literary examples. They indicate much more movingly than the often dry and obscure – gruesome even – theories of psychoanalysis the widespread occurrence of the character traits my tales recount. I hope the urgency of transforming therapy and politics will thus become obvious.

I

Childhood Fixations

I

Virgin Birth

The mother, who satisfies the child's hunger, becomes its first love-object and certainly also its first protection against all the undefined dangers which threaten it in the external world – its first protection against anxiety, we may say. In this function [of protection] the mother is soon replaced by the stronger father, who retains that position for the rest of childhood. But the child's attitude to its father is coloured by a peculiar ambivalence. The father himself constitutes a danger for the child, perhaps because of its earlier relation to its mother.

Sigmund Freud, 1928[1]

At its most extreme, fear of the strength the father represents, leads some to both augment and banish him in entertaining the fantasy of virgin birth. Others, disillusioned in the fathers of their children, choose to live without them.[2] Yet others get rid of them either physically or figuratively and look to someone else to embody our society's idealised notions of manhood. A classic example is Mrs Morel in D. H. Lawrence's autobiographical novel, *Sons and Lovers*. Disenchanted with her husband, Mrs Morel treats him as though he were not there and instead seeks in her sons the male paragon he so evidently is not.

It takes madness, however, to absent not only the father but the very idea of him as well. Negation of 'the paternal metaphor', Lacan insisted, is the hallmark of psychosis.[3] By contrast, most therapists and caseworkers today – in so far as they draw on Winnicott's version of object relations theory – characterise schizoid states of mind as reversion to what they take to be the initial state of infancy, namely that of imagining ourselves one with the mother as though nobody else existed. They overlook the fact

15

that, once we know of the biological contribution of the father to our creation, we can never return to this uterine fantasy without repudiating him.

The psychoanalyst Marion Milner is virtually alone among Winnicott's followers in recognising this aspect of schizoid regression. She attributes the fantasy of an adult patient, Susan, of being all in all to her mother not only to the fact that the latter constantly addressing her daughter as 'Oh Moon of my Delight', and inciting her to love her – 'Yes, the whole world',[4] – but also to her mother's refusal to acknowledge that the lodger was Susan's father. Paradoxically, this had the effect of making men so fascinating to Susan that, as a child, she readily acquiesced in an elderly neighbour's exhibitionism. It was so reassuring to see his penis as evidence that not all power rested with her mother and herself.

Adults often remember their childhood as though, like Susan, their mothers had made their fathers absent from their lives.[5] But we seldom see this just as it is happening. The following case is therefore particularly illuminating. It shows a woman, Tessa, in the very process of cultivating the idea that she was sole origin of both herself and her child.

Tessa was in her mid-twenties when I met her. She devoted herself to belittling her father and her son Tom's father as mere children – as no different from herself. To realise the 'oceanic illusion',[6] of continuing placental union with her child, she waged constant battle to do away with any potential male intruder. She barricaded her house and garden: hers was the only garden in the street thus fenced off. A bell on her front door pealed out a nursery rhyme jingle, announcing her world to be a mother-baby universe – no grown-ups allowed in.

Soon after I rang she appeared: wan face, long crumpled hair, over-large jumper dwarfing her, bare feet made tiny by the clown-faced slippers in which they were encased. She took me through the hall, explaining its emptiness: 'I don't want anything belonging to anyone else.' Since moving in four years earlier she had refused all offers from her neighbours to help decorate and furnish her empty home. She was determined to have nothing from outside. She exhausted herself keeping it away, rising before dawn every morning to clean and rid her house of all invading dirt.

16

One grimy piece of furniture had escaped her vigilance. A friend had managed to offload an old sofa on to her. Tessa left it – an uninvited guest – stranded in the middle of her otherwise empty lounge. Its stay was strictly temporary, Tessa assured me; she had insisted its donor remove it as soon as possible. Meanwhile, she said, it served merely as a toy in her son's make-believe desert-island games.

My visit, like the sofa, Tessa indicated, could only be accommodated on a fleeting basis. She kept the kitchen, into which she took me, empty of chairs lest I or any other caller park themselves too long. A plastic seat had somehow drifted in from the garden. Otherwise there was no furniture, not even a table. 'It is my kitchen,' Tessa asserted, for herself and Tom alone.

She offered me chocolate fingers – covered in clingfilm, she explained, to prevent cigarette smoke getting in. She herself ate nothing. Indeed she took in so little – food or money – that she seemed to be hardly there. She was so poor that she could only afford to heat the room with the two tiny front burners of her stove. They flickered between us.

Nothing solid. I found myself losing my bearings, and wandered in my questions. Twice I forgot to switch on the tape recorder I used for interviewing, so fusingly confused, projectively identified, did I become with her ungrounded state. For Tessa I remained an outsider, signalled by her extending her arm to shake hands formally at the end of my first visit.

By then she had made the story she told me of her life as untethered as herself – a blur of misty recollections, everything uncertain, no firm dates or facts. The only thing she made perfectly plain was her ousting anyone or anything signifying adult men. She started by telling me that her mother was the same. Immediately after she gave birth to Tessa, a year after Tessa's sister, Amanda, was born, their mother threw out their violent father and moved south to live with their grandmother. She too, Tessa insisted, had no men in her life. True, her Nan had married twice. But her first husband disappeared; and her second husband was killed in the war.

As for Tessa's father, he was 'too pathetic' to stay up north alone. He followed his wife south. Over the next five years she

17

bore him three boys – James, William and Charles. Her mother rejected the last two, or so Tessa claimed, because they were two more males than she could abide. By the time I visited, all three were grown up. But Tessa still treated them as babies, particularly the rejected ones, whom she referred to by diminutives – Billie and Charlie.

Running and ruling their childhood home was Tessa's doing alone. She kept everyone in order, her father included. She recalled tearing up his pay slips to prevent him cashing them in for drink. Denying his power (evidence of which sometimes slipped through her defence against it) Tessa told me that he left it to the women to sort her out when she destroyed his invoices; he left it to her mother to march her down to the post office to tell her off in front of the postmistress for shredding the proof of his income.

'I never had a father,' Tessa insisted. She characterised him as an oaf who looked to her to baby him, to drudge, skivvy, cook, and generally look after him when he returned late, night after night, raddled with drink. She kept him as a child in her eyes – someone she had to mollycoddle, and whose household affairs (including his council tax) she had to manage.

When she herself was a child, she said, it was harder to infantilise and dispose of him. So she escaped into books:

> I'd read even though I wouldn't know how. They were such big words. They were so much harder than me. But I read and read. I kept doing it. The books were so full of different words, of another atmosphere and world.

But books proved too adult: try as she might Tessa could not figure out the letters.

She tried another tack. She ran away to her Nan, despite her father forbidding her, and beating her when she returned. She answered by making him into a fairy-tale figure, a big bad wolf with herself as Little Red Riding Hood defying him. One Easter she carried a basket of eggs to her grandmother's house. When she got there she would clamber into her Nan's bed and sleep at her feet, or to remain one with her Nan, she would ask her endless questions to keep them both together and awake.

She made her Nan her whole world – father, mother, children, all rolled into one. She hated her father intervening, and her mother's sister for separating them by putting her Nan in a nursing home when she became old and frail. Tessa went there only once. Her grandmother forbade her to come again because, said Tessa, muddling who was whom, she could not bear to see her wasting away.

When her Nan died Tessa did not go to her funeral: 'I wouldn't see her go down in that hole, and that mud go on.' She could not face the world outside. Instead she turned her mind inward – 'I see her as she is, not when she was ill' – seeing herself as the rag doll her Nan used to have. Tessa planned on becoming exactly the same as her Nan, even to the extent of having twelve children like her.

As a child, whenever she was apart from her Nan, Tessa recreated the illusion of their self-sufficient togetherness with her younger brothers, Billie and Charlie. Perhaps she was driven to it as a defence against her father's preference for their older sister, Amanda. Whatever the reason, she told me he was utterly useless, and in his place she became her brothers' sole keeper: mother and father, breadwinner and cook, provider and judge.

She earned money by babysitting for single-parent families whom she painted as being as fatherless as her own, and through babysitting she met Billie's friend Eddie. It was not Billie but their older sister Amanda who had the gumption to suggest Eddie ask Tessa out. Eddie was Tessa's son's father, although she never accorded him that status. She treated him as just as much of a baby as Billie.

Sexual intercourse was not Eddie's doing. It was just fate, Tessa said. She always knew it would happen. Nothing phallic was involved. Tessa depicted their sexual union as leaving her *virgo intacta* – an innocent babe. 'He took what he wanted,' she told me, just as I took her words into my tape recorder. It was an oral – not a genital – matter of platonic sibling affection.

Tessa also mistook the first symptoms of pregnancy as oral, the result of food poisoning, little different from the medicine and nostrums with which, she said, her doctors fed and sickened her. She could not countenance the idea of a man or boy inside her. She dreaded having a son. But equally, she could not bear any intrusion to stop her pregnancy, so she went along with her family's Catholicism and carried the baby to term.

Throughout, she repudiated her growing foetus's father-to-be, Eddie, as a nonentity. Or she treated him as no different from herself: he suffered the same symptoms, she said. He was quite incapable, just as her father had been, of supporting her, so she managed it all herself – from immaculate conception to virgin birth.

In this she was not unlike the pregnant heroine of Milan Kundera's novel, *Life is Elsewhere*. Fending off her disappointment in her husband's hostile indifference to her, Kundera's heroine finds in the Virgin Mary:

> her model of motherhood free of the need for human fructification ... an ideal of mother love in which the father does not interfere. She felt an intoxicating longing for the child to be called Apollo, a name that to her meant the same as 'he who has no human father'.[7]

As soon as Tom was born, Tessa instantly banished his father from her life. She wrote him a poem the same day, entitled 'Too much, not both':

> There is a new life born today.
> Who he, this Tom, is
> He is here to stay
> He needs me more
> We will grow together
> And learn
> Just me and him

Tom was *her* child, she insisted. He would be brought up *her* way. No room for Eddie. Anyway, Eddie was no father. He was just a kid. To prove it Tessa told me how, when his parents left town, he immediately moved in with another woman who would baby him just as Tessa had.

Now she was actually a mother Tessa would have no more to do with him. On leaving the maternity hospital she returned to her childhood home, just as her mother had returned to her mother's home when Tessa was born.

But Tessa did not stay long. The more she got rid of the men the more they seemed to plague her. She had long negated her father and her younger brothers, and now felt unbearably intruded upon by her oldest brother, Jim. The pressure built up as he repeatedly came into the kitchen when she was cleaning it until, exasperated by her fussily telling him to get out, he threw a chair at her, kicked her in the face, and rammed a stool into her stomach. It left her with no alternative. Grabbing baby Tom, she left.

Anything was better than the threat of invasion by Jim, even though it meant a succession of dismal dwellings. First she camped briefly in another lone parent's house. Then her movements became vague: a mother and baby home; institutions for down-and-outs and addicts being 'weaned' off drugs; sheltered housing with the elderly, where Tessa recalled with horror the flats' 'buzz in, buzz out' open access to any passer-by.

Then, at last, nirvana – a room, plus kitchen, for herself and Tom alone. To celebrate the occasion Tessa got rid of their father's names by choosing from a collection of black singers' names, copied from record sleeves and put together in a hat. She picked one at random – Jimi Hendrix – and she and her son became Tessa and Tom Hendrix.

It was like a wedding, she said. Not, of course, she added, that she would ever marry for real. Marriage was too much like being owned. To get away from any such idea she had also thought of getting rid of the first name her parents had given her: Tessa. She would change it to something stronger.

But that proved unnecessary. Something much more substantial turned up – a council house of her own. It was an ordinary two-up, two-down affair, but almost immediately Tessa converted it, at least one room, into an extraordinary womb-like nest. Downstairs, as I have already mentioned, remained bare. Upstairs was equally empty, with stripped floorboards, unpainted walls, damp ceilings, no lights, furniture, carpets, nor any other fittings.

Nominally she assigned the front upstairs room to Tom. She papered every surface with an army of grotesque Batman figures reminiscent of the gargoyles mounted on church spouts, signifying the horrid male figures she strove so hard to keep out. She could not have more clearly signified her intention never to let Tom sleep in this, his so-called 'den'. To emphasise the point she told me, 'He must never have an empty room.' So she kept it void.

Instead she created a cocoon-like inner sanctum for the two of them at the back of the house. Nobody else was allowed to stay. She even kept the sun out. The curtains remained drawn day and night with a red lamp always on, blurring all distinction of time and space. Here, in this uterine chamber, walled with beds, carpeted, and fitted with television, video and hi-fi, she and Tom lived, ate and slept next to each other, just as she used to sleep, as a child, with her grandmother.

Tessa did everything she could to prevent anyone coming between them. When Tom was younger she would not even let her own family see him. Later she relaxed this embargo. She let Tom go to her father's house, consoling herself with the thought that her father would never seduce him away from her: he paid Tom no more attention than he did herself or her two younger brothers.

As for her own house, she kept it as though she were an orphaned Snow White surrounded by a crowd of indistinguishable dwarfs. No visitors were allowed unless she could reduce them to uniform sameness with herself. She did away with their individuality, making them into an anonymous throng of 'waifs and strays', as one hapless visitor told me, reminding me of the Beatles' 'Eleanor Rigby' chorus, 'All the lonely people, where do they all come from?'

Previously Tessa had included her younger brothers, Billie and Charlie, within this dispossessed crew. She had even let them look after Tom when she was hospitalised (for what, I never discovered), but she stopped them looking after Tom when she discovered they had let their girlfriends in to 'infect' him, as she put it, with their drugs. The next time she was ill, and again had to go into hospital, she had Tom fostered.

By the time I visited, both brothers were gone. Billie had long been in trouble with the law – in the first place, according to Tessa, who reduced his offence to mere childishness – because he stole some chocolate. Whatever the reason, in prison Billie was sexually propositioned by a fellow prisoner. Of course, Tessa asserted, Billie resisted. It was outrageous. Billie was quite right not to let this man in. It would have utterly changed him. She knew. After all, she had spent her whole life keeping out all male intruders for precisely that reason. Billie was also quite right, she went on, after being released from jail, to join others in beating up a man who seemed bent on soliciting him in the park, even though the ensuing brawl resulted in the man's death.

Billie took the rap. Of course. He was too much of a child to stand up for himself, so she took charge, or so she said, when his case came to court. Then, rather than let Tom know anything of the authority of the law, she told him, when Billie was sent to jail, that he had gone away on holiday. She herself could not forgive Billie for allowing himself to be banged up with the men, so she punished him by refusing to visit.

In his place she devoted herself to their kid brother Charlie. But now another figure threatened to intervene – Charlie's girl-friend, Sally. Tessa tried to do her down: she derided her as having to bribe Charlie to keep him home with her and getting at Tessa by hitting Tom and not giving him sweets as she did his cousin, Amanda's child.

She consoled herself with the thought that Sally and Charlie were 'together but apart'. Indeed they were. Like Billie, Charlie landed in jail, not because of any male *machismo* or mugging, Tessa stressed, but because of his childish addiction to drink and drugs. She had tried to scare and wean him off them, through her own example, as though she were interchangeable with him, by becoming so addicted herself that she nearly died, but Charlie refused to learn from her. So she exiled him too, for having thus asserted his independence, for being a man, not a 'boy', as she dubbed him. Despite his pleading letters (ending in pitiful baby X-kisses on one she showed me), she punished him, just as she had Billie, by not visiting him in jail.

Having repudiated both men, she made her son her all. Until Tom was three she had never let him out of her sight – not once. Even when he went to playgroup she stayed with him rather than join the grown-ups. But she could not stay with him when he went to school. So she got a puppy. Like Tom, she experienced the pup as her sole creation: from choosing its parents to selecting from their litter a female, as likely to be 'more faithful' than a male.

Tom endowed his drawings of the hound with a phallic knife to protect them. Perhaps he got the idea from Tessa calling the bitch after a protective sleuth, the TV heroine, Miss Marple: she characterised the detective as 'putting her whole mind's body into her work'. Tessa kept Miss Marple's namesake, Missy, constantly with her. She was 'always here for me – asleep and awake. She would never go.' But she did. Ever fearful of men and their sex, Tessa had Missy spayed to stop other dogs sniffing and getting into her. The wound became infected and Missy died.

Tessa could no more bear to know that the dog was gone than she could bear to know of her Nan's death. She dreamt they were both still alive, that nothing could separate her from them. She wanted to dream herself with them for ever. She would rather die than wake up to their not being there. Twice she nearly killed herself. She overdosed with sleeping pills: once when her sister Amanda took Tom out for the day; another time because she was so upset when her friend Deirdre was battered by her boyfriend.

Tessa concentrated her whole being on excluding any such threat, even life itself. She wanted to be free of everyone, she declared. Perhaps that was why I found it hard to keep a conversation going: she either pushed me away so much that the gulf seemed unbridgeable, or she treated me as so much the same that there was no space, as Julia Kristeva might put it, for words.[8]

It was the same with food. Tessa either refused to take it in, or she so identified with what she ate that she slept to preserve the food, like herself, from being used up. It nevertheless remained alien, something, she said, that could have choked her to death several times while she slept had Tom not woken her up, as a mother might a baby to save it from cot death.

Tessa was more than happy to remain an ever interchangeable mother-infant duo with Tom. He babied her – she babied him. She still held his hand, even though he was eight, when she took him to school, skipping and playing 'I-Spy' as they went. She still kept his father away because, she said, 'he messed up Tom's head'. Nor would she let any of Tom's schoolfriends in lest they interrupt his train of thought; it must be kept continuously on his school-work from one day to the next. Like her, she insisted, he could only bear to be with one other thing or person at a time.

Yet by the very process of eliminating all external intrusion, because of the gap she feared it might open up between herself and Tom, she jeopardised his learning to read and write the words that would bridge the gap. As Lacanian theory would predict, Tom failed to acquire 'full speech'.[9] At the age of eight he could still scarcely add numbers or string two sentences together to tell a story.

He did, however, try to use speech to separate himself from Tessa, but she dismissed his attempts as 'lippy ... all mouth'. Perhaps she was right. Faced with a similar dilemma the fatherless French philosopher, Jean-Paul Sartre, asserted his independence from his childlike mother, or so he says, with words. In this he was helped by his grandfather and, when he was only eight, wrote his first novel, *The Banana Salesman*.[10]

Tom had no such patriarch to help him. He had none of Sartre's verbal wherewithal. Instead, modelling himself on his uncles, aggrandised in his eyes by the fact that his mother had exiled them for being too manly, Tom resorted like them to fight and flight. When he was a toddler he would hit the dolls at the playgroup he went to. At school he bit the girls and thumped the boys, especially when they called him a 'bastard'. Being taunted with having no father made him utterly miserable.

Tessa, by contrast, gloried in his fatherlessness. It sanctified Tom. It made him the same as Jesus. Christ, she reminded me, was the child of a virgin birth. She planned on Tom becoming a priest – celibate, neither husband nor father, her own for ever. She wanted him to know, but certainly not to experience, everything – to be eternally hers just as she said Leah kept Moses for herself, hidden in the bulrushes. It was Tom's favourite picture, Tessa declared, in the Bible she had given him that Christmas.

Tom had other ideas. He was naughty: perhaps that would free him from his mother, as it had freed his uncles. Or he ran away to join them. He began running when he was six, when his mother's Nan died. Without her, Tessa had kept him closer to her than ever. But fleeing her for the road outside put his life in danger.

At first Tessa was not worried. She assumed he ran away, just as she fled into sleep, because his head hurt. Then it occurred to her, after he had been gone for hours, that he might have fled to get away from her. Perhaps, she hazarded, he wanted more than her: two parents, not just one. That was when she first sought help, not from the police, but from the more motherly-seeming social workers. It was through them that I met her.

As for Tom – when I saw him, fleetingly, so successfully did Tessa keep all outsiders away from him – he was full of rumbustious energy. Tessa had told me it gave him colic. But he seemed completely relaxed, togged up in football gear, lounging happily on the kitchen sideboard where Tessa and I had so gingerly perched when we first talked.

Now he seldom ran away. Perhaps the horror of 'abjection', as Kristeva puts it,[11] of disappearing into his mother, had abated now that she had let someone in from the outside world – a boyfriend, Julian. True to form she belittled Julian too, likening him to a pathetically crying cartoon clown she had stuck to her fridge door; sometimes, fearing that he might divide her from Tom, she made him stay away.

Ironically, in thus absenting him, as she did all other male figures, Tessa only glamorised him in Tom's eyes as the solution to his ills. He missed Julian dreadfully when he was not there, and again became torn between staying and going himself. Graphically he acted out the conflict by hiding away all day from his mother in her kitchen cabinet, leaving her to think he was gone when all the time he was there, inside her, as it were, in the cupboard's womb-like space.

I felt similarly torn. Tessa seemed utterly bereft and at sea, worn out with the effort of keeping everything male out. How could I leave her in that state? In going, she indicated, I would be no better than a counsellor she had seen at the hospital who, after promising like a fairy godmother always to be there, abruptly ended her sessions when they had scarcely begun.

Tessa consoled herself with the thought that her words would remain with me, in my tape recorder. To put it more theoretically, she experienced them not as an abstract Lacanian mark of our separateness, but as a concrete Winnicottian 'transitional object' or security blanket, signifying our continued mother-child togetherness, like that she hoped to sustain with Tom by belittling all the men in her life.

Her story shows only too plainly the phobic avoidance of men involved in remaining fixated to the myth of virgin birth. Yet paradoxically, as her tale also indicates, the very attention devoted to getting rid of everything signifying men has the effect of magnifying their importance. So too does Don Juan glamour.

2

Don Juan

At the height of the course of development of infantile sexuality, interest in the genitals and in their activity acquires a dominating significance which falls little short of that reached in maturity. At the same time, the main characteristic of this 'infantile genital organ-ization' is . . . the fact that, for both sexes, only one genital, namely the male one, comes into account. What is present, therefore, is not a primacy of the genitals, but a primacy of the phallus.

Sigmund Freud, 1923[1]

In contrast to Tessa's technique of rejection, some people glorify men by remaining fixated to the childhood equation of the boy with his penis. Freud theorised infancy as progressing from the baby centring his interest first on his mouth and the breast, then on his anus and faeces, and subsequently on his penis. Entering this third stage of 'phallic monism', as Freud termed it, the boy is at first too much in love with himself and his penis to turn his attention to Oedipal rivalry with his parents.[2] Or, as Kleinian analyst Jane Temperley puts it, he may defend against any such rivalry by identifying with the phallus, as though he could thereby control and not have to know about his mother's sexuality, specifically her sexual involvement with the father.[3]

Fixation to the illusion of phallic power and control occurs in both sexes. Freud's sometime colleagues, Wilhelm Reich and Helene Deutsch, claimed that in both boys and girls this stage of development involves 'identification of the total ego with the phallus . . . characterized by a proud, self-confident concentration on their own genital',[4] and 'passive-exhibitionistic being gazed at'.[5] To this the feminist writer Simone de Beauvoir later added that this phase involves the boy projecting himself into his penis as

28

'symbol of autonomy, of transcendence, of power', whereas the girl learns to project herself into her whole body to secure her self-esteem.[6]

Fixation at this stage, Reich indicated, is a means of defence against recognising sexual inadequacy. Children first resort to it, he suggested, to stave off disillusion in themselves when the parent doesn't applaud their phallic exhibitionism and display as 'His Majesty the Baby'. As adults they may then take their revenge by arousing desire in one lover after another solely to disappoint them.

In Lacanian terms the endless phallic quest of the Don Juan or *femme fatale* is rooted in an infantile fantasy of being everything – symbolised by the phallus – the mother desires as defence against recognising that neither she nor anyone else can be anything of the kind. In women it may involve adopting a masquerade of femininity, of being the phallus the other desires.[7]

Marlene Dietrich in *Blue Angel* is a striking example: primped, manicured and positioned by her lover and director, Von Sternberg, to be the very picture of what men, young and old, desire.[8] Her complement is the man who inflates himself and his sex generally by 'over-valuing', as Freud put it,[9] the woman for whom he wishes, so as to find himself reflected in her, again in Lacanian terms, as phallus.

Chris was a case in point. He imagined himself the apple of his mother's eye, her pride and joy. His blond good looks seemed to make him the incarnation of Aryan masculinity he assumed she most desired. He felt she had always been besotted with him, that she had never had any other interest.

He dismissed her own parents as violent, and 'gone to the bad'. He depicted his father, a roofer, as nothing, a mere shadow; there was no way his mother could have desired him. It was a complete mystery to Chris why, after his home town Liverpool suffered an appalling disaster, when many of its football supporters were killed in Sheffield's Hillsborough Stadium, his mother did her utmost to find out whether Chris's father, with whom she had long lost touch, had survived. On the other hand Chris perfectly understood her similar enquiries to make sure he himself had not drowned in the Zeebrugge disaster in which, as a seaman, he might well have perished.

As a child he refused to countenance the fact of his mother's continuing sexual relations with his father. The birth of his sister Eileen, when he was seven, profoundly shocked him. He accommodated it only by recalling that Eileen's birth made his mother more dependent, since she then became crippled with thrombosis. She accordingly looked more to him, not to his often absent father, to be the man of the house, and to the God of the religious sect they now joined together.

Chris refuelled his self-esteem by believing that his mother sanctified him, but this also trapped him into emasculating dependence on her idolising him. Having figuratively absented his father, there was no third figure to intervene and make room for him to escape psychologically. Like Tessa's son in the previous chapter, Chris resorted to running away. When he was only four he started going off on the buses alone. This voyaging improved his well-being. So too did the recollection of a fellow-passenger, a man, drawing railway trains especially for him on the steamed-up bus windows.

Otherwise no one seemed to care or come between himself and his mother to provide the separation he needed to gain the necessary distance from his experience so that he might represent it through pictures, words or figures. Chris, like Tom, also had difficulty in learning to read and write. He was still somewhat dyslexic and innumerate when I first met him, and found it hard to remember dates, birthdays and telephone numbers.

Not for him even the most simple things of the mind: his perception was confined to the body. He corresponded to the characterisation, by the Danish philosopher Søren Kierkegaard of Don Juan.[10] As opposed to Faust's commitment to self-reflective intellectual enquiry, wrote Kierkegaard, Don Juan is nothing but 'flesh incarnate'.

Certainly Chris, who remained a playboy into his late thirties, sought as a child to realise himself not spiritually but through his body. At school he concentrated all his energy on sport; football and climbing became his chief means of asserting his independence

from his mother and later from his girlfriends, on whom he otherwise depended to sustain his infantile phallic grandiosity.

When he was eighteen, as soon as he passed his driving test, he
sought his freedom, like the image evoked by Kristeva of the
perpetual traveller fleeing absence and insufficiency in himself,[11]
through non-stop travelling from one country and woman to
another. He worked as an itinerant disc jockey. Music glossed over
the gaps that might otherwise have disrupted his fantasy.

The *roué*, wrote Kierkegaard,

> desires in every woman the whole of womanhood, and therein lies
> the sensuously idealizing power with which he at once embellishes
> and overcomes his prey.[12]

Prose is too punctuated to express the continuity sought through
such smoothing-over idealisation. The list of Don Juan's conquests
in Molière's play, *Don Juan*, says Kierkegaard, is laughable. Only
through Mozart's music in *Don Giovanni* – including Leporello's
aria cataloguing his master's thousand and three conquests – is the
seducer's would-be undivided and unindividuated desire rendered
seamless. Nothing else, insisted Kierkegaard, conveys the seducer's
endless repetition, which no more tires of seducing than the wind
of blowing, and the sea of billowing.

Hence the centrality of music in Chris's life. He made the
doormen on the gigs he ran his Leporello. They kept a tally of his
women. Unlike the fictional Don Juan, however, Chris also made
some attempt to settle down. In his mid-twenties he met and
married Nina. Like his mother, she was religious, and on the
rebound from another man. They married and moved to Spain.

From there Chris continued his travels and philandering, but it
became increasingly hard to sustain the illusion of himself as
phallic *conquistador*. Availing herself of his frequent absences, his
wife took a lover – her boss. She had already humiliated Chris, he
said, by always reaching orgasm before him in sex and then refusing to continue so he could prove himself a man by climaxing too.
More galling still, as soon as their first and only child, Kylie, was
born Nina replaced him with her. Kylie seemed to Chris to become

the sole object of Nina's desire, just as he imagined he had been of his mother when he was a child.

Far from gratifying his narcissism by making him a father, Kylie's arrival threatened to weaken still further his inflated idea of himself as phallus incarnate. Worse was to come. Not only was Kylie's birth accompanied by Nina banishing Chris from her bed, but his most recent business venture collapsed. Chris could not take in or process these assaults to his virility.

Without psychological mediation, observes the psychoanalyst Joyce McDougall, there is nothing to prevent stress afflicting the body directly in the form of psychosomatic illness.[13] Just as it was in his body – his penis – that Chris had vested his self-esteem, so now it was on his body that the assaults on his narcissism took their toll. He was hospitalised with ulcerative colitis: this diminished him still further in Nina's eyes.

They separated. Chris returned to England. From there, he continued travelling – first as a ski instructor, then as a merchant seaman. Ashore he spent every evening picking up girls in the pub before going home to an older woman, Pam, whom he had met through work. She became his lover-cum-landlady – a quasi-maternal figure – whereupon his mother disowned him for betraying her and their religion's ethic of sex only within marriage.

As though for the first time, it dawned on Chris, then nearing forty, that he might not be the godlike figure his mother had seemed to see in him. Or it would have dawned on him, had it not been that he defended against disillusion, like Don Giovanni, by feeling so 'grand' about himself that he could court hell and damnation with impunity.

Defying the anti-suicide teachings of the fundamentalist sect to which he still belonged, he decided to drown himself. Despite her phobia about the sea, Pam first offered to join him, she loved him so much, but then, dreading losing him – he was, she said, 'such an impressive lover' – she urged him to seek medical help. Hence his referral for psychotherapy.

Perhaps he was depressed. When he arrived at the clinic he was certainly not the proud young Adonis he might once have been. He was middle-aged and balding. Yet he still seemed to embody the phallic sexuality women are bred to want. He exuded the sensuousness that is traditionally the essence of Don Juan's charm. Languidly, he sprawled in the clinic's waiting room in his city suit or, more casually, in shorts and open-necked T-shirt, exposing a silver chain inviting onlookers to admire his bronzed chest.

Flirtatiously, he flattered and attracted the clinic's women employees. Not the men. Perhaps they found his sexuality discomfiting. Certainly they tried to deflate him, calling him nothing but an overgrown child – *puer aeternus*. And it was indeed an eternal boy, an *ersatz* Peter Pan, who eventually emerged in therapy.

But not at first. Initially Chris seemed the embodiment of Don Juan, as first seducer then seduced. He no sooner inveigled me into sympathising with his plight than he told me he would soon be going away – overseas – making me the one to invite him to stay; making me suggest he commit himself to longer-term therapy.

The same thing happened a few months later. He returned from holiday telling me how much he had longed to see me, then announced that, because his job often took him abroad, he would have to quit therapy. Again he put me in the position of supplicant. Contrary to my usual practice, I found myself offering him fortnightly sessions. It seemed I was no different from all his other women, into whom he projected his longing rather than recognise it in himself.

His success as seducer was surprising since, right from the start, like Molière's *Don Juan*, there was something ridiculous and quite unprepossessing about Chris's phallic swagger. He was such a dandy, foppish, a spiv. One day he arrived sporting the braided blazer and cap of his latest job. He had become a hotel porter. His workmates, he went on, had been measuring the distance between their thumbs and forefingers to estimate the size of their penises. According to this index Chris was very well endowed, so much so that his colleagues teased him mercilessly about it. And about his uniform. 'Is your cap screwed on?', they jeered. 'Do you even wear it in bed?'

It was no laughing matter for Chris. His seriousness on this point made him all the more ludicrous – absurd, childish. He seemed to be no more advanced than three schoolboys I recently overheard:

A: How could somebody have a dick 30 centimetres long?
B: You're lying, Neil.
C: But you could dream it.[14]

Chris would not rest content with dreaming. He was more like the six-year-old who brags he is King Willy, repeatedly draws pictures of himself as a gun- or rocket-wielding Titan, or rigs himself up as a Ninja Turtle. Chris had done something of the sort himself as a boy, but more self-seriously. When he was scarcely more than a toddler he ran away from home to buy his mother a long-nozzled hoover to prove himself her man.

For an adult to mistake, without a trace of irony, the insignia of masculinity for its realisation is nonsense. Paradoxically, by concretising himself as a man (through ostentatiously clinking his car keys during his sessions with me, for instance) Chris made his maleness seem nothing but an empty symbol. Perhaps that was why he so wished, as he put it, 'to be more able to distinguish image and reality', not least because in collapsing the two – himself and his penis – he made others uncomfortable. It made them laugh, but it also made them uneasy. It lost him his job. He was fired.

His phallic brag was not only disquieting: it was frightening. Not for nothing does *Don Giovanni* start with rape and murder. These are the counterpart of the libertine's comedy. As for Chris, he told me his penis was so big it hurt and damaged his wife in sex. It was the main reason, he said, why their marriage had broken down.

Nor did this seem an idle boast. He certainly made me nervous, instilling in me the very anxiety his aggressive version of masculinity otherwise evoked in him. Was I worried? he asked. It seemed I was. I found myself dreaming of him as the murderer in the film *Jagged Edge*. In my nightmare he became the embodiment of his account of himself as a 'hysterical firecracker' who 'left a trail of devastation' as far back as he could remember, and also of his father as a drunkenly violent womaniser always in and out of jail.

Chris recalled his father as someone who only occasionally appeared, and then only at night, in his childhood home. He would engage Chris in rough horseplay and abrasive unshaven hugs. Then he presumably went to bed with Chris's mother, but all Chris remembered of their getting together was his father physically attacking his mother and kicking the furniture.

At other times Chris reversed this brutal image of his sex. It was not his father or himself but the women who were the attackers and violent intruders. It was their and my penetration he both dreaded and desired:

> At first with you, I wanted to keep it superficial. It was like duelling. I feared assaults on my male ego, that you were really trying to probe into me. It made me feel uncomfortable. But then I decided to let you get inside, and I've really appreciated it.

In keeping with Reich's account of the phallic narcissist, fixated to a stage when the child identifies both his mother and himself with the penis, Chris endowed me and all the other women in his life, even his eight-year-old daughter Kylie, with phallic attributes. He complained that Kylie had threatened to decapitate him with the way she threw the boomerang he gave her. Nor was his sister Eileen any better. She said she had been raped, and that that was why she was pregnant. More likely, Chris insisted, her alleged assailant had been assailed and ravaged by her.

A woman at the hotel where he used to work, 'really penetrated' into him, he complained, the way she went on about his crowding her. His landlady, Pam, was the same. She was 'a double-edged sword'. She mortified him by intercepting love letters from his Italian girlfriend, Lisa. Pam was 'a space invader', the way she came into the dance hall he frequented to stop him picking up other women. Back home, he said, she left sharp knives in the washing-up water, ignoring his repeated pleas not to do so in case they cut into him. He was too crippled, physically as well as emotionally, to get away. A leg injury prevented him from mountaineering, his usual excuse for leaving his women. Pam was as bad as his mother. When he was a child, his mother constantly threatened and undermined his masculinity by 'dissecting' his every move, and ever since he could remember there had always been some 'penetrating female getting under my shell'.

Women, he said, were like quicksand – lethal in their unpredictability. He could never tell from one moment to the next what they would do. He felt I was the same, at best uncertain, at worst a knife-wielding surgeon. What I said really 'got into him'. It hurt. I drained him of his manhood. Since seeing me, he complained, he had lost all interest in sex. He could no longer pull the women. Instead they had to do the chasing, they had to persuade him into bed, and even then they had to make all the running. He just wasn't up to it.

He compared his state to that of dolphins whose dorsal fins are cut off, he informed me, to make aphrodisiacs. Or they are wantonly gelignited: what a waste. Dolphins are so sensitive to the needs of others, he went on, that simply being with them relieves depression. He wanted to be like them, to help others, to work with the handicapped. By looking after and rescuing this species he would put right his own sense of being wounded and castrated: he joined societies for animal protection and for saving the planet.

At other times he indulged his view of himself as world saviour by reviving the infantile 'oceanic feeling'[15] – of himself and his girlfriend Lisa endlessly conjoined. He basked in the 'warm glow' of recollecting their spiritual togetherness, at one with each other's love of drink and sport. At such moments he felt totally superior to others and their sordid rat race. Or he recalled himself, aged eighteen, sitting in his car, godlike above Liverpool and its 'mortal combat' below.

Now, however, he was unemployed. It would have made him feel hopeless had it not been that he mocked those in work as driven by a contemptible 'killer instinct'. He despised their destructiveness: whether it be the global pollution wreaked by his fellow-men or the crude male gutter talk of Pam and myself referring to his sexual peccadilloes as 'screwing around'. No wonder, he said, he could never achieve 'peaceful coexistence' with women.

They all seemed out to emasculate him, his ex-wife Nina included. Far from thanking him for leaving her his car when their marriage ended she crashed it. Then she added insult to injury by selling all the tools with which he had equipped it. 'You ask your husband,' he complained to me. 'He could tell you how long it takes to get these things together. All for nothing.'

His mother had likewise annihilated him. She 'reduced him to pulp'. Just as the psychoanalyst Karen Horney noted that the little boy fears that his mother will deride his penis as too small for her,[16] Chris never showed his mother the things he made as a child lest she do them down. For instance he did not bring home a drawing of a train he did at school, although he was particularly proud of it: it was so long it stretched over yards of paper. Anyway, he said, he had every reason to dread his mother's scorn. She used to go on at him for losing his money and his house key; she belittled him by kissing him in front of other boys when they fetched him for school; she babied him by telling him, when they were out visiting, not to touch the furniture.

These injuries to his masculinity surfaced as Chris's therapy continued. He became increasingly disillusioned, and likened himself to a sick and damaged car sent for diagnosis. Or he was a vehicle without a driver, he woefully announced the day his girlfriend Lisa wrote, finally ending their affair. It left him void – a man who wasn't there. Nobody at home. Just flotsam, buffeted every which way, or a small boat with no one at the helm. In this state, he feared, he could all too easily be seduced into taking any job, provided it came with the promise of a car.

It seemed now that he had never had any masculinity. It was not its surfeit, he now realised, but its lack that had driven his exhausting journeying from one country and woman to another. None assuaged the yawning void. Each, he said, was just a 'carbon copy' of the last. He began to experience all too painfully 'the end of internality, the death of the Ego', of which Kristeva writes in explaining why, when 'phallic power is put into play' it can exist at best, as in *Don Giovanni*, only as 'musical fascination . . . Everything else is fantasy.'[17]

Nobody, said Chris, had ever helped him fill the emptiness. His childhood home lacked all trappings of masculinity. No television, even. Worst of all, he claimed, he was the only child at school not to have a father at home, the only boy not to have someone to teach him football or how to swim. He had only learnt by teaching himself. True, his mother had tried to make good his want of a father. She had made him arrows to go with his bow. But they quickly broke, unlike the ones the other boys' fathers made them.

Chris's fatherlessness pauperised his childhood, he said. It made him the ignominious recipient of free school meals, and there was no money to pay for school trips abroad. His mother could not fund him. When Chris was sixteen she had a nervous breakdown, which put paid to her continuing her work as a charlady. Chris had to leave school and get a job; he bitterly resented the other boys who had fathers to finance their staying on to gain themselves 'a fistful of qualifiers'.

Since he blamed the women, beginning with his mother, for his not being the man he wanted to be, he looked to them to repair the damage. Having unmanned him, he reasoned, his ex-wife Nina might at least look after him when he visited her and their daughter in Spain. He was completely nonplussed when, far from providing him with bed and board, she expected him to find them for himself. In England he looked to his landlady Pam to provide him with everything he needed, car included. He was dumbfounded when she not only failed to do so but looked to *him* to help provision her and her home.

He retaliated by moving out as soon as he could afford to by getting a job, but he still enviously felt that the women had everything and he had nothing. He grumbled that they had all the 'gadgets'. His sister Eileen, he told me, who was then planning to move out of their mother's house in Liverpool, would have no difficulty getting everything necessary by way of hi-fi and so on. By contrast he despaired of ever acquiring the things he needed to fill his unfurnished flat. Perhaps, he mused, he should advertise for someone to share and help equip it. Failing that, when he eventually moved into an apartment on his own, he got a radio to keep him company. Looking to the continuity of music, as he had always done, to fill his otherwise empty sense of himself, he kept the radio on all night. It warded off the dark desolation he had previously sought to evade by always having a woman in his bed.

What a contrast to his former Don Juan glamour, the bedraggled 'little boy lost' who now emerged. Had he previously felt he could attract the care and affection of others, as he believed he had excited that of his mother as a boy, only through phallic display? Did he fear that, if his underlying eunuch-seeming Peter Pan self was revealed, women would ridicule and lose all interest in him?

Certainly it seemed to have had that effect on Nina and Pam. Pam lost faith in him and no longer saw him as an impressive lover. She called him 'a hollow cardboard cut-out'.

Nor did Chris any longer credit his former self-publicity as 'a bit of a lad with the ladies'. He might get a woman into bed, but once there the initial excitement instantly dwindled into indifference. Everything felt futile, 'like the drum of a washing machine going round and round'. He had lived his life at such a pace, he said, he feared it would speed up and run out altogether.

At other times he felt he was a baby. He described Newhaven, where we met, as an 'embryonic sac', and me as a quasi-maternal container, 'a carrier' into whom he could put whatever he had to say to keep it safe. I was no longer a potential sexual conquest. To him I was a 'life-belt'; he saw me as someone uncluttered by dogma, unlike his mother, and understood him completely. In a couple of sentences, he said, I summarised feelings of which he had been unaware. I made them come alive by putting them into words. Even better, he said, I transformed his talk – his 'waffle merchandise' – into thoughts. In his eyes I had become the mother defined by the Kleinian analyst Wilfred Bion, who takes in, digests and transforms the baby's raw experience into thinkable ideas.[18]

Previously Chris had been impervious to my mood, certainly to any horror I might feel at his remorseless seduction and betrayal of all the women in his life. Like the doormen where he worked, I had once figured as his Leporello, the figure into whom, according to the Freudian analyst Otto Rank, Don Giovanni splits off and disowns the guilt of his philandering.[19] Initially Chris had tried to seduce and elicit in me his own pressing, anxiety-laden desire. Now he was more concerned to monitor my state of mind to find out if I was attending to him as a mother might to her child. Was I ill? Had I got a cold? There was a penny on the floor. He picked it up and gave it to me. He hoped, only half-joking, it would revive my fortunes. He suggested I have an early night, I seemed tired. It was true. As he became more 'becalmed', more obviously empty, I found it harder to stay awake. How different from the alert vigilance he had aroused in me with his earlier threatening phallic show.

He no longer felt the same need to prevent its hollowness being exposed. He was better able to face the absence in himself. No longer did he defend against it by cultivating an image of his father, as of himself, as brutal seducer. Now he recalled his dad as a forlorn figure, breaking the window of Chris's childhood home and plaintively pleading with his mother to let him in.

Having previously believed his mother had no need of his father, that he himself was more than enough to fulfil her every wish, Chris now longed to remember his parents lovingly together. He wished he had got to know his father better before he died, that he had taken up his invitation to work with him. He regretted giving in to his mother's threat to disown him if he joined forces with his father. He wished he had kept contact with him; that, instead of a sister and daughter, he had had a brother and son like himself.

With this, Chris became more friendly to the little boy he had once been. An image recurred to him of a child at a football match whose mother comes over to tell him how much she misses him. Previously Chris had fled all such memories – including those of himself, as a tiny mite, feeling empty and cold in the dark of winter. Whenever possible, as a grown-up, he would flee to warmer countries, as he emphasised by wearing an Oz-emblazoned T-shirt to his sessions with me. Now, however, after one last climbing expedition to Nepal, he no longer felt compelled for travel.

It was the same with work. Before, he had avoided the career ladder. It seemed so unmanning: a spiritless 'treadmill'; an imprisoning 'ball and chain'. But work had lost its terrors. He enjoyed his new job as a company representative, and would even risk his masculinity by using his (limited) knowledge of Spain and its language to stand up to his boss and suggest ways of improving the firm's Spanish operation.

Similarly with sex. In the past he had charmed one woman after another: rather than know about his dependence on them, he had made them do the wanting. He aroused their interest, as he had aroused mine, only to play hard to get. His ploy, he said, 'was to turn women from the hunted into the hunter'. He used to number his conquests – ticking them off to other men. It was a mechanical accounting matter, without feeling lest that put him off his stride.

Recently both chase and conquest had lost their allure. He no longer needed the women as repository into whom to split off and project his dependency and phallic insufficiency. He recognised them in himself. Therapy left him feeling he had 'lost a limb', he told me when we last met, but disillusion made him feel more confident of achieving something real. I had made an enormous difference. Or so he said. Now he had just one girlfriend. They lived apart but saw each other whenever they wanted. Nor did he travel solo any more; instead they went places together.

He was no longer a lone predatory wolf. Why? Because, he told me, I had pointed out the absence motivating his previous relentless seducer's quest. He openly admitted it. Before leaving for the very last time, he looked me full in the face, as he never had before, and confidently held out his hand to shake mine.

Did I make him better? Or were his concluding compliments just another ruse whereby, Freud claimed, men regularly overvalue the women they desire? Was it just another move in the age-old Don Juan game of awakening the woman's desire by inflating her importance to inflate his own? Whatever its cause, fixation to such narcissistic fantasy is much more captivating than its developmental successor. It too magnifies men – through envy of their sex.

3
Penis Envy

The first step in the phallic phase ... is not the linking-up of the masturbation with the object-cathexes of the Oedipus complex, but a momentous discovery which little girls are destined to make. They notice the penis of a brother or playmate, strikingly visible and of large proportions, at once recognize it as the superior counterpart of their own small and inconspicuous organ, and from that time forward fall a victim to envy for the penis.

Sigmund Freud, 1925[1]

Never did Freud outrage feminists more than with his theory that as soon as the first stirrings of genital desire are followed by discovery of the penis girls envy boys on this account. The feminist-minded Berlin analyst, Karen Horney,[2] immediately countered Freud's theory, as first formulated by her analyst Karl Abraham,[3] with the claim that it was an instance of men's general defensive disparagement of women out of envy of their mothering, which they also counter by excluding women from public life.

Feminists have since pointed out that women do indeed want to enjoy the same privileges as men. To this extent they do envy the penis as symbol of what men have and they lack.[4] Indeed such envy is a major driving force of women's liberation.

But feminist struggle can also become paralysed by envy in so far as it involves tearing men apart; this then rebounds against us, as Klein described the baby becoming torn apart by internalising the fragmented bits into which he enviously spoils, wrecks and tears to shreds everything he most loves and yearns for in his mother.[5] In detailing the fantasies involved, Klein enormously advanced our understanding of envy beyond its equation, by both Abraham and Freud, with acquisitiveness; with simply wanting what others have. On the other hand, Klein and her followers attend so much to mothering, to which they assimilate penis envy, that they overlook the force of the latter, not least its effect of psychologically shoring up an over-inflated image of men.

It has been left to others to demonstrate penis envy's devastating effects. A recent example is Deborah Warner's 1992 production of Ibsen's *Hedda Gabler*. In it Fiona Shaw portrayed particularly well the nervous debilitation to which Hedda is reduced through enviously tearing apart the work of her husband Tesman and that of her erstwhile lover Lovborg. In its place she substitutes the empty romantic images of Lovborg dying 'with vine leaves in his hair', and of shooting herself with her father's pistol to escape another admirer, Judge Brack, becoming 'the only cock in the yard'.

Rachel, a woman in her mid-forties, whom I saw in therapy some years ago, was similarly racked by the lacerating envy with which she tore not only men but also herself apart, making men seem all the more enviable by contrast. It was envy, I learnt, that had eroded her self-confidence. She arrived immaculately coiffured and glamorously dressed. Inside, however, it soon transpired she was a fraught bundle of nerves. Agitatedly she twiddled her car keys. Anxiously she avoided my eyes lest I 'scrutinise' her as relentlessly as she did herself.

Then she disparaged my boss, Dr Brown. She told me that some years before, her husband Simon had consulted him. Rachel had gone to see him too, to ask what medicine he had prescribed for her husband. What a pompous man! Rachel expostulated. Stupidly and without an ounce of feeling, Dr Brown had dismissed her with 'Typical woman, always wanting to know the names of everything.'

She tore into him and every other man in her life. Why, she asked, did her husband seek treatment? Because he had a phobia about death. What a ninny. His mother was quite right, Rachel said, to deride Simon and his worries as absurd.

Rachel likewise decried her brother, Tim. He was two years older than her, and he too had had psychotherapy? Why? For impotence. Mercilessly Rachel told me that Tim's psychoanalyst attributed it to their mother ridiculing Tim, as a boy, when he had an erection on stepping out of the bath. Rachel gloated in the memory, just as she gloated in recalling their mother babying Tim in front of his classmates by telling him to put his coat on in case he catch cold.

Rachel's memory of this incident, however, came later – after she had recounted the early years of her life. Both she and Tim were adopted. She never met her natural father, whom she lauded in his absence. It was virtue, she told me, his love of his seven legitimate children and his Catholic faith, that stopped him divorcing his wife to marry Rachel's mother. But he would certainly have supported her financially, she was sure of that. By contrast she characterised her mother as utterly callous, as having doubtless lied to the adoption agency and told them she had no financial means, to persuade them to take Rachel on.

Her adoptive mother, Martha, was no better. Too mean and cowardly to admit that she could not have children herself, Martha put the responsibility on Rachel. She got her to lie about her birthday – to say she had been born on a date when Martha's relatives were not around to see she was not pregnant. Rachel hated Martha for making her carry the burden of her own defects, and for Martha's undoubted disappointment at her not being a boy.

Martha must have wanted a boy, Rachel reasoned. Why else did she idolise her older brother Tim so much? Perhaps Martha valued him as replacement for her own older brother who had died of TB when she was sixteen. Certainly Martha became completely distraught when Rachel was six and Tim fell grievously ill with meningitis and pneumonia. It was the only time, Rachel claimed, Martha ever broke down. Otherwise, attributing to Rachel her own hatred of feminine weakness, Martha rigidly defended against it by presenting herself to the world as 'a tower of strength'.

As for Rachel, she looked to God for help. She wrote to Him to save Tim. He must have heeded her prayer. Why else did the letter disappear from the dining-room table where she had left it for Him to see? Overlooking the possibility that her mother had done the good deed, Rachel went on to excoriate Martha for keeping her and Tim off school after his recovery to prevent him from falling ill again. Martha taught them herself, but she made

Rachel feel a fool compared to Tim. Rachel loathed his intelligence, which eventually won him a scholarship to Harvard. 'Short of a brain transplant,' she told me, she would never become like him.

Doubtless, Rachel added, I too found her utterly tedious. I obviously preferred men as patients – people more 'exotic' and clever, like Tim. She expected me to punish her as her mother had done, out of hatred at her not being the male genius she assumed Martha wanted her to be. To prove it Rachel told me her mother hit her as a child for doing badly in a maths exam, and another time humiliated her by making her stand in the hall waiting to be caned. Then, attributing to her mother the phallic attributes she wanted for herself, Rachel characterised Martha as ruling with 'a rod of iron', as 'a mobile bed of nails'.

Martha would also get Tim to do Rachel down. One day he asked her point blank what it felt like to be an idiot. Other times Martha belittled Rachel in front of Tim. She made her look 'only half an inch high' by pointing out to him that Rachel was so frightened of the bathroom geyser exploding she dared not light it. Martha seemed bent on attacking Rachel for not being a boy: she cut the fingers off her gloves, tied them round Rachel's fingers to stop her biting her nails, and then sent her to school for all to see.

The only self-esteem Rachel could glean from the situation, as Freud's colleague Karl Abraham once wrote of depression,[6] was to magnify her suffering as the worst ever, as 'unutterable misery punctuated by extreme unhappiness'. Her distress was made worse when she threatened to run away only to have her mother heartlessly hand her her coat to speed her on her way.

If only her adoptive father had intervened. Rachel believed only men had the power to help. She deplored her father for not being a proper 'man'. He was a timid, frightened mouse, she said, so scared of offending his own mother that he did not dare marry until after she had died. By then he was middle-aged, yet still childishly terrified. Fearing his wife Martha would be the death of him, he wrote his will the night they married. Rachel told the story with such biting wit that unwittingly I found myself smiling. Attributing her own savage envy of her father to her mother, Rachel told me that Martha took his tennis balls away from him to stop him playing tennis with Rachel. Other times Rachel referred to him as a boorish bigot, 'full of utter bilge'.

Very occasionally, however, she let slip the admiration that caused her envy of him. She told me of his fair-mindedness, openness, flexibility and generous financial support of her family. She also mentioned an occasion when he was obviously concerned for her welfare: she had broken down at school and lost her memory (as her brother lost his when he had meningitis); her father fetched her and, as they were driving home, asked her what was wrong.

But it was more than Rachel could bear to know of his love for her, since it made her feel so hateful by comparison. So she did not tell him what was bothering her. Indeed she never confided in him: never told him about her worries when she tore her dress; nor when she had nightmares full of snakes and trees.

She preferred to keep her woes to herself, as more often than not she did with me. She could no more bear to credit me than her father with compassion, so badly did it reflect on her heartless cynicism in tearing him and other men apart. Instead she insisted he had no sympathy for her, that he was indifferent to her distress, for example when she saw a child drown in the local swimming pool. Yet she subsequently admitted she had overheard him later that evening talking with her mother about how upset she must have been.

Even if he was concerned about her, which Rachel doubted, she belittled him as too hopeless to help. He could do nothing to prevent her mother venting the spleen Rachel herself felt against women: by cutting Rachel's hair short like a boy's; buying her clothes that were far too large; blaming her for menstruating when she could not get sanitary towels because the shops were shut. If only Rachel had not anorexically starved herself, Martha stormed, her periods would have been regular and she would not have been caught unprepared.

Womanhood, Rachel declared, made her mother no better than herself. If Rachel was anorexic, her mother too rigidly controlled what she herself ate. She allowed herself only two biscuits a day, out of spite at everything enjoyable. Rachel sneered at her mother's obsessiveness: she still rose at the crack of dawn to scrub the house clean, as she did when Rachel was a teenager, chivvying her out of bed early every morning by noisily hoovering under it. Martha also regimented their meals, timing them to start exactly half an hour before those of everyone else.

Every summer, Martha mercilessly frog-marched the family off to watch cricket, against which Rachel rebelled by stripping men's things of meaning. Compulsively she found herself unpicking their words into their constituent letters, pointlessly translating them into those of the Greek alphabet. She dissected them, made them dead and gone.

As a child she tried to repopulate the killed-off emptiness by inventing a crowd of imaginary friends. She did not give up this illusory crew until the age of seventeen, when she began training as a dental nurse. She decided on this career when she was fourteen, after having an operation on her jaw. Identifying with her surgeon as aggressor, as Freud's daughter Anna might have put it,[7] she decided to take up allied work.

She did not choose the work because of the caring involved. She hated the very idea, found it 'embarrassing' and 'nauseating', contaminated as it was by notions of femininity and of weakly being cared for. Anyway, she warned me, if you care too much, patients never get better. Perhaps, she added, she should have pursued a more obviously male career – banking or lorry driving, she suggested – not dental nursing with its idiotic pettifogging female colleagues always picking one up for every tiny fault.

Fittingly, given the burning envy that inspired her destructive dissection of others, Rachel first met her husband Simon at a fireworks party. Hating the idea of becoming dependent on him, she left it to him to do the wooing. She also left it to him to write when they were apart and would only reply intermittently.

On the eve of their wedding her father told Simon she was adopted. What an idiot! She had already told him. She would no more risk unguarded exposure than Ibsen's Hedda Gabler risks it from Judge Brack. Nevertheless, she dreaded lest marriage and dependence should put her at Simon's mercy in other ways, by making her vulnerable to his illness or death. She would hate to be like her friend, she told me, who shook like a leaf when her husband was hurt.

Fortifying herself against such eventuality, Rachel told herself on her wedding night that if she ever lost Simon (through death or divorce) she would never remarry. Meanwhile she warded off any envy Simon's love might arouse in her by scorning his care, reliability and predictability.

As for pregnancy, she loathed it. She also detested knitting for her baby son, Richard. Later, when he was a teenager, she hated his valuing and clinging to her when, for instance, worried by his father being late home, he asked her to stay with him while he did his homework.

She much preferred her younger son, Luke. She marvelled at his harum-scarum ways, his cocking a snook at authority and getting into trouble with his teachers and the police. She loved his being such a carefree madcap, absentmindedly careering on his bicycle into the village pond. But it rankled that her parents accepted his mischief when they had been completely intolerant of hers as a child.

Allying herself with Luke's cocksure confidence buoyed up her self-esteem. But in therapy she felt it all too readily drained away in unseemly dependence on me. She derived some comfort from hearing a well-known TV personality talk of his dependence on therapy, but mostly she despised such dependence as unnerving, humiliating, sickening and misery-making. It made her feel such a 'wimp', a term she used again and again to deride the men in her life. Repeatedly she turned against herself the contempt with which she jeered at them.

Or she felt it was I who was contemptuous of her. She saw me as a godlike figure sitting in critical judgment, training a spotlight on her, sadistically forcing her to confess all – including her fear of dogs biting her in the street, and of men attacking her when she was out alone at night. She feared I too would savage her, just as she savaged herself. Heartlessly, she felt, I sat back waiting for her to bare her soul. She hated being subject to my male-seeming domination, to my holding 'the whip-hand' over her, as she put it, regarding the timing of sessions and holiday breaks. If she became really depressed, she thought, I would kick her in the teeth.

Therapy became an 'ordeal'. Getting me to say what I thought, she complained, was like getting blood out of a stone. Her envy poisoned whatever help I might give, just as it envenomed the love she felt from her father and husband. It reduced her to tongue-tied silence. Just as she shredded all care and affection, she was terrified that putting herself into my hands risked my mentally shredding her.

I tried to make things better, but my efforts were in vain. It reminded me of how all those years ago, when she broke down at school, she had dismissed her father's concern. She was too proud to accept any sympathy without tearing both it and herself apart. She sneered at both her husband's support and mine. She picked holes in whatever I said. Most of all, she picked herself to pieces.

Just as she had feared letting herself down in front of her father as a child, so now she was terrified of lowering herself in my esteem. She never told me how throughout the first year of her therapy she replaced dependence on me with dependence on something more readily available and under her control – drink, antidepressants and sleeping pills.

I only learnt of her growing addiction from her husband, Simon, after the first summer break. In my absence, she had heaped back on herself the embittered envy with which she had previously lambasted the men in her life. Filled with self-loathing, she felt she had no right to dissuade Simon from going away to Newcastle to comfort their friend, Irene, when her husband left her. The inevitable happened: Simon and Irene began having an affair. This provided Rachel with external foes, as alternatives to those gnawing her from within. It proved she had been right to beware dependence on men: it always ended in disaster. She mocked Irene for being unable to cope on her own. Simon, in turn, worried lest Rachel might collapse were he to leave her. Anxious about her well-being, he wrote to me.

Characteristically, Rachel could not bear to know of his concern, which left her feeling so nastily empty by comparison. So she told me that, even if he did care, he was too much of a weakling to help. She also derided him to his face. He retaliated by visiting the clinic and telling me in front of her how, when he was making love to her that morning and cried when he was about to come, she told him to shut up.

49

I could well believe it. Certainly, in the following weeks she attacked him as someone whose presence she would never miss. She deplored his depression about the failure of their marriage as pathetic, and his dithering prevarication about whether to stay or leave. She attributed his indecision to cowardly fear that her mother would disapprove, and to the expense of divorce. More fool him, she said, he should have thought of that before. Her sons were quite right, she added, to castigate him as 'an interfering twit' for going to help Irene in the first place.

Rachel then began to worry that Simon might likewise do her down: that he might expose her as a fraud to the Inland Revenue; tell her mother she was a bitch; gossip maliciously about her with Irene. Fearing the worst, she redoubled her attacks on him.

Who was he – this man? He was getting nowhere in his job. When he moved to Newcastle and married Irene he would have no work at all: the unemployment rate there was notoriously high. As for him and Irene, she went on mercilessly, Simon only got together with her because he was fed up with Rachel and fell feebly into the arms of the first woman who happened along. He was the fraud, not Rachel. Nineteen years she had stayed with him, only to have him throw their marriage to the winds.

No sooner was he gone, however, then her envious dismantling of everything good in him rebounded against her. Echoing Sartre, she remarked bitterly: 'You think hell is other people, only to find it's hell without them.' She felt shell-shocked, completely destroyed by Simon's rejection, sure that the badness was in her, not him. The memory of their arguments made her feel so vile that she tried to drink herself into oblivion.

But alcohol made her feel even more deplorable, too unworthy to ask Luke, her younger son, whose masculinity she had long vicariously enjoyed, to stay with her rather than go to Newcastle with Simon. Losing him would be like death, she said, like the loss her mother suffered when her brother died of TB. Typically, however, she could no more let Luke than his father know how much she valued them and wanted them to stay. It would be blackmail, she said, to ask her son not to go, and as for Simon, she would not do him the favour of grovelling.

Without any word from her to make them stay, they both left.

But Rachel could not get Simon out of her mind. Previously, she had told me how useless he was about the house, how when the pipes leaked he left them to fix themselves, but such derision no longer served. She wished he would return and mend everything. Only a man, only Simon, could fix it all; without him the house became as old, cracked and tumbledown as herself.

Nor was this mere metaphor. Believing she really was dilapidated – drooping and unsexed – she decided to spend the little money left over from the divorce on having a facelift. Simon feared the surgery might do her more harm than good. Although she dismissed his worry, as she did mine, as wanton obstructiveness, something got through and she cancelled the operation.

Taking in, rather than caustically rubbishing, our sympathy was not enough to cure her of her envy of Simon's relationship with Irene. What did they expect her to do, she asked with withering scorn, 'Remain a nun the rest of my life?' She would show them. Defiantly she had a succession of one-night stands. But her promiscuity, and telling me about it, left her feeling more ruined than ever under her hair tint and make-up façade.

Ruination turned to triumph when Simon and Irene's marriage collapsed. But triumph has a nasty habit of turning against its victor. Anyway, both Simon and Luke were still miles away – in Newcastle. Following the ending of therapy, when she went for alcohol counselling instead, Rachel no longer had us to hate, so she turned her loathing on herself. It made being alone unbearable. She tried to stifle the battle raging within her by drinking still more, until she had to be hospitalised for detoxification. No sooner was she discharged than she again turned to drink, even more so after it lost her her job, thereby reducing her to virtual solitude both day and night.

She tried to fill the emptiness with lodgers, but they provided little solace, so much did she belittle them, at least the women, as shameless hussies, as no different from herself. Feeling so wretched she would rather be dead, she took a massive overdose. It would have killed her but she fell out of bed and the noise alerted her older son Richard, who was still living with her. He got to her just in time.

Survival left her still hating herself, this time for botching up her suicide attempt and making herself indebted to Richard. Yet again she tried to spoil his and the rest of her family's concern for her. Undaunted, they all visited her in hospital, even her brother Tim, whom she had so long dismissed out of envy because their adoptive mother Martha had seemed to value him so much more on account of his sex. This time, Rachel surprised herself by both recognising and appreciating his love.

Who then could she now make the repository of the clamorous vestiges of her hatred, which now peopled her dreams with hideous black maggots and creepie-crawlie sleeping pills? Who but my boss, Dr Brown, the psychiatrist she mocked when we first met six years before? How sad she must have felt, he said after her suicide attempt, when her younger son Luke left. At that she burst into tears. She hated his sympathy. She tried to turn it around, by ridiculing him as heartless for making her cry like that. 'I ask you,' she added. 'Men!'

There was a time when her sarcastic derision of men had made me smile. But laughter had had its day. Recalling our sessions, I despaired at how little we achieved in relieving her destructive envy. It still so evidently tore her apart under the proud figure of a woman she presented to the world. Men seemed all the more enviable by comparison, and she was all the more desperate to have them fill her bed.

Her tale painfully reveals the extent to which 'penis envy', as Freud so notoriously called it, inflates the importance of men it seeks to destroy. It does nothing, save in fantasy, to unpick their overvaluation. Instead penis envy ruins its bearer, so much so that neither therapists nor feminists want to know about it. Yet know about it we must, if we are to treat its devastating effects, just as we must know of the ruination often done by its Oedipal successor.

4
Oedipus

So far there has been no question on the Oedipus complex, nor has it up to this point played any part. But now the girl's libido slips into a new position along the line – there is no other way of putting it – of the equation 'penis-child'. She gives up her wish for a penis and puts in place of it a wish for a child: and with that purpose in view she takes her father as a love-object. Her mother becomes the object of her jealousy. The girl has turned into a little woman.

Sigmund Freud, 1925[1]

Three-cornered rivalry with others, derived from Oedipally idolising the father and his successors, is the stock in trade of romantic fiction – from *Anna Karenina* to Mills & Boon. Contrary to Tolstoy's famous dictum, 'All happy families are alike but an unhappy family is unhappy after its own fashion', unhappy families are remarkably similar in the triangular conflicts which tear them apart.

Today, however, therapists and caseworkers generally ignore the Oedipal origins of these conflicts, and their revival (long ago pointed out by Anna Freud)[2] by the bodily changes of adolescence. Arguably the Oedipal rivalry and desire of teenagers is revived not only by biology but by other contingencies. They may be alerted to being excluded from their parents' coupling, for instance, by one or the other taking another lover. But this is often overlooked, with social workers attributing the ill-effects of what they call 'the reconstituted family' to the disruption of attachments formed with the mother in infancy.

Sexual violence is likewise often explained in dyadic maternal terms as resulting from insecurities in the protagonists' earliest relations with their mothers,[3] to the neglect of the triadic Oedipal factors also involved. Yet these Oedipal factors are brutally apparent in abusive couples, if only one could bear to look, as in the case of Celia whose story highlights the harm done by defensive fixation to this stage of development.

Celia was in her mid-thirties when we met as a result of her involvement with social workers over the custody of the children she had borne to her mother's boyfriend, Roger. She staked her all on wresting him and other men from others. She made men the most – indeed the only – important figures in her life. Without a man she felt she was nothing.

Her surroundings were enough to make anyone feel empty and forlorn. She lived in a rubbish-strewn, bleak, half-deserted council estate. Many of the houses were up for sale. Hardly anyone ever bothered to visit. No need, therefore, for a door knocker or bell.

I tapped on the window instead. It brought the sound of several locks being unfastened. Celia had had them fixed, it turned out, because she feared being the butt of the neighbouring children who, in the past, had always been on the prowl, ready to break in or taunt her with being a whore.

She was certainly sexy. At times she was positively beautiful, in sharp contrast to the ugly broken-down kitchen she took me into, with its battle-torn cupboards and smashed-up fittings. She offered me coffee, gave me a chair, and then retreated to a bench in the corner. There she huddled, nervously puffing a cigarette, a desolate waif, the picture of destitution.

Beside her her youngest child, three-year-old Ryan, sat squashed into a high-chair silently munching. He might as well not have been there for all the notice Celia took of him. Her children left her feeling utterly alone, she later told me, all her life with them had been a void of 'being on my own waiting for somebody to come'.

She hoped I might fill the emptiness – that I might take her place as excluded third person, as Oedipal spectator to the stories of her men, with which she immediately regaled me. She could not bear any interruption from Ryan. His bag of chips finished, he began clambering out of his chair. I watched, worried that he would topple over the chair and himself. Instantly, sensing she had lost my attention to him, Celia whisked him upstairs.

Within seconds she was down, ushered me into the sitting room, and resumed her tale, deaf to Ryan's noisy thumping above, utterly absorbed in telling me, another woman, about her love life with the men. Everything else was immaterial, at best a muddled blur.

If only she could have disentangled it all, I thought later, when I tried to unscramble her account of her life into a chronological sequence. Had she been able to think it through she might have been less in thrall to the male brutes she said had made her life such a misery. She turned them into the ogres that plagued her from within. It was these internal nightmare monsters, I learnt, that made her look so hunted when she first opened her front door to me. In getting rid of them into the men she knew she became increasingly animated – until, as I have said, she became quite beautiful.

It was, however, a precarious basis on which to found her self-esteem. Fearing lest she lose it if her tale of sexual conquests was interrupted by Ryan, she stopped her ears to his shouted unhappiness, anguished crying and head-banging upstairs. I had no such cause not to hear his distress. Like Dolly in Tolstoy's *Anna Karenina*, appalled by her sister-in-law Anna's indifference to her baby, I found myself horrified by Celia's unconsciousness of Ryan. I was just about to offer to fetch and hold him, when he quietened. Perhaps his rocking and weeping had tired him out.

Noisy or silent, Celia seemed hardly to notice him at all. Later she told me, with no trace of sympathy, that all her children were head-bangers, adding incongruously, 'I love Ryan to pieces.' Yet she was completely numb to him. Her stupor reminded me of the New York publisher, Hedda Nussbaum: so obsessed with securing the sole love of her lawyer lover, Joel Steinberg, she was completely insensible to their daughter Lisa's misery, and even to Lisa's eventual death at Steinberg's hands.[4]

Steinberg also battered Nussbaum, and Celia's lovers battered her. It proved they loved her: at least when they hit her they were not attending to anyone else. Battering, in Celia's case, returned her to an Oedipal scenario in which, as a child, she remembered winning her father John Potter, 'her hero' as she called him, from her mother.

Perhaps she remained fixated to this wish because Mr Potter

had so seldom in any way requited it. His attention always seemed elsewhere. Even when she was first born, Celia complained, he was preoccupied with others, specifically with the death of his own father, a gypsy who used to beat him as a child for seemingly being the product of his wife's adulterous liaison with another man. Why else, he asked, was John left-handed and fair-haired, unlike his other eight children?

Celia too was blonde. But her physical similarity to her father did not stop him beating her just as his father had beaten him. The beatings, however, came later. Celia's earliest memory was of sitting high up on Mr Potter's shoulders, his attention riveted on her. It made her feel wonderful. So did the photographs in which she saw them as so wrapped up in each other that her father had no time for her mother (in whom, Celia added, he lost all interest when he went away to fight in Korea).

By the time Celia was four, just after her brother Tony was born, her father's adoration of her turned to abuse. He thrashed Celia just as he later belted his girlfriend's daughter, Lucy. His violence left Lucy 'brain dead', Celia said. Had it also stupefied Celia? Was that why her account of her life was so incoherent? Or was it because her father preferred to beat her rather than listen to her and thereby help her decipher herself to herself? Certainly it was of her father's lack of interest in her, not of his violence, that Celia most complained.

He clearly had other things on his mind. When Celia was eight his sister-in-law beat her baby Keith so badly that Celia's grandmother had to look after him. When she proved too old to cope, Mr Potter took over the baby's care. He adopted him.

Faced with this second sibling rival Celia felt she could regain her father's undivided attention only by being naughty. It was the time of the Moors murder trial. Fearful lest his children suffer the same fate as the Moors murderers' victims, not least because he met someone in the doctor's surgery whose child had gone missing, Mr Potter forbade Celia to go out on her own. So that was precisely what she did.

It gave her a moment of glory. Against her father's wishes she went alone to her friend's house, and then ran out after her dog when it bolted into the road. An oncoming truck hit her. It was headline news – because the driver was involved with the Mafia. Celia savoured the memory. Even better, she remembered trouncing her mother by asking for her father, not her, when she awoke from a three-week coma during which Mrs Potter had kept day-and-night vigil by her side.

Celia's triumph did not last. Her headmaster thought the accident had sent her 'round the twist', and her classmates teased her. They called her 'jamjar' (because of her surname, 'Potter') and 'four eyes' (because of the glasses she now had to wear). They even beat her up.

Was it to protect her that her father decided to take her and the rest of his family away from his native Birmingham? More likely, Celia assumed, he decided to leave because he had been discovered embezzling the petty cash at work. Whatever the reason, after the move, she felt that he briefly favoured her. She was now in her early teens and her father was still glamorous and young enough to be mistaken for her boyfriend when he took her out.

Perhaps he did indeed want that role. Certainly her talk about boys made him jealous. He taunted her with her alleged affairs, and got her brothers, Tony and Keith, to call her a 'slut'. If that was what won her his interest, she concluded, that was what she would be. She was not attracted to boys, to the army cadets, for instance, with whom she and her friends hung out. She only found them appealing to the extent that she could use them to excite her father's attention.

It also won her her mother's jealousy. Mrs Potter was so unable to face growing old, crowed Celia, jubilant in her youth, that she pretended she was Celia's sister. She stole Celia's boyfriends, or acted as her procuress. It was with this that Celia had begun her tale, telling me how her mother first introduced her to Ryan's father, Roger, when he was twenty-six.

Mrs Potter first met Roger at work and pestered Celia to go out with him to cheer him up after his girlfriend had jilted him. It was hardly the stuff to arouse Celia's desire. He seemed nothing but a spoilt brat, babied and doted on by his mother ever since birth when his twin brother died. But then Celia's mother took him as a lover. That was when Celia began to want him for herself.

At first, however, she was more concerned to secure her father's undivided love. She was eighteen. His mind was still elsewhere, beset with worries not only about his wife's infidelity with Roger, but also about Celia's brother Tony who had just been discovered to have cancer. If only, Celia lamented, her father had confided his troubles in her she might not have felt so abandoned when he devoted himself to Tony. Nor would she have felt quite so rejected when he vented his anxiety on her. This culminated when he angrily threw her out of home because of the mess she was making – no different to that made by Tony and her other brother.

Denounced and rejected by her father, she returned to Birmingham to live with her maternal grandmother. The house was full of gratifying memories of her grandfather preferring her to her mother; he always gave her much better presents, for instance. He even gave Celia the privilege of being the last person to see him before he died. Perhaps it was his death that triggered her mother's adultery. 'She would never have dared,' Celia explained, 'had the old man been alive.'

As for Celia herself: the loss of Roger to her mother compounded her upset at her grandfather's death, and at losing her father's love to her brother. Her grandmother was no help, babying Celia and insisting she be back home early every evening. Celia's only solution to the loss of the patriarchs in her life was to find another man, so she moved in with the first man she met, Graham, whom she bumped into in the dole queue.

Like her father, he proved to be a thug. He too expressed his interest in Celia with physical violence. Within a week he had given her a black eye. Appalled at his brutality, the fellow-residents in the squat where they were living threw him out. Celia felt too bereft to stay on without him, so she left too. Her grandmother would not have her back. So, egging herself on with 'better the devil you know', she trailed after Graham from one dilapidated household to another.

Two months later they married. Briefly it won her her father's attention. He came to the wedding. But his interest soon waned, and he did not seem in the least bothered by the fact that Graham continued to ill-use her. He was too preoccupied with his wife deserting him to live with Roger, and with his own new girlfriend

Tina. All the more galling to Celia was the fact that Tina was the same age as her.

Having yet again lost the interest of her father, with whom she had been besotted, to someone else, Celia had to make do with her husband, Graham. At least he attended to her. His jealousy knew no bounds. He locked her up for days when he was away, and when he was there he repeatedly assaulted her. The battering continued for two years. When Celia became pregnant with their one and only child, Emma, the Council rehoused them, but the move led to yet more rows.

Pets were not allowed in their new flat, but Graham insisted on keeping his bull-terrier. He had acquired it from a dogs' home, and perhaps he identified with its unhappy orphan state. There was no doubting its misery – the dog even ate its own shit. It was more than Celia could bear. It made her feel she too was filthy, especially when the dog defecated in the room she had prepared for the baby growing inside her.

She called in the RSPCA to take the terrier away. To Graham this seemed tantamount to ousting him in favour of their expected child. Furious, he threw Celia downstairs, again and again. Each time she picked herself up and went off to the neighbours to complain, only to return to be thrown downstairs again. The next day, however, she left Graham for good. While he was out her mother came round with Roger to collect her; Celia grabbed everything that had ever taken Graham's fancy away from her, including his stereo, which he had always forbidden her to touch.

Three weeks later she gave birth to Emma, but her daughter gave her no sense of comfort. Celia's self-esteem depended entirely on getting a man; now she wanted to get Roger away from her mother. He looked after her and lavished her with affection, but it did not last. Her mother saw to that. Pretending Celia was unrelated to her – the condition necessary for the Council to provide Celia with alternative accommodation – Mrs Potter engineered her removal.

Again Celia was alone. Baby Emma was no company. She was, and remained, nothing in Celia's eyes. Thirteen years later, when we met, Celia still had not put her picture on the sitting-room wall alongside those of her younger brothers. When she was a baby, Emma left Celia feeling shamefully old and worn out: her brother, she said, quite understandably would not even acknowledge her in the street.

She looked and felt utterly hopeless. She could not cope. Neglecting her house, she let it become a cesspit of mess and filth – walls scrawled all over with Emma's scribbling, floors soaked with the cat's urine – so squalid that Emma was taken into care. She was eleven months old. Five weeks later the Council returned her to live with Celia after she had gained some measure of self-confidence through getting herself a man. Roger had moved in. Soon Celia was pregnant by him, but at once Roger deserted her for her mother.

Losing him left Celia again feeling desperately alone and helpless. And again the welfare services stepped in, arranging for Emma to be fostered while Celia went into hospital to have her next child, Jason, and fixing for her to move from her damp prefab.

For Celia, however, the greatest comfort came later: Roger again left her mother to live with her, when Jason was three. In much more luxurious and peaceful circumstances Tolstoy's Anna Karenina, attributing to her lover Vronsky her own inordinate desire for his single-minded love of her, refuses to have more children by him lest this would drive them apart. For the same reason Celia would not at first contemplate having any more children by Roger. Every time she got pregnant she had an abortion. Eventually feeling more secure in Roger's love, she decided to go ahead with her next pregnancy. But Roger seemed no more able to abide diversion of her interest from him than she could stand diversion of his interest from her: she assumed he blamed her attention to the baby for her refusal to have sex with him every night as he demanded.

Again, as in an endless cycle, he left her for her mother. Was it her mother, Celia asked herself, or her mother's eleven cats who drew him away? Whatever the cause, being without a man left her desolate. Looking to her long-adored father to fill the void, she contacted him. But he still seemed to have no time for her. His continued rejection left her feeling so forlorn that she decided to have the baby adopted when it was born. Just then, however, another man turned up – Trevor.

Nervous of telling me how, in effect, she had stolen Trevor from her friend, Tracy, his wife, Celia offered me a cigarette. Anyway, she added by way of self-justification, she only gave in to Trevor's advances because he was so miserable at Tracy deserting him. Nevertheless, it was great having him look after her. True, he did not accompany her to the hospital when she gave birth to Ryan, but he did get the ambulance. No man had even done that much for her before. But then he too left, to return to his wife because, said Celia, she told him she would have their children taken into care if he did not come back. However much Celia tried to reassure herself, Trevor's departure was mortifying. Yet again she had lost a man – the *raison d'être* of her life – to someone else.

Trevor's wife had blackmailed him: now Roger blackmailed Celia. Without Trevor she lacked the strength to withstand him. Before he had threatened to commit suicide if she were ever unfaithful to him; or to beat her if she wouldn't have sex with him. Now he said he would not give her money for their children's support unless she sucked him off. He insisted he had to come, even though it often took hours; otherwise he would suffer awful stomach ache.

Prostituting herself with fellatio left Celia feeling abject and, paradoxically, all the more beholden to Roger, especially since he further diminished her by telling her that no other man would ever look at her, now she had children. Or, echoing her father, he derided her as a whore. Her mother had told him of her loose ways. Like Leporello in *Don Giovanni*, but with quite opposite intent, Roger annotated his disdain for her by keeping a record of her supposed liaisons.

He scoffed at her for her imagined affairs, and got her children, Emma and Jason, to do the same. They denounced her as a tart. Soon all the neighbourhood children joined in. They jeered at her. They tormented her. They even took her cat and killed it. Why? To attack her, Celia assumed, just as she attacked herself for being nothing without a man.

At first I found myself sharing her self-perception as useless. Obviously, it seemed, she was far too hapless a victim to be able to mend her windows, for instance, when the local children broke

61

them, even though it meant that her heating bills sky-rocketed so that she had no money to buy food.

But having me as a third-party Oedipal witness of her couplings animated her, until I became aware that she did have the energy to cope, that she was just as capable of fixing her windows as the woman welfare worker who happened to visit some months previously had been in immediately getting polythene to cover them.

Celia clearly enjoyed talking to me. She hoped I would call again. In the interim, however, she became more wary. Perhaps the demons she had shaken off by 'being of service' to me, as she put it, had returned to make her feel too ragged and disadvantaged to want to be seen by me.

At my next visit she looked dispirited and haggard. As before, however, she quickly cheered up as I listened to her affairs. Again they revolved around having or not having a man. Without Roger, after Ryan was born, she told me, she felt so vulnerable to being scorned by others for her single state that she stayed home all day. She became agoraphobic. Or she would only go out, and then only to the shops, by keeping her children away from school to accompany her and scare off her feared detractors.

Perhaps that was what alerted Emma and Jason to how empty and beholden to others their mother felt without a man. They filled her up with the booty they now stole, succeeding, where all else had failed, in securing her belated interest. Proudly she told me they were such good thieves she could write a whole shopping list of Christmas goodies and they would steal the lot. Her mind became full of them – of their thieving and of worries that it and their truancy might get out of control.

Their exploits, their always being on the rampage, however, soon backfired. Feeling unable to cope or manage her children's mayhem, Celia again washed her hands of them. She decided to free her mind of them by sending them to live with her mother and Roger even though this meant going through the ordeal of seeing the couple together at the social work meeting formalising the arrangement.

She consoled herself with the thought that Roger agreed to having the children so that he could see her. She certainly wanted to see him, yet the children did not seem to secure his attention so much as excite his jealousy. Didn't he always ask her what she had done when he went away, in case she had been having sex with someone else? Didn't he even accuse her of having lesbian affairs with her women friends? Assuming she could only win him by seeing others, she made the most of it. No wonder she felt guilty when he accused her of being unfaithful. For that was precisely what she was bent on seeming if not being.

Roger, she said, used to want her to sit beside him as a passive 'ornament' in the pub all day. He would not allow her to look at, let alone speak to, anyone else. So what did she do? When his interest waned, she phoned one of his drinking pals, Greg, just for a chat. It had the desired effect. Her call regained Roger's attention: he followed them, scared Greg off, then beat her up. She even dreamt of Roger standing by her bed berating her for going out with one of her girlfriends.

Imagining his jealousy was not enough to sustain her that Christmas. Emma and Jason were now living with him and her mother. The only person she had with her was baby Ryan. He was no company, and Jason was no comfort when he returned to be with her on Boxing Day. Neither boy filled her emptiness. So she took up with the next man who came along, just as years before she had taken up with Emma's father, Graham. Late on New Year's Eve, as she drunkenly tottered home, she bumped into a passing stranger, Pete, fell into his arms, and invited him home. He had stayed ever since.

He protected her, mended the windows, and took a night-time job to be with her all day to keep away the marauding children. His presence stopped their attacks, she felt, because it meant she was no longer an empty nobody. His being there was crucial to her well-being.

When it came to choosing between him and her children, she chose Pete. Nine-year-old Jason was devastated. True to form, Celia anaesthetised herself to his misery: it reminded her too painfully of her own on losing her father's love. Jason was not unhappy, she told me. He was just angry with Andrew, the social worker who took him away, and taunted him for being black.

Celia joined in with her son's racism. It felt so good having

63

someone else to pick on for a change. She called Andrew a 'shit', the epithet she often used against herself. What a fool this so-called 'do-gooder' had been, she went on, accusing her of not loving her children. Of course she loved them; Jason was a real 'mother's boy'.

But he was a boy, not a man. As for Ryan, he was not even a boy. He was just a baby, the same as her – a brat, a messer, a wrecker, someone who screamed for her man's attention. Ryan gave her the nightmares which left her exhausted when I visited for the last time. Rather than face herself in him she kept him out of sight. I never saw Ryan again after that first glimpse in the kitchen. Even his eating there had been unusual. More often, Celia told me, she left him to have his meals alone – breakfast, lunch and tea – in his cot or stuck in his high-chair in front of the television. His company, like that of her other children, made her feel bad. So did Pete's baby whom she was even then expecting. Her pregnancy made her feel sick. As for childbirth, it was just a matter of 'blood and snot'. Nothing could come of nothing. She could never produce anything good.

The only reason she felt half-way all right when we last met was that she had a man with whom to arouse others' jealousy. Roger had begun phoning again. Trevor was once more following her around. Better still, even though she had seemingly lost her father's interest for ever, Pete's father was evidently concerned. He had given her his sweater, for instance, when Pete's mother insisted they all go for a walk in the freezing cold.

Best of all Celia had triumphed over this high and mighty woman – matron at the local hospital – by becoming her son's one and only desire. She had proved Peter's mother wrong in predicting that he would soon tire of her. Not only had he devoted himself exclusively to her for over a year, he was going to marry her as soon as her divorce from Graham came through. Meanwhile he was buying a house for them: she cancelled one of my visits because she and Pete were going to see the estate agent. It buoyed her up, putting off a woman in favour of her man, but it could not match her delight in telling me how she had wrested Pete from his adoring mother.

At long last, it seemed, Celia had won herself the happy-ever-after ending of three-cornered romance – the prize of persisting Oedipal fixation by which she, and countless others, inflate men's importance through the fantasy that having a man (whether idol or brute) is all that is needed to solve life's ills. But whatever its allure, making one's life work the task of winning a man from others is more likely to undermine than to boost one's self-esteem. As Tolstoy warns cryptically in his biblical preface to *Anna Karenina*: 'Vengeance is mine; I will repay.'

5

My Father Myself

The Oedipus complex offered the child two possibilities of satisfaction, an active and a passive one. He could put himself in his father's place in a masculine fashion and have intercourse with his mother as his father did, in which case he would soon have felt the latter as a hindrance; or he might want to take the place of his mother and be loved by his father, in which case his mother would become superfluous.

Sigmund Freud, 1924[1]

The corollary of the Oedipal three-cornered romance of Celia's story is identification with an idealised image of the father as 'phallus'. Wanting to take the father's place in intercourse with the mother, as indicated in the above quote from Freud, is not confined to men. Freud described, as not at all unusual, the case of a young woman who revived this wish in her late teens. He claimed she was defending herself against jealousy of her father's continuing sexual relations with her mother, evident from their recent baby, by identifying with him, and sexually desiring older women as he did.[2]

Identification with the father is, of course, no more a cause of lesbianism than maternal identification is a cause of male homosexuality. Gay, lesbian and heterosexual desire involves a variety of different identifications, as Freud emphasised, and as his followers point out in countering the surprising homophobia of many of today's psychoanalysts.[3]

In this chapter I shall be concerned with just such an identification with the father, triggered by evidence of his licentiousness: an identification startlingly like that of the father in a book Freud referred to as 'the most magnificent novel ever written'[4] –

66

Dostoevsky's *Brothers Karamazov*. In it Dostoevsky magnificently described not only the damaging effects of rivalrous idealisation of the father but also its parallels with his century's defensiveness against loss of faith in God and in Russia.

The craving for authority, the Oedipal fantasy of equalling the father's supposed phallic prowess, still wreaks havoc in personal lives and in the lives of nations. Yet therapists and caseworkers almost entirely neglect this aspect of their patients' and clients' disorders in focusing on mothering instead – all, that is, except a few Kleinians. After years of concentrating on our psychology's pre-Oedipal (paranoid-schizoid and depressive) determinants, Kleinians are now increasingly attending to its Oedipal aspects.[5] In keeping with their mentor Melanie Klein, they recognise the early occurrence of the Oedipus complex but focus on its oral and anal rather than its phallic aspects.

Nevertheless the latter persist. They were particularly apparent in the case of Mark Davies – a man in his early thirties when I saw him in therapy some years ago, still riveted to glorification of his father. Like Dmitri Karamazov, Mark was one of three brothers, and wedded to the goal of beating his father's boasted sexual conquests.

Mark impressed his doctors. Their case notes and letters to each other showed how over-awed they were by his personality and high-status City job. They exaggerated his qualifications. They inflated his symptoms – diagnosing them as evidence of manic depressive psychosis, for which they prescribed lithium carbonate.

Previously, Mark complained, they gave him drugs which stopped him having erections or ejaculating. At least lithium carbonate did not make him impotent; it did not take his masculinity away. Now his doctors confined themselves to reducing him symbolically. They wrote to each other about the length of his hair, which had been cut short, as though, as with the mythical Samson, this was evidence of his dwindling power. Or they bragged about their authority over him. One doctor, taking on the mantle of Victorian *paterfamilias*, reported to his colleagues that he had told Mark in no uncertain terms that, were he ever to arrive drunk for his appointments, he would be summarily thrown out of the clinic.

Mark responded in similar vein. Rivalrously he questioned his

doctors' status and prestige. He derided them as 'so-called pro-
fessionals'. He said he longed to hear 'their words of wisdom'.
Yet despite his continuing rivalry with his father, now played out
with them, his physicians attributed his symptoms, in the now
orthodox fashion, to a 'mother complex'. They concluded that his
problems were due both to his pining for his dead mother and to
his hatred of her endless knitting, loneliness, and depression when
she was alive.

Certainly Mark soon spoke of his mother to me, announcing
challengingly:

> This will play right into your hands. My earliest memory is of her
> washing me. I was standing on the laundry basket in the bathroom.
> And I said, 'You aren't my mother. My mother never smacks me.'

His pronouncement should have alerted me to the denial by which
he kept his illusions going. Yet these denials were connected less
with mixed feelings about either his mother or me than with
continuing idealisation of, and competition with, the men in his
life. Indeed, even before he spoke of his mother, his memory
produced an image of the magical resolution of this rivalry – a
childhood idyll of himself and his brothers making a giant snow-
ball together.

As for his father, Mark boasted of his lechery, just as Dmitri
Karamazov does of that of his father Fyodor. Mark both hated
and emulated the sexual lawlessness of his father, Mr Davies, while
also lauding him as a paragon of order and propriety whom he
sought to copy and model to his own son, Nicholas. Mr Davies,
Mark said, was not unruly. He kept a regular timetable. He would
never cancel appointments (as I did his therapy sessions over
Easter).

Mr Davies, Mark emphasised, was no mere therapist. He was
much more important – a nuclear physicist – brilliant, and so good
with his hands. Retired from laboratory work, he was now a
freelance carpenter. He could mend, build or make anything. He
never failed. When Mark was a child he seemed ten feet tall, divine,
someone Mark looked up to with the *credo*, 'Trust in God and
keep your powder dry.' His father was 'omnipient', Mark said,

all-knowing all-powerful omnipotent omniscience combined. He was no tinpot dictator, Mark added, not like Idi Amin or Colonel Gaddafi.

True, like them, Mr Davies had been in the army. But he resigned his commission on moral grounds. He disapproved of applying his scientific knowledge to military destruction. Or so Mark claimed, glossing over the nervous breakdown that had caused his father to quit the army for a relatively low-status civilian job. Eventually, however, he became boss of his own petrol station, more through luck than effort. He bought it when Mark was six, with money he won on the football pools. Mark marvelled at his father's windfall. It so swelled his bank account, Mark said, that his father could buy the family a vast house, equipped with a seemingly endlessly long lounge and a colour television well before anyone else could afford one. Anything his father wanted he could get. He ran the best 'zocker' car on the block and took them all on fabulous foreign holidays.

But grand living had its day. However much Mark exalted himself by magnifying his father as being as rich as Croesus, he abruptly learnt that, compared to his father, he was only a child, forever excluded from his sexual relations with Mark's mother. This was suddenly brought home to him one night, when he was eleven. Woken by the noise of his parents arguing, Mark went downstairs to see what was happening. They told him they were going to separate. Who would he like to live with? they asked. Hardly had he answered than, ignoring him, they fell into each other's arms. He felt totally belittled, not least because, in the course of their row, they had berated each other for their affairs with others. Until then Mark had grandly believed himself to be 'author of all the sins'. Now, he learnt, his parents had outwitted him in this.

He consoled himself with being made much of by his brother, Matt, who was five years older and let Mark tag along with him when he went out. At home Matt invited him to share his bedroom when their older brother Andrew joined the army, as their father had before him. Most of all, however, Mark buoyed himself up by having an affair, when he was thirteen, with a girl his father fancied. Doubtless, Mark reasoned to himself, his father would succeed over him. Mr Davies was so eligible, or so Mark said, that his 'ministrations' and 'wicked ways' must have made Mark's own 'adolescent fumblings' seen utterly paltry by comparison.

Mark depicted his brother Andrew as a lecher equal to their father. Army life curbed his womanising, drug-taking and boozing, but before that, Mark indicated, Andrew too had idealised and competed sexually with their father. Mr Davies had stolen Andrew's girlfriends, even his wife: he had an affair with her when she was sixteen and pregnant with Andrew's first child.

Mr Davies's lust for Mark's own girlfriends proved to Mark his own sexual worth. He was delighted to discover that his still 'debonair' father, as he called him, had propositioned Dawn, when she moved into the Davies household to live with Mark. He was not in the least annoyed with his father for flirting with her, but he was annoyed with Dawn for discomfiting his father by refusing him. Yet Mark courted similar embarrassment, pursuing the same wanton debauchery that had earned his father Dawn's contempt.

He was the personification of the jaundiced dictum, asserted by Dostoevsky's Grand Inquisitor, that man prefers aping and subjecting himself to the patriarchs of the Church – with their promise of material wealth, magic and mystery – to struggling to achieve the adult freedom, individual liberty and moral responsibility preached by Christ. Waving away the limitations of such struggle, Mark preferred to succumb to his father's devilry. He drank it in – literally – arriving 'plastered' at his end-of-school exams. But by some 'miracle', as he put it, he passed them all.

He would not however stay on and work – as his brothers Andrew and Matt did – for university entrance. Ridiculing their degrees as mere bits of paper, he left school in the hope of winning himself a fast buck, as his father had on the pools. At first he proved lucky. He enjoyed a meteoric rise in the City. After only two years' menial work, during which he effortlessly passed a couple of exams (equivalent, he assured me, to his brothers' A levels), he earned such good money that he easily bought himself the same luxury his father's gambling bonanza had won him.

No longer would his father poach his girlfriends. By the time he was eighteen Mark could afford to buy himself a house, to marry and live elsewhere. He and Dawn embarked on a life of bliss: good jobs; 'loads of dough'; flash cars; eating out every night; weekends in Paris, and, best of all, an 'open marriage' in which Mark could act out all his Oedipal 'three in a bed' fantasies.

Repudiating any law to the contrary, he proclaimed that he followed the Japanese edict: 'Anything goes so long as it's physically possible'. Whatever Japan's teaching on the subject, Mark no sooner discarded one girlfriend than he acquired another. His only goal was to match his mother's account of his father as sexually tireless and irrepressible. Mark conjured up an endless succession of lovers for himself and for his wife, and hence an endless fund of stories of sexual conquest to flatter each other's narcissism.

The promise of such *Liaisons Dangereuses* delights did not last. 'The bubble burst,' as Mark put it. It proved impossible to invent ever more titillating triangular scenarios. Not that he and Dawn did not continue to have affairs, but sexual licence threatened to settle into dreary routine. It got too cosy. He and Dawn became 'a comfy, elderly Darby and Joan pair', more like brother and sister than husband and wife.

He tried to renew the excitement by moving in yet another lover, Camilla, hoping she would 're-inspire' him. She too had been a victim of paternal seduction, by her first father-in-law. But it did not do the trick. The fun with Dawn was gone. Mark quit. Dawn stayed in their house, while Mark went to live with his parents, and then with Camilla, whom he later married, in a new house in Sheerness.

Now Mark turned to drink in earnest. Losing Dawn, the woman his father had wooed, started him on the road to alcoholism ('if I *am* beset by such a beast'). He developed a taste for 'being out of it'. Anyway, he asked himself, why should the loss of Dawn clip his wings?

He let his mother take the blame. As though he were still in need of the pampering she bestowed on him when he suffered asthma as a baby, as though he were still a youth entitled to sow his wild oats with impunity, she castigated herself, not him, for his marriage breakdown, just as she had blamed herself when he crashed his car. It was her fault: she should never have pressed him to learn to drive, nor to marry Dawn. Mark was only too happy to let her take responsibility. It left him free.

But the restrictions of manhood caught him up. Camilla became pregnant. Not wanting to know, Mark cavalierly went on 'playing the field'. He continued to indulge his boyhood fantasy of taking his father's place with the girls. He had 'a blossoming romance', as he put it, with Christine, a girl barely out of school. She was sixteen, the same age as the wife and mistress of Dmitri Karamazov's father, Fyodor, when he first courts them. Mark met Christine through work, and when the affair aged and lost its charm, he entertained *Dallas*-style tycoon fantasies of engineering her dismissal.

What he hated most was that he now had the necessary status to do so. At first he hyped his promotion to managerial rank in the inflated terms of schoolboy epic. He described himself as having been put in charge of 'a troubleshooting bunch' to 'ginger up' the office. In reality, his elevation risked ending his adolescent dream of riding roughshod over the regulations of the adult world. Now he was one of its rulers: no longer could he enjoy the boundless hedonism of youth – 'running around, getting pissed, flinging money on frivolity, and driving fast cars'. Undaunted, he went on playing the libertine, and when senior colleagues ridiculed him, he reacted peevishly by impugning their masculinity. They were nothing but 'sterile, schoolmarmish, pettifogging, cubbyholing bureaucrats', he said, so hidebound with pedantry they even had rules for when one could go to the toilet.

Hating the constraints of work, he retreated to the limitless enchantment of childhood dreams. He stayed in bed all day. By the time Camilla gave birth to their son, Nicholas, Mark had been on sick leave for several months. Fatherhood drove him even more into sleep, as escape from this further indication of adulthood and its confines.

Compared to the threat that becoming a father posed, the news that his mother had cancer left Mark blank. So did her death some months later. Her dying could not stop his persisting dream of possessing her as his father had. Of course, her death meant he could never actualise this wish so he resorted to fantasy. He imagined her still alive – as a ghost – rattling at the door: his three-year-old son, Nicholas, saw her, or so Mark claimed. It kept her living, even if only in spectral form, and so did Mark's new-found interest in parapsychology. It kept his mother ever available to him, in the same way that he refused to take in the fact that I would not be in the clinic over Easter, somehow imagining an identikit therapist would be there in my place.

Very occasionally he acknowledged his mother's loss. He recalled her emaciation as she lay in bed, waiting to die. At such moments, as though it had only just occurred to him, he felt incensed at the 'merry dance' his father used to lead her. Usually, however, her death left him mawkishly self-pitying. He pictured himself as a hapless war orphan or as a starving Ethiopian refugee – deprived, evacuated, driven for ever from his parents' life together.

More often he evaded any such nightmare with more inflated notions of his masculinity. It was these that drove him to seek therapy – specifically thoughts of killing his father, as Dostoevsky's Dmitri boasts of killing his. Or he bragged that he would murder his wife, Camilla. Either way he hoped he would acquire the same fortune his father had won: he planned to kill his wife for the insurance money, and, as for his father, he blustered, he could kill him and anybody who got in his way with no qualms or guilt. It would be cathartic – 'cleansing'. It would secure him his father's possessions, including the 'antiques' he made.

It was all planned in chilling detail. Mark frightened himself with his 'clinical, malice aforethought, cool and clear' plot. It seemed easy – 'as simple as riding a bike'. He could put his scheme into action all too readily. There was a risk that, 'like a business project', he would get away with it. He so infected one woman doctor with tales of his cunning that, seeking more to reassure herself than him, she announced that were he ever likely to give vent to his murderous impulses she would have him hospitalised 'at the drop of a hat'.

Perhaps he had frightened her with the same bombast with which he sought to intimidate me. At our first meeting he bragged about the enormous sex drive that, he said, caused his wife such 'chagrin'. He boasted that he was the life and soul of the party, and went on to tell me, as though he were Marvel Comic's Incredible Hulk, that when he was angry he hit cookers, doors, freezers and fence-posts. He even broke his hand, his punch was so tough. Then, further straining credulity, he said that he was once so

73

enraged he hurled his wife's washing machine, full of laundry and soapy water, out of the kitchen door. It was an absurd caricature, Grand Guignol.

Yet his violence seemed real to him, frighteningly so. He looked to me, or so he said, to deflate his self-aggrandising delusions, 'to sock it to him'. Similarly he looked to his son, to jump on him every morning to wake him up. He grumbled that a previous therapist had not roused him in this way, that she had been insufficiently confrontational.

Soon I understood why. For, despite the graphic detail with which he recounted his sexual and physical exploits, they became a monotonously repeated formula – dreamlike and, perhaps for that reason, soporific. Was I suffering the same drowsiness he said he suffered between sessions when, as he put it, he became an 'aut-o-mat-on', akin to the round-and-round, going nowhere cycle of the 'laundr-o-mat'?

Valiantly he tried to shock himself and me awake by recounting ever more dramatic symptoms. He arrived one day to tell me he had succumbed to gambling again, stuffing money into a one-armed bandit. He likened it to a woman, to the gadgets his mother played at the beach when he was a child. Not casino, cards, or horse-racing. They never gave him the same buzz.

Onlookers in the pub had marvelled how, in a single evening, he could ram over £150 into the fruit machine. His audience, he said, credited him with being a veritable '*machismo* Svengali'. Others were provoked. His older brother, Andrew, threatened to haul him off to Gamblers Anonymous.

Mark hoped that his women would respond, as his mother had, by babying him. He hoped that, by recounting his latest spree, he would get me to look after him as his mother apparently had before he was shocked into discovering his father's prior sexual claim on her. He hoped his gambling would also elicit Camilla's sympathy. After his latest jaunt he had gone home and pathetically told her he was no good, that he had lost all their savings, that she should take their son Nicholas and leave before he did them any more harm. It had the desired effect. 'Poor lamb,' she cooed, just as she and his previous wife Dawn had so often done before when he regaled them with tales of his betting.

Like other therapy patients, he wanted me both to shore up and expose the fantasies involved. If his previous therapist failed him by being insufficiently active, he dreaded I might be the reverse. He likened the threat I posed his dreams to his fear of his soldier nephew being killed in the Gulf War. Then, Mark said, he would have 'nothing to believe in but the daisies'.

Often he left angrily. Worst of all was the time I disabused him of the idea of ever recapturing and realising his 'negative' Oedipal wish, as Freud termed the boy's homosexual desire to supplant his mother in bed with the father.[6] Mark still found Mr Davies 'physically beautiful, and mentally wonderful'. He longed to be filled with him, with his intelligence. 'I love him to death,' he told me. He then recounted an occasion when, baulked in displacing his mother in his father's desire for her, he instead displaced his wife Camilla in imagining himself to be the sole object of his brother Matt's sexual longing.

Matt had come into a fortune, just as their father had. He owned an enormous house in Hampstead. The previous week he had come to stay with Mark and Camilla. Mark loved it. It was just like old times when, as teenagers, they shared the same bedroom. They were such soul mates. 'Like a flower', Matt, usually so closed to others, opened up to Mark. It was marvellous, especially as Camilla obviously felt excluded, like a discarded puppy, said Mark, hopelessly seeking its master's affection. Mark glowed in recounting the scene to me. Yet it also made him feel it was my doing that his Oedipal wish could never come true, that he could never realise the bliss he wanted with his brother, just as he unconsciously wanted it with their father.

He hated me for being this killjoy wrecker. He started missing sessions. Then he came back, to insist he was no dreamer. He had half a mind to see me the previous week, he said, just to prove to me that it was no fantasy but reality, an abscess on his hand, that had kept him away. Nevertheless his attendance became more and more sporadic – until, like the schoolmarm bureaucrats he had earlier derided, I delivered an ultimatum: either he show up regularly or we would have to stop.

He chose to quit. Therapy, he wrote to me, had exposed 'some of the dark corners of my mind to considered thought'. Ultimately, however, he felt unable 'to face up to the issues raised'. Instead he preferred to sink back into what he had once referred to as his Walter Mitty reveries.

He was still prey to being angrily awoken to reality, as I learnt when we met many months later. One time, he told me, a chap in the pub had bragged to him how, when his first child was born, he would still expect his wife to feed him first. If she didn't, the man said, he would leave her and go back home to his mum. Irritated by this mirroring of his own childish demanding self, Mark told the man he would want to look after his son when he was born. Mark knew, he was a father himself. At this his drinking partner guffawed, 'You! You're nothing but a drunken layabout.'

Mark was outraged. How dare this man question his sense of himself as patriarch? The chap might be physically bigger, but Mark would not stand for his slights. He took him outside and 'demolished' him. Repeatedly he hit, punched and kicked him; he would happily have unmanned the fellow altogether and broken every bone in his body so that he would not be able to move, let alone walk away.

Nevertheless, it left Mark fearful of being bested by other men in any future fights. He worried he might have his teeth knocked out, as he had once before. With this he drew my attention to his newly capped incisors – twice the size of their originals, he told me.

He settled for proving himself a man symbolically. He had been threatened with eviction. His brother Matt's marriage to Lucy had collapsed, and to pay her maintenance Matt would have to sell Mark's Sheerness home (which Matt had bought for him when he quit work). Sheerness, Mark admitted, was certainly no Mayfair, but living there was nowhere near as humiliating as being turfed out into council 'bed and breakfast' accommodation. He decided to get a job, but his search proved futile; he was not shortlisted, let alone interviewed, for anything, high or low. It made him so angry he attacked his head. He shaved off his hair. Like a teenage punk, he acted the coxcomb. 'Puffed up like a cockerel', he strutted up and down, staring people out, frightening them into thinking that, given half a chance, 'he could knock anyone off their perch'.

His 'Neanderthal pose' and phallic brag might have convinced others, but did not convince him. Perhaps it was done to get others to gratify his Oedipal wish, like that of Freud's Wolf Man patient,[7] to become the masochistic object of his father's punishment. He was, he said, 'dying for someone to whack him, to give him a good spanking'. This gave way to another wish: to do away with his brother Matt's ex-wife Lucy so he could again enjoy Matt to himself. Anyway, he reasoned, Lucy was never any good for Matt, neither as wife nor homemaker; Mark hated her and her 'sparkling intelligence'.

He started writing a murder mystery, in which Lucy would be principal victim. He would make it funny, like the stories of his hero, the manic-depressive comedian Spike Milligan. But Mark's novel became too serious – a tale in which Lucy would be gruesomely killed, and readers persuaded it was he, Mark, who had done the deed. 'Horrible' was an understatement, so dreadfully would he, the narrator, mangle 'his brother's keeper'.

At first his rivalrous hatred of Lucy fired him with energy. He wrote day and night. Then he lost heart. He could never finish or submit anything for publication lest it fall short of the ideal by which he sought to emulate the men in his family. If only he could settle for less – send in a snippet – as Matt apparently had to a distinguished scientific journal, on the strength of which he had been elected to the editorial board. Mark, by contrast, could never complete anything, even the clinic's routine questionnaire.

All he had were dreams of becoming one with his godlike image of his brother and father. He wanted me ritually to cleanse and absolve him of the sins that tarnished his self-image. He wished I could look into a crystal ball and tell him when he would stop being crazed.

His recourse to religious and magical metaphor was in keeping with that favoured generally by men, according to Dostoevsky's Grand Inquisitor, when faced with the threat posed to their faith in God by the reality of evil. Wrongdoing certainly did Mark no good. His father was still indulging his lust for young girls. Sunk to the level of peripatetic odd-job man, Mr Davies still harassed teenagers he met at work. With mixed admiration and contempt Mark dubbed him 'a wolf bunged in among the chickens'.

Only the other day his father had shamefacedly admitted that he was having an affair with another virtual child, Rosie, whom Mark had first met when she worked in Mr Davies's garage (just as Dmitri Karamazov meets the girl who is his undoing through her working for his father). Dmitri ends up paying with twenty years' hard labour in Siberia for his folly in never outgrowing the child's wager of inflating his self-esteem through phallic rivalry with his father. Mark's outlook was similarly bleak. He was still marooned in the Oedipal dream of equalling the glories he attributed to his sire. Ideally, Freud once wrote, we are woken – indeed this fantasy is destroyed – once we construe the mother's absent penis as signifying the danger that our Oedipal desire will be punished with castration. Or, like my next character, we perversely disavow her lack.

II

Acting-out Rebels

6

Pervert

> This abnormality [fetishism], which may be counted as one of the perversions, is, as is well known, based on the patient (who is almost always male) not recognising the fact that females have no penis – a fact which is extremely undesirable to him since it is a proof of the possibility of his being castrated himself. He therefore disavows his own sense perception which showed him that the female genitals lack a penis and holds fast to the contrary conviction.
>
> Sigmund Freud, 1940[1]

Therapists and caseworkers, influenced by the work of US psycho-analyst Robert Stoller,[2] often attribute perversion to eroticised hatred of the mother for not being 'good enough', as Winnicott might have put it. Men, it is argued, may then take out on others their hatred of the mother for failing them, while women take it out on their own bodies or on their children.[3]

Other analysts, adopting a version of Lacanian psychoanalysis, attribute perversion and homosexuality in both sexes to refusal to acknowledge the mother's vagina – her phallic lack – as signifying the place where the father comes into his own, as phallus.[4] This may involve defensive retreat from phallic to anal eroticism.[5] Or, as Kleinians put it, perversion involves enacting the fantasy of projectively identifying with, or intruding into the parents' sexual union out of envious hatred of their creativity, thereby losing the distance from them necessary for symbolic thought.[6]

But this means an entirely unwarranted conflation of, and reduction of homosexualities and perversions as if they were all the same. It also fails to explain the greater frequency of fetishism in men, which Freud attributed to their having more reason to fear the castration seemingly signified by women's phallic lack.

Arguably similar disavowal occurs in sexual abusers in so far as they attribute to their victims the phallus they disown in themselves. Why, though, does their abuse often only begin in middle age? Klein's account of the depressive position is, I think, helpful here. Generalising from the case of a boy she treated during the war, she argued that men may retreat from sexual rivalry with their peers because they imagine themselves to be castrated and too empty of anything good to repair the ill-effects of such rivalry.[7] I suggest that the same dynamic sometimes occurs in the sexual abuser who, depressively fearing and hating his own masculinity, aggrandises it in his victim, whom he then perversely experiences as victimising him.

Mr Benn was a case in point. He was in his late fifties, and was most particular I protect his anonymity. I never learnt his first name. I came to think of him as Mr Benn because his fastidious, suburban respectability reminded me of the eponymous hero of a children's TV series about a Mr Benn who fetishistically looks to the shopkeeper of a fancy-dress store to equip him with a variety of heroic garbs to cover up his felt lack of manliness.

My Mr Benn was just as punctilious. His manners were impeccable. On receiving my mid-December letter asking to visit he phoned to confirm the date I had suggested, and to wish me Happy Christmas. When I arrived at his gate, the fence augured a paragon of respectable good citizenship. Placards pinned to it declared CHILDREN SHOULD BE SEEN AND NOT HURT, and NO MORE COSMETICS TESTING ON ANIMALS.

Mr Benn himself was a model of decorum as he welcomed me in, ushered me through the hall decorated with a poem by one of his daughters, and into the kitchen where he offered me a cup of tea. A washing machine noisily declared his dedication to keeping everything clean. Apart from a discordant Ninja Turtle poster, the room was exemplary in its propriety, with respectable though faded Christmas decorations, soft-focus animal pictures, and an old-fashioned solid-framed wireless. In talking to me Mr Benn exuded a similar air of old-world solidity, caution, precision and courtesy. Recounting his tale, he often paused to correct a word here, a phrase there. He regularised it all. He sought to make everything just right.

His major objective was to convince me of his probity; that he was more sinned against than sinning. True, he acknowledged, he had had sex with his daughter Rebecca when she was thirteen. But the school had indecently over-reacted to her disclosure, after she had calmly kept quiet about it for over a year. Would that others had been so circumspect. Instead the headmaster, police and social workers had impetuously intruded. They never stopped to think before rushing in: the headmaster immediately informed the police; the police in turn misled Mr Benn about getting a solicitor; the social workers instantly whisked not only Rebecca but also his other daughter into care.

The authorities had virtually destroyed him. They had left him 'gutted', voided of himself, castrated, 'as if half my body had been chopped off'. He likened their emasculation of him to that of a teenager, once he turns eighteen and is suddenly deemed man enough to become a soldier and die for his country.

Perversely disavowing generational boundaries, as though he too were still a boy, Mr Benn projected all responsibility for his abuse of Rebecca onto others, first and foremost on to those who most accused him of it. Everybody but himself was at fault. Then, confusingly, he insisted that he was always even-handed in apportioning blame, that he held himself just as responsible as others for anything that went wrong.

Given this contradictory account it was hardly surprising that Mr Benn sometimes experienced himself as irrational, as 'muddle-headed and therefore dangerous', as his doctor once summed him up. He worried that, being a psychologist, I too might judge him crazy. At the same time he courted, or perhaps more accurately pre-empted, this opinion of him with a notice stuck to his front gate announcing to outsiders: BEWARE – LOONIES INSIDE.

It completely contradicted the sane child protection and Greenpeace posters beside it. But there they were, next to each other. He experienced himself in the same divided way. Most of the time he felt he was a pillar of the community, absolutely irreproachable. Then another figure would creep up – an alien demon – and, with 'yippee' whoops of glee, take him over. That must have been what happened, he reckoned, when he abused Rebecca. Someone invaded him or he must have stepped outside himself.

Surely, he insisted, others must have realised the situation was dangerous – a 'mother' looking after three children on his own. So saying he disavowed not only his responsibility for abusing Rebecca but also his sex. In all seriousness he several times referred to himself as a woman. Or, in excusing himself, he elided the sexes. He was no worse, he implied, than the Liberal Party leader, Paddy Ashdown, just then accused of having an extra-marital affair. It was not Ashdown but the public who were at fault, with their prurient interest in his supposed mistress. They probably also wanted to know 'her inside trouser leg measurements', Mr Benn added, as though she were a man. Another time Mr Benn referred to God – as 'he, she, or it' – forgiving him his offence. Then he lauded the band of 'unsung hero housewives' with whom he allied himself.

He was not a man, he emphasised, certainly not the man to abuse his daughter, even if the prominent macho insignia and bulky key ring attached to the thick leather belt of his jeans told a different story. Meticulously stressing the middle syllable, he told me he was 'im-*po*-tent' – a cripple. When I first arrived he made much of his disability. He leant on a crutch as he opened the front door to me. When he sat down, he kept his stick prominently in view, hung over the back of his chair. If this were not enough to keep me mindful of his infirmity, he added that his doctor said he was 'not man enough' to go through hip replacement surgery for his arthritis. He then told me of yet another of his disabilities, his 'stress incontinence'.

His relatives and friends saw him as a self-pitying coward. He was, indeed. In his more depressed states of mind he likened himself to an empty marmalade pot, or a spent elastic band. It was the same with his dreams: in one he featured as a broken-down car; in another as a vehicle filled with water, reminding him of a woman he knew who suffered housemaid's knee, and of a neighbour's paraplegic daughter.

Making much of his own handicaps, he sought to blind both himself and me to the potency and power as a father that he had exploited in seducing his daughter into having sex with him. In the process, he distanced himself from a host of hated childhood images of masculinity.

His story began with a memory of street urchins noisily intruding into his sleep, when he was a baby, with their jangling bicycle bells. Later, as a schoolboy, he claimed, a gang of boys put him into a moving cement mixer. His father acted with similar disregard for his well-being. He put him and the whole family in danger during the Blitz by dragging them all to London, week after week, and down 'Bomb Alley'. Another time he terrified his son by getting him to swim miles out to sea.

His father, however, also taught him how to use ill-health to avoid the hazards of masculinity. He got himself invalided out of the Navy just in time to avoid being sent overseas in a ship that, on the very next voyage, was torpedoed and sank with all its men on board.

Closer to home, Mr Benn's father introduced him to the risks of male sexuality. Often men came to the house threatening to murder his father for sleeping with their wives. As a boy Mr Benn used to '*cringe*', he said, insinuatingly drawing out the vowel, when those ferocious cuckolds came to the door. No wonder he grew up to opt for sex with his daughter rather than with grown women; the latter might embroil him in dangerous sexual rivalry with other men of his own age. After all, such competition had endangered his father's very life.

He never learnt to be a man, he said; his father was too busy womanising to teach him. He was never around. He had 'too many other fish to fry' even to play football with him. Worse still, his father's repeated sexual imbroglios resulted in his being eventually ousted for ever from Mr Benn's childhood home by his irate wife.

She too might have been having affairs, but Mr Benn did not want to know anything about that. True to Lacanian accounts of perversion,[8] he would not countenance the fact of his mother's phallic involvement with his father. Yet she must still have been having sex with him, since she gave birth to yet another child, Mr Benn's second sister, just after they parted. She must also have been sexually involved with other men, the man she married, for instance, after divorcing Mr Benn's father. But Mr Benn preferred to think of his stepfather asexually, as a woman like himself who, Mr Benn added, just happened not to be as good at making tea.

He was thirteen when his parents separated, the same age as his daughter Rebecca when he abused her. When his parents divorced he identified so closely with his mother's assumed grief that he broke down in tears. It had been absurd, he complained, the way people told him off, saying it was not manly to cry. Of course he cried. He was still a child. Yet everyone unreasonably expected him not only not to weep but also to be the man of the house, now his father was gone.

One cannot be forced into masculinity, he insisted, especially given a father like his who never taught him how. As a worker, Mr Benn went on, his father was 'jack of all trades and master of none'. As a lover he made a mess of things to the end. He even made 'a balls-up' of his death. He died of a stroke in the house of a woman whose child everyone assumed was his, but it later transpired he was not the child's father, he had never had sex with the woman and his relations with her were purely platonic; an utterly unselfish matter of him looking after her.

Weakly his father had let himself be misunderstood, just as Mr Benn often was. He too, he complained, had always been mis-judged as a hopeless incompetent. As a boy his school reports described him as useless. By contrast, the headmaster seemed to him to be perfection itself. A monumental figure of strength, he ruled with a rod of iron. Mr Benn remembered him as at least fifteen feet tall and as many stone in weight. In keeping with the character type ascribed by Freudo-Marxists to those who most readily become prey to fascist authoritarianism,[9] Mr Benn both deplored and marvelled at this man's rule of law. He left school for a similar regime in the army, after first working on the railway.

His military job took him overseas, and it was there he met the first of his three wives. With their entry into his story it became clear that, disowning the abusive side of his masculinity, Mr Benn projected it into the grown-up women in his life, just as Nabokov's paedophile narrator in *Lolita* projects his own heartlessness into the mother of the twelve-year-old 'nymphet' he seduces.

Mr Benn had always hated women. He was a misogynist long before he met his first wife. Ever since birth, it seemed he repudi-ated his mother. He said she was 'terrific', but mostly he let me know how dreadful she was. It was not he who was the dangerous uncaring parent; it was women. Having babies no more made his mother maternal, he maintained, than it did any of his three wives. His mother completely botched up the job. Damagingly so. When he was a baby she skewered him with a nappy pin, sticking it right through his gut. Not only did she put his nappy on, he added sarcastically, 'she literally attached it to me'.

She was no lady. She was a cantankerous old bag, a dragon, a foul-mouthed fishwife. She shrieked at the boys who woke him as a baby, berating them as 'noisy sods'. Mixing up and reversing who most abused whom, Mr Benn went on to emphasise what a *'pain'* he must have been to her, never going to sleep. Did he think he had masochistically invited her abuse? Several times, he said, she tried to drown him. She even threw him over a bridge into the river, he claimed, because his crying irritated her so. Only his father's timely intervention saved him.

Later Mr Benn infuriated her with his schoolboy 'slugs, and snails, and puppy-dog tails' masculinity, and with the tadpoles he insisted on bringing home. Had he wanted to provoke her wrath? Whatever the cause, Mr Benn indicated, she was often virulently angry.

She was also a dreadful cook. She burnt the toast so often the sink was black with its scrapings. The family would have starved but for the marvellous Sunday lunches his father cooked – traditional British roast beef, deliciously drenched in its juices, topped with Yorkshire pudding. Other men also came to his rescue. The grocer, for instance, made good his mother's deficiencies and those of wartime rationing by supplying under-the-counter provisions.

By contrast with these men's munificence, Mr Benn recalled his mother as barren and empty, emaciated and so ill that her body became rotten with boils. If she had been left to her own devices he would have been deprived of everything – knowledge of sex included. If what he learnt was smutty and the result of filthy kerb talk, it was her fault. She tried to keep him totally ignorant of sex, even hiding the newspaper when it carried a story about the use of frogs in pregnancy testing.

She, not he, was to blame for his warped sexual ideas. Warped they certainly were. Above all anti-female. Telling me for instance how 'peeved' he had been at his sister's wartime birth (not least because it coincided with the end of the baskets of Easter eggs he enjoyed before the war began). Mr Benn described how, as a child, he thought hens' eggs were delivered by squeezing their necks. Imagine, he said, all the throttled chickens it took to make the reconstituted eggs they ate during, and just after, the war.

Just as he overlooked the role of the cock in chicken reproduction, so he negated that of the penis in human sexuality. It was not the genitals – male nor female – that he remembered giggling about with other boys as a child, but tits and bums in which, of course, the sexes do not essentially differ as children.

As a grown-up he disowned his own genital sexuality. Instead he located it in women. He groused about the King's Cross prostitutes flaunting and imposing their sex on him when he worked on the railway, and deplored his first wife as a whore. It was undeniably as much his doing as hers that she fell pregnant almost immediately they got together, but he blamed both their children on her. They were no responsibility of his, he insisted. When the marriage ended he did nothing to support or keep in touch with them. Anyway, he said in self-defence, they would not want him to intrude.

His second wife was no better. Attributing to her the same lack of sexual interest to which he himself pretended, he castigated her as an absolute bitch, who showed her indifference to him by reading the newspaper while they were making love. She also squandered all his money.

His third wife was a slight improvement. But not much. She too never adjusted her spending to his meagre earnings. 'With due respect to the ladies,' he added, 'she was one of those women who was a "mum" but not a mother'. She gave birth, that was all. She was completely incapable of looking after children. Mentally and physically she just was not up to it.

Good riddance, he said of her departure. She left him their three children to look after – Leon aged seven, and two pre-school daughters, Rebecca and Imogen. Lucky she did. Otherwise she might have dragged them down into the gutter with her. True, his having to care for them put paid to his taking the exams necessary to gain promotion in his accountancy job. Indeed, he had to give up work altogether. He became a full-time housewife – a much better mother, he assured me, than his third wife had ever been. Nor did he ever remarry. The children came first.

Not for his wife, he maintained. Even when their children were tiny she kept wicked company. Then, as though she were prone to the same disavowal of sexual difference as himself, he told me she left him to have a succession of affairs with lovers of either sex, regardless of their gender.

No sooner did her older daughter, Rebecca, become sexually mature than she too became the repository of Mr Benn's hated, disowned and split-off sexual appetite. When she was thirteen, he said, she became 'an absolute pig'. It made him think all children were 'a pain in the arse' – always ready to take advantage of their parents. Rebecca stayed off school. She spent all day at the park, a well-known drugs haunt for everybody and everything suspect and no good. Before, it had been her mother and now it was Rebecca who went to the bad and risked dragging her sister Imogen down with her.

Mr Benn was not the man to stop it, or so he claimed. He called in the police, but they were no help. A policewoman did come round, but her only advice to Mr Benn was to keep the girls at home. That was a fat lot of use: if he had been able to control his daughters he would never have had to call in the police.

The authorities had only themselves to blame, he went on, when he subsequently took things into his own hands by sexually abusing Rebecca to teach her a lesson – to shock her into going back to school. It worked: within a week she had returned to class. She recognised the worth of his strategy. That was why she did not disclose his abuse until eighteen months later, and then only at the instigation of her 'namby-pamby' boyfriend. What a sap. He wasn't even heterosexual.

The foster mother to whom Rebecca was then sent was no better. Without wishing to be 'deleterious' to the lady concerned, Mr Benn censoriously judged her 'rough and ready ways' as making her as bad as all the other women in his tale. He hedged his misogyny about. His son Leon, at least according to Mr Benn's account, was a straightforward male chauvinist. Not so Mr Benn. He was much more mystifying.

It was yet another ruse to prove himself the innocent. As for abusing Rebecca, although Mr Benn acknowledged planning to do it, he also insisted he remembered nothing about the actual abuse. He lodged all knowledge of it in her. He congratulated himself on accepting her word for what had happened.

He himself denied any participation – as a man. It was a matter of oral sex – not her on him, he emphasised, but him on her. Not fellatio but cunnilingus, the recourse, as Lacan once observed, describing the impotent lovemaking of Freud's patient Dora's father, of men without means.[10]

In Mr Benn's estimation it was not he but the women, including his daughter, who had the means, the potency. He attributed to them the aggressive sexuality he disowned in himself. He called Rebecca 'Mate'. Obligingly she took on his projection. She became the leather-clad macho biker he wanted her to be, as I could see when we happened to meet.

He soon cast me in a similar mould, as an agent of phallic intrusion and attack. We had hardly started talking at our first meeting when, with smug outrage, he said, 'Hello? Is that a dog I see in my garden?' Guiltily feeling responsible for this canine intruder, I jumped up, went out, shooed the dog away, and shut the gate I assumed I must have left ajar on entering. Yet I still remained the baddie. On my next visit, Mr Benn told me he had not been able to sleep – my questions had so upset him. They really troubled him, got him down, left him feeling quite ill. He hoped it would be better now we had got the 'shitty bit' of the abuse out of the way. It had all been my fault for raising the subject in the first place.

He worried that my visits might spoil his relations with Rebecca – as if he had not done enough on that score himself. Again he made me feel the wanton intruder. I found myself apologising for visiting when she happened to be there. Not for nothing. He made this – Rebecca being home – a reason to cancel our next two appointments, at the very last moment. He made no apology for any inconvenience he might have caused me. Quite the reverse: he relished making things difficult. He felt I deserved no better. With malicious glee he smiled when I arrived in heavy fog, shaken after witnessing a horrific traffic accident, and was fooled by his broken doorbell.

Yet it was again I, not he, who ended up feeling the sadist for exposing what he called his 'can of worms'. He made me feel I was no different from two WRAC officers who he said raped him and his cousin when they were thirteen. The two boys stood no chance against these viragos. They had grabbed hold of the lads, sat on them, masturbated them, thrown them into a ditch, and left them there, without their trousers. I was no different. Why else had he only just remembered this incident after all these years?

It marked the climax of what he had all along sought to persuade himself and me: that it was others, me included, who were the abusers – not him. It was as though I were the whiplash upper-class heroine of Strindberg's *Miss Julie* with Mr Benn as my abject valet. Yet however much he played the part of downtrodden servant, he also forcefully made me mind my step. He made me careful not to mention his abuse of his daughter again, to humour him instead with talk of his sufferings.

Unwittingly – unconsciously – I found myself colluding. The more I went along with his masochism the more he confided in me. He became increasingly intimate. So much so he warned me to watch out: it could lead to sex. Was this the way he had wormed his way into his daughter's bed? Certainly, he told me, they often engaged in heart-to-heart chat in which she pitied him just as I found myself doing.

Given the see-saw of his story between innocent victim and guilty abuser, with one perspective readily eclipsing the other, perhaps the whole story would never emerge. But one thing was apparent: no sooner did Mr Benn feel secure in winning me over to his image of himself as completely lacking in masculinity, no sooner had he successfully evacuated it into others – letting me know, for instance, that unlike other men he had no interest in pornography – than he confidently teamed up with the great and the good.

He ended by reminiscing about George VI, or 'Dear Bertie', the name by which, Mr Benn reminded me, the Queen Mother used to belittle the late King. He talked about this royal personage as though he were a close friend. Once, he said, he had been within touching distance of him when the royal train passed through the railway siding where he was working. Since the King's death he noted it every year in his diary: there it was, by the date of our last meeting. Mr Benn remembered, as though it were only the day before, the billboards announcing his end.[11]

Mr Benn too could have died. The newspaper exposure of his offence nearly killed him – this man whose moral watchword was not guilt in his own eyes but shame in the eyes of others. So he was thrilled when, as I left for the last time, I caught sight of a certificate on the wall announcing he had been voted 'Super Dad' by a local TV station. What a contrast: with his being on probation for sexually abusing his daughter that had first brought me to his home. Testament indeed to Freud's diagnosis of perversion as 'now you see it, now you don't' phallic disavowal.

7
Wimp

> I would say that it is in order to be the phallus, that is to say, the signifier of the desire of the Other, that the woman will reject an essential part of her femininity, notably all its attributes through masquerade. It is for what she is not that she expects to be desired as well as loved.
>
> Jacques Lacan, 1958[1]

Contrary to Lacan's observation, women more often pretend to femininity, to having no masculinity, just as Mr Benn did. It can be fetching. Indeed, that is its intent, as Kleinian analyst Joan Riviere observed regarding women who seek to avert others' hostility to their seemingly stolen male professional success by playing the incompetent, the castrate.[2]

In men this tactic is more risky. The homosexual, for instance, may, according to Anna Freud, deny his masculinity in courting and exaggerating that of his lover.[3] But he thereby chances rejection. For, by contradicting his own sex, he makes others feel uneasy in theirs.

Or men avert such anxiety by guying their bruited lack of masculinity. Examples include *Portnoy's Complaint* in which Philip Roth's anti-hero makes comedy of his endless whingeing, kvetching and masturbating as futile gestures towards proving himself a man. Protested lack of masculinity is likewise the subject of Woody Allen's films and, in real life, denial of his status as her father was used to excuse his alleged sexual abuse of his adopted stepdaughter.

By contrast, the following case, stripped as it is of any veneer of self-parody, highlights the harm done by such acted-out self-emasculation in inflating the male authority of others. It concerns a twenty-four-year-old, Barnie, who was so gawky in his manner that he seemed an overgrown child. With his gangling figure and long thin face, still baby soft with no apparent trace of beard, I took him for a boy. His probation officer, Derek, who had already known him for some time, made the same mistake. He told me Barnie was the youngest in his family. In fact he was the oldest by several years.

Like a toddler, however, Barnie whined, albeit about grown-up matters. When we first met, while Derek was on the phone, he moaned to me about his rent. It was so high, so unfair. Perhaps he griped in the same way to others, with some measure of success. The next time I met him, awkwardly carrying a hoover along the street, he had been rehoused.

He took me indoors, then sniffled noisily as he recounted his woes. His lack of masculinity was mirrored in the meagreness of their telling – his speech inarticulate and hesitant, quite unlike that of the fast-talking Woody Allen. He took ages to absorb what I said. The cogs of his mind slowly ground into motion as, under his breath, he reformulated my questions to himself. Eventually he found something to say, but his responses were so sparse that I despaired of them ever amounting to a story. The empty silence with which he greeted my comments often led me to reword them, rooting around how best to make contact, like Philip Roth's Mrs Portnoy quizzing her son as he jerks off behind the closed bath-room door.

Barnie was not averse to my attention. He craved it. Happily he told me what to others might seem too shamefully embarrass-ing, about the baby details of his life. 'I was never spoilt,' he said, 'I never had toys bought for me – just the basics. All my other mates had everything bought for them. Matchbox cars, toys, everything. Not me.' His parents, he said, never took him out. They kept him in or only let him play in the garden. 'I was the type of child that never went to other people's houses. They came to me.' He depicted himself as an *ersatz* Walter the Softie, from the children's comic the *Beano*, playing in his paddling pool. It was a far cry from the Action Men toys the other boys owned.

Then, he grumbled, when his sisters were born, four and five years after him, whatever playthings he had were all thrown out.

Barnie too: he was evicted from his upstairs room and sent to sleep in a much smaller room downstairs that had once been the family kitchen. Now, he groused, it became a lumber room into which the family discarded not only him but all their other unwanted rubbish.

Barnie wallowed in being mistreated. He fondly recalled his father swinging him in a baby-bouncer: 'It was pinned to the ceiling by a sort of rubber band. He used to pull me down to the floor and let it go so I hit the ceiling.' But his mother stopped his father jigging him up and down, telling him Barnie was too much of a baby to stand it. Later she similarly infantilised him to his friends, telling them they had to go home early because Barnie had to go to bed.

Like Freud's Wolf Man patient,[4] Barnie oscillated in middle childhood between naughtiness and obedient conformity and sub-mission to others in the hope of winning their male attention. Like the Wolf Man he also suffered phobias, nightmares, which made him 'shiver and twitch', of 'fights or animals, particularly foxes' coming after him.

As a child his endless going on about his fears and timidity failed to secure its goal. Far from gaining others' masculine affirmation, it repelled them. Barnie tried to ingratiate himself with the boys at school. He made efforts to join in their 'rough and tumble' play – in French lessons, for instance – but they rejected his advances. So Barnie stayed away. He 'bunked off', spending his days with younger boys from another school. He remembered joyriding with them on a motorbike over rough ground and fields. But his teachers caught up with him, and punished him.

Barnie revelled in being thus recognised by male authority. He became positively loquacious when detailing its rules:

> On report you get given a card. You have to go to the teacher after each lesson is finished. He has to sign it. Then you have to go to another teacher. And at the end of the week you have to go to the headmaster. If there's any spaces – or you get a 'bad' in there – they want to know why you've been bad.

His teachers, however, soon excused him. Perhaps he irritated them in their masculinity as much as he did his fellow-pupils. They told his parents they could do no more for him, that he should go somewhere else. Barnie's parents accordingly sent him to boarding-school. This did not bother Barnie – or so he said. He loved the school's macho pursuits, the more authoritarian and rule-bound the better: cricket, football, cross-country running, riding, Highway Code, cycling proficiency test. Free of his usual hesitation, he reeled off its system:

> You lived in the house with sixteen people and a housemaster. You got set homework. And you had to do jobs around the house – chores. You had to make your bed. If it was not satisfactory, they stripped it. They made you do it again. If you were naughty you were sent to bed early, or you were made to stand under the stairs.

Barnie gloried in the school's military discipline: it was the first thing he mentioned in itemising what he most liked about this period of his life. The only problem, as he saw it – and he also phrased his reservations in terms of rules and regulations – 'was not being allowed to smoke unless you didn't get caught by the teacher', and having to get special permission to go home more than once a fortnight.

Tailoring oneself to an inflated image of male authority, however, is a precarious means of sustaining one's self-esteem. Barnie's was soon utterly undermined. Perhaps it was his infuriatingly cringing unctuousness – like that of Uriah Heep in Dickens's *David Copperfield* – that provoked his mother into telling him, when he was fourteen, that he was not her son, that he was adopted. She told him she had wanted a boy, but had been unable to bear one herself, so had adopted Barnie instead.

Evidently, Barnie concluded, he had disappointed her expectations of his sex. Why else had she told him then of his adoption? Taking himself to indeed be lacking in the masculinity he assumed she wanted of him, he told me how he wished he had never been born. He despaired of what would become of him and became convinced that there was now no hope that he would ever become brainy like his sisters. He felt he was nothing but garbage, like the clutter his mother was sorting through when she came across his certificate of adoption and first told him about it. He had pleaded with her to tear the document up – but that would not make him her son.

Perhaps he should try to find his real parents. He assumed, however, that they too would not want to know him, since they had not wanted him in the first place. He told himself he could never be a man now. He had lost the only father he had ever known. He was sure his biological father was no use – just someone who got into trouble like he did – perhaps he was even then imprisoned, scruffy and tattooed. At this Barnie told me he had a tattoo, on his shoulder. He had had his name printed there. He hated it. No respectable institution, he informed me, ever allows people in with marks like that. He loathed riff-raff – the dirty, smelly, unwashed company his misdemeanours had landed him with.

The Freudian analyst August Aichhorn attributed delinquency to failed superego identification with the father.[5] Certainly Barnie emphasised the lack of any such magnificent figure inside him. Once he knew that the man he had taken to be his father was not his real dad, he said, he felt he had no reason to forgo acting out his grievances against him and his mother – against their having deprived him of his birthright, his upstairs bedroom, and so on.

He stole and pawned his mum's jewellery, took money from his dad, and emptied the savings account they had opened for him. Why not, he asked, again stressing his emptiness: 'I didn't have nothing for myself. I just wanted something. I wanted to get my own back.'

He spent the money trying to win other boys' approval. He joined another lad in stealing his father's home-made wine. Walking the streets alone later that evening, Barnie was stopped by the police. 'When you're young,' he explained, 'you like to get into trouble.' He relished telling me the policeman's words: 'What are you doing with that wine?' he asked. 'Drinking it. Have you any objection?' Barnie retorted. His cheekiness earned him still more gratifying attention from the officer: he took him down to the station.

Cheerily, quite unlike his habitual petulance, Barnie stretched animatedly while telling me about this and another occasion which also culminated in his being apprehended by the police. He had been shopping. Returning home through the grounds of a local hospice he had started to clamber over a summerhouse in its grounds. Suddenly his foot went through the gazebo's already vandalised plasterboard ceiling. A woman walking below noticed and told him to come down; she said she had phoned the police. But when Barnie reached her, no police were in sight. Typical woman. It was a wind-up. Disgruntled that she had no more respect for him than he had for himself, he walked off.

Just then, however, joy of joys, three police cars *did* drive up, transforming Barnie's spirits from misery to excitement: 'I dived over this fence into someone's garden. I done a run.' The officers caught him and pulled him into their car. He climbed out of the window. Again he ran. Again they caught him, put him under arrest, and imprisoned him. The thrill was short-lived: the police soon let him go, with only a warning. They treated him as a mere boy.

Officially, Barnie was nearly grown up. Soon he would be sixteen, could leave school and go to work. His mother told him he would have to earn his own living now she would no longer be receiving Child Benefit for his upkeep. But, he protested, he was not fit enough to get a job. He then recounted the litany of minor ailments keeping him at home – nose-bleeds, bad back, veruccas.

Eventually, however, he was well enough, and got a job with a packing company. But he soon lost it. 'Provocation,' he said, leaving it unclear who most provoked whom. Boxes of aftershave went missing, and Barnie bought some from the lads who stole it. He wore it to work. Usually the manager ignored minor thefts, but when Barnie flaunted the evidence under his nose he had to do something about it. He did. He gave Barnie the sack.

It did not faze Barnie. Being noticed by the man – even if it meant being fired by him – endowed him, in Lacanian terms, with the phallic completion he craved. But the thrill evaporated quickly when his adoptive father – whose work as a commercial salesman had earned the family a big house, fast cars, and other bonuses – was made redundant and became a pen-pushing clerk (not much different from Portnoy's father) who ignominiously toadied to others and obsequiously did his boss's bidding, even though it meant crippling himself with overtime. More than ever Barnie felt the want of a man to bestow on him the affirmation for which he longed.

He tried to bolster himself by looking to other authorities to give him significance, and found it through the episode that led to his referral to the probation hostel where we met. The incident started innocently enough, on Barnie's birthday. He had been drinking in the pub with some other lads, and afterwards they walked across the surrounding country looking for a tractor to steal. Barnie lost his mates and, finding himself alone, wandered through the fields into a greenhouse in the lame hope of finding cannabis growing there.

Then he came to a barn. The door was fixed with a heavy lock. Barnie yawned complacently as, with growing confidence, he went on to tell me how he smashed the bar holding the lock in place. When he left, he could not make the door fast to cover his tracks. It made him nervous, so he lit a cigarette and, without thinking, or so he said, dropped the match. Next thing he knew, the straw on the floor was alight.

Hopelessly he tried to extinguish the flames. Giving up, he ran away, thinking all the time of the police. He kept glancing over his shoulder, looking and listening for them. Then he caught sight of what he had done. The barn was 'a massive fireball' in the distance, a nightmare realisation of an inferno wish. Gripped with excited horror, he felt physically sick. He shook. Hardly knowing what he was doing, in panic he ran across the motorway. Anything to escape. He tore his hands on a barbed-wire fence.

When he eventually got home he explained away the blood by bragging to his mother that he had got into a fight. Next day he could not resist boasting some more. He told the truth to a chap he knew. 'Silly prat,' was all his mate said, but he promised not to tell. Within the week, however, it was headline news: the conflagration was vast. Perhaps that was why his pals 'grassed' on him.

It gave Barnie satisfaction to know they recognised the immensity of his deed. It was the same with his adoptive father. he talked to Barnie about the seriousness of what he had done. He backed him up. So did the lawyers. The men all paid him due respect for the severity of his crime. Not so his woman probation officer: she got him excused prison, the usual punishment for arson. The court treated him, as he had been treated so often before, as a child. It was an anticlimax: he had committed an atrocity and all the recognition he got was infantilising probation.

He was being babied all over again. The probation officer was no different from his mother, he griped. She did not credit him with being man enough to have done the deed: 'She still reckons there's someone else involved. She doesn't believe I have the brain to have done it.' If only she had believed in him, he would have had the grit to study and get the qualifications necessary to go to university like his sisters.

Failing that, he tried to gain some self-esteem from the male authority represented by the punishment's curfew restrictions. With animation he recounted them, then went on to enumerate the Outward Bound programmes he had been sent on (a means by which probation, far from exposing and undoing the myths of masculinity that do such harm, reinforces them by sending its supervisees on quasi-military assault course training). True to the authoritarianism by which Barnie sought to boost himself, he delighted in the regime, including abseiling. He was sure it was his having abseiled that persuaded Mike, the probation hostel warden, to accept him as a resident.

Proudly Barnie also plied his probation officer, Derek, with details of the Outward Bound expeditions, and of a building course he wanted to do. He hoped to win Derek's approval, but his mewling calf-love had the opposite effect. Irritated by Barnie's fawning, Derek distanced himself by stressing that, unlike him, Barnie had no staying power, that he childishly flitted from one thing to another, and only wanted to go on the course to tag along with another boy who happened to be doing it.

Barnie's fellow-residents found him equally exasperating. Knowing his tendency to whine, they discounted his story of being adopted as yet another instance of his crying 'Wolf'. They stole his milk from the kitchen, he grumbled; he now kept it on the window-ledge of the room where we sat.

They also took his money. An Afro-Caribbean boy, Leroy, had

just intercepted a five-pound note Barnie's mother had sent him through the mail, and he had broken the lock on Barnie's bedroom door, got in and taken Barnie's radio. It gave Barnie another excuse to see the police, this time as victim, and he was at the station, telling them about Leroy's crimes, the next time I was due to see him. Leroy was sent to jail, but Barnie had no sympathy for him.

He kept all the sympathy for himself, cravenly cultivating self-pity. He made it and his timidity visible for all to see, emphasising his fear of intruders, for example by barricading the door of his room with his bed. The last time I saw him he had a hangover from a party the hostel warden had given the night before. Again Barnie had tried to provoke the men, this time the warden, by taking his beer and stashing it in the toilet. He added pathetically that a girl at the party had teased him, pinched his bottom, and run away before he could catch her.

It was the same in his home town of Durham. He told me how his girlfriend there infantilised him, treating him as though he were her baby brother. His younger sister did the same. She told him he was so pesky, such an irritating brat, that she would not let him come to the pub with her because he would only let her down in front of her boyfriend. She never gave Barnie a chance. Even when he did prove himself in male company by beating her at snooker she ruined his success by storming off.

Barnie went on to tell me that he wanted to become a commercial traveller like his father. Then he would be able to go places and have a business car, petrol, expenses, perks. But this image of himself soon relapsed into his more usual crybaby mode. Sadly he recounted how he would have to learn to live on his own. His parents would not always be there; already they went off on holiday without him. One day they would be gone altogether – dead.

He tried to buoy himself up with the thought of the lads both in Newcastle, where the hostel was, and back home in Durham. He told me they had all pleaded with him to stay with them over Christmas. Best of all, the police in Durham still had him in mind. Why, only the other day the constable on his parents' estate had stopped him in the street, when he happened to be delivering a summons to another chap, and asked Barnie what trouble he was into now. He had a reputation all right – with the men in Durham. He would go back there for New Year's Eve and when he returned to Newcastle he would be only too happy to see me again.

But it never happened. True to the emasculating portrait he had painted of his mother, she phoned to cancel our appointment. Barnie was not up to it, she said. Anyway, she added, there was no reason for him to be on probation. He was just a child – and crippled too. His troubles were all due to a deformity with which he had been born. It caused him so much pain. What he needed was nursing, not policing; she was taking him to the hospital that very afternoon.

Her talk reminded me of the feelings Barnie had evoked in me a fortnight earlier. Like Celia in Chapter 4, he had convinced me he was a victim who could not possibly look after himself. Someone, I had thought, should mend the lock on his bedroom door to protect him from the hostel's intrusions, from his barbaric-seeming fellow-residents, the torn and jagged furniture and floor-boards, the noise of the cars outside. Quite unlike my next character, he had convinced me he was a nothing of a man.

8

Tough Guy

His breaking open of cupboards and taking out articles, as well as his other destructive tendencies, had the same unconscious causes and symbolic meaning as his sexual assaults. This boy, feeling overwhelmed and castrated, had to change the situation by proving to himself that he could be the aggressor himself. One important motive for these destructive tendencies was to prove to himself again and again that he was still a man.

Melanie Klein, 1927[1]

Unlike the wimp, the 'tough guy' relentlessly drives himself to banish any lack of masculinity through ever-escalating acts of macho derring-do. But these actions can never achieve their object, since the male ideal they strive for is a fiction.

It was this self-defeating impulse that drove Melanie Klein's twelve-year-old patient, described in the above quote. Klein's explanation was that as a toddler he had seen his parents making love and wanted to displace one or other of them in the act, a desire for which he dreaded being punished with castration. It was in this mould he internalised them, as punishing, guilt-inducing figures. This was particularly so after his father died, his mother fell ill, and his older sister tyrannised over him; in self-defence he sided with these castrating figures by becoming aggressive himself. Hence his delinquency.

Freud too drew attention to the father-based superego determinants of law-breaking,[2] factors now often forgotten by today's counsellors. Instead, influenced by the work of Bowlby and Winnicott,[3] therapists tend to neglect the male element and attribute delinquency to thwarted maternal attachments resulting, for instance, from parental discord.[4]

103

Acting out our culture's masculine stereotypes is not of course confined to those who break the law, but it is often more obvious in them. I have accordingly selected the case of an offender, Keith, to illustrate this form of rebellion, which, like the other defences described in this book, only exacerbates the problems that cause it, by accentuating masculinity.

Keith's story reminded me of James Dean as Jim Stark in *Rebel Without a Cause*. The film took its title from a case history by the Freudian analyst Robert Lindner.[5] In the movie Dean is fearful of losing his manhood – a loss represented by his emasculated henpecked father, Mr Stark. He feels especially vulnerable when taunted by others calling him 'moo-cow' or 'chicken', and to prove himself he wrestles another teenager, Buzz Gundersen, to the ground and then races cars with him, as a result of which Buzz is killed.

Cars cost the real James Dean his life. But his tough guy act lives on, in men like Keith. He was twenty-five when I first met him with his probation officer, Bob. He confronted Bob just as Jim Stark confronts his rivals in *Rebel Without a Cause*, and just as the biker Marlon Brando confronts the sheriff and his men in *The Wild One*. Doubtless Keith modelled himself on some such romantic hero. He arrived at the office wearing oil-stained jeans, leather boots, a black cap and dark insignia-stamped T-shirt, reminiscent of Brando's leather gear and 'Black Rebels Motor Cycle Club' embossed jacket.

Keith made it his business to face down anyone, especially any man, who implied he was not the full-blown bully boy he cracked himself up to be. Was he into hard drugs? Bob asked. 'What, me? Not likely. That's for wimps.' The very idea of injecting heroin (of being penetrated as though he were a woman) appalled him. As for the spots on his arm, no. They certainly weren't due to any needle jabs. Far from it. They were scars from the broken glass of his most recent crash.

Then, talking man to man, Keith told Bob of the money he made from drug dealing, and of recent scientific research proving the medicinal value of cannabis. True, he did not like the idea of those Pakistani hands kneading it. 'You never know where they've been,' he added, as though they were no better than shit. That was why, he went on, he always smoked, never ate, cannabis. His racism, like his sexism, was a foil for his terror of becoming emasculated through ingesting or identifying with those whom white male society puts down.

He became enraged when Bob implied he was a pusher. Not him. No way. He would never be one of those wheedlers who wait outside schools to ponce off children. They had no manhood to lose, he indicated, when the police 'grabbed them by the balls and took them off'.

Then, suddenly, his tough-guy talk collapsed. Bob asked Keith how long it had been since he last saw his baby son, Jake, now living with Keith's estranged girlfriend, Nicola. At this Keith, who was adopted and for whom Jake was his only known blood relative, almost cried. Tears started to his eyes. It was months since he had seen Jake, and then only for an hour.

At this, and again like Brando brought to the point of weeping by a woman in *The Wild One*, Keith fended off his grief with macho display. He would abduct his son, he threatened, right away. He was not going to wait for any official court order to see him. After all, he was just about to be 'banged up' for drug dealing. By the time he got out Nicola might well have moved and taken Jake away from him for ever.

He would not stand for it, nor for being hurt or played around with by her. Take this for an example. She wanted a fridge. Right. He got her the biggest money could buy. He paid hard cash for it. All for what? When he took it round she told him she did not want it till the next day. He would not stand for that. He left it outside. She never took it in. Instead, he expostulated, she gave it to someone she knew he hated. Not content with that, she concocted a report with another woman, the welfare officer, making him out to be 'the biggest cunt under the sun'.

He fixed with his solicitor to have the report quashed. Women could really get you down, he went on, hoping to engage Bob in shared male misogyny. He would much rather go to prison with its devil-may-care male company than do community service, painting and decorating elderly women's homes. The work was OK, he added, but he hated it. Last time he had to paint an old biddy's toilet. He stood on the loo, to paint the ceiling, when along she came and told him to get off. Her pestering and the lavatorial context didn't do his manhood any favours – even though he tried to restore his self-esteem by asking her how the hell else she expected him to paint her ceiling.

But what a demeaning battleground. He wanted to get as far away from it as possible, back to the manly clashes of the street. He went on to recount one incident, as a finale to the story of aggression with which he sought to erase from his mind, and Bob's, his 'unmanning' unhappiness at the mention of his son.

Bob had asked him about his non-drug-dealing offences. By way of explanation, Keith launched into a tirade against a car driver who, some months earlier, had swerved and cut into him on his motorbike. The man damn near killed him: it was a matter of life and death. Worse still, he made Keith damage his bike. He had had to lay it on its side, away from the road, to prevent the man's car bumping into it. Being laid on the ground never did a bike any good, so as soon as he could, Keith got it back up, mounted it, and chased the guy. As soon as he got level with him – at the next set of traffic lights – he put his crash-helmet through the chap's windscreen and dragged him through the broken glass. He could happily have murdered him. 'Well,' he went on, 'you would want to kill someone if they tried to kill you.'

Having attempted to restore his masculine reputation in Bob's eyes, he left. Several months later I learnt more of the force impelling his act, the superego figure relentlessly driving him to prove himself a man, to prove himself different from his adoptive father who, like James Dean's father in *Rebel Without a Cause*, seemed to him an utter sap.

Keith had expected and almost wanted to be sent to prison. He served bail and was tried, but was then let off with a non-custodial sentence, which he served living first with his adoptive mother and then with her long-estranged husband, Mr Wood, because it was easier to get to his job from where Mr Wood lived.

Keith got work stacking slabs of stone in a local cement factory. While he was out his adoptive father acted as his minder and amanuensis. It was Mr Wood who phoned to arrange when it would be most convenient for Keith to see me; it was to him that

Keith handed the phone to give me directions, and it was he who opened the door to me when I arrived, like a welcoming housewife.

Like Mr Stark in *Rebel Without a Cause* Mr Wood was baby-faced, and tall but pudgy – a fitting figure on to whom Keith could readily project any unmanly unhappiness. Mr Wood's large stature belied an almost wilful femininity. Nervously anxious to keep in his son's good books, he jittered, asking if I would like something to drink. He winced when I replied I would like coffee, black without sugar. 'Too strong for Dad,' Keith added. Meanwhile Mr Wood put on the kettle and fixed the drink. Was it too hot, he worried, as he gingerly handed it to me in a dainty teacup. Then, still agitated, he shuffled from foot to foot in the kitchenette behind us, not knowing whether Keith wanted him to stay or leave. Finally he took himself off to a tiny back bedroom, and only felt at liberty to come out when Keith had finished.

Keith sought to distance himself as much as possible from this shambles of a man. It was the motor of his delinquency. His father's effeminacy – including his being ignominiously thrown out by his wife when their marriage had ended ten years before – was the main factor in the 'marital discord' contributing to Keith's lawlessness.[6] Through law-breaking he hoped to escape any similarity with him. In this Keith resembled the ex-con John McVicar who, in his autobiography, attributes his self-appointed cult of *machismo* to the desire to get away from the abjection of his father, signified by his wife throwing him out of their marital bed when John was six.[7]

McVicar vigorously denies being like his father. So did Keith. It would be too humiliating. Mr Wood cut such a sorry figure: he was not man enough to stand up to his wife; he had never owned a car; he couldn't teach Keith to drive. Instead, Keith added,

> He rides a pushbike . . . and very little else. When I go out, I tell him, 'Don't do anything I wouldn't do'. 'Why son,' he replies, 'if I did anything you did I'd be having a whale of a time.'

Left at home, like an abandoned housewife, his father cooked Keith's meals and made his packed-lunch 'sarnies'.

In the past Mr Wood had worked. He had been a bus conductor

for thirty years until he was laid off ten years ago, about the time his wife divorced him. Now he did not even have the bottle, or so Keith said, to stand up to the Jobcentre and refuse their offers of 'Re-start' work. He was so servile. Why else, Keith asked himself, did his father agree to subject himself to this exploitative scheme whereby the government massaged the unemployment figures?

Keith had been offered a job through a similar project. Unlike his dad, however, he refused even to go to the interview. Being paid little more than dole money for construction work for which other gangers were paid £290? It was a mug's game. 'I can graft as hard as the next bloke – but not for £90 a week.' Keith sure grafted. He shifted hundreds of concrete slabs every day – as fast or faster than the other men. Indeed, Keith boasted, it was because he was so strong and quick at the work that he was taken on permanently.

Keith stressed his similarity with other working men. That was why, he said, he had never been roughed up by the police. When he was a youngster he used to provoke them – bang around in the cell, and so on. Now, however, he treated the police as men with a job to do, just like him:

> The way I see it I'm just part of their work. You treat them like your mates. Anything to make your job easy, to make your life easy. If you eff and blind at them of course they beat you up. Not that I'd ever invite one in for a cup of tea. Don't get me wrong.

But he respected them – as blokes.

It was only idiots he had no time for, like the wally who served him with a summons for a bunch of minor motoring offences. 'I ask you,' he said, fishing a document out of a jamjar stuffed with glorious memorabilia – so different, he bragged, from everything else in his father's flat. 'Here it is,' he announced, reading the policeman's statement:

> At 4.30 p.m. Thursday 22 August, I was proceeding along Mill Street, approximately three quarters of a mile west of London Road,

when I saw a black Mercedes resting on its roof. It appeared to have been in a motor accident.'

Keith had been giggling on and off throughout my visit. Now he guffawed uproariously at the folly of the officer stating so pompously what was so blindingly obvious. Of course the car had been in an accident. Why else was it upside down in someone's front garden?

Keith made it his business to prove to himself and me that he was in no way an authoritarian wimp – like the policeman who booked him, or his father. Perhaps that was why Keith painted one of his cars maroon – to be different from the crowd. It was an old BMW. He had crashed it too. Taking off fast in a busy street he had collided with a delivery van that was backing round the corner. Daft really – the maroon. The police could spot him a mile off. The only BMW of that colour in all Norfolk. Not flash, but unusual. It certainly stood out from the cars of other, more slavishly conformist men.

As for his own get-up: in defiance of the midwinter cold, he kitted himself out in a sleeveless vest to display to best advantage to me, a woman, his hairy chest and tattooed arms. He made much of his physique. It was the same with his son, Jake. When I asked after him, he replied by boasting about the toddler's height and girth.

Meanwhile he lounged seductively in an easy chair, every bit the cool dude, lighting his cigarettes with a pistol, which emitted a flame at every press of the trigger. At first I was alarmed, not realising it was a toy. Keith repeatedly clicked the mechanism on and off to light and relight one roll-up after another. Heavily and sonorously he drew in their smoke to add weight to his words.

Ridiculous, really. But at the time it didn't seem a laughing matter, especially when Keith told me of a real weapon he owned – a spring-loaded, telescopic truncheon. Expensive. American. 'The game I was playing,' he added, 'you don't fool around. I might use it to whop someone who tried to take my girl. Or, if somebody tried to turn me over to the police, I'd sort them out with it.' But when I asked whether he had in fact ever assaulted anyone, he stalled angrily, inhaling long and loud. His weaponry was proof of his sexuality. How dare I question it or put it on the line? I had done it quite unconsciously.

Immediately I became aware of the threatening annoyance I had provoked. Keith soon let me know, telling me how, if anyone crossed him, he always exacted 'retribution'. I backed off. Fearful that he might act out against me the violence by which he sought to fend off his sexual insecurity, I tried to cool him down, to restore his confidence by inviting him to tell me his latest cops-and-robbers story.

He readily took up the challenge. A whole troop of policemen had been involved:

> Eighteen of the bastards came storming through the door. Eighteen! They turned the house upside down. There were seven in my room, seven down in the sitting room, and four turning the rest of the house over. I was up top doing the larger amounts of dope. The bloke downstairs was knocking out little bits. They busted me of whizz [amphetamine] that time. My mate was with us. He'd just come out of the Scrubs. Just done five years inside – for armed robbery. He had some stuff on him. But, to prevent him being sent down again, I told him, 'Give us it here.' So he got off. I took the rap.

Honour – sticking up for his mates – the watchword of male chivalry, even if it meant risking jail. Anyway, being locked up held no terrors for Keith: 'Prison? It's a doddle. Food's awful. Screws are awful. But the company's great. Live for the day. And who gives a toss for tomorrow?'

More even than his fearlessness he sought to prove his riotous male excess. He drove faster than anyone else, cut corners; took loads of whizz; got drunk. He pushed himself to the limit to show himself how far he could go. He had told his probation officer all about his driving. Now he regaled me with stories of his boozing. He put down any man who would not recognise his prowess: the effete doctor, for instance, who, following an unusually hard-drinking New Year's Eve, attributed Keith's loss of voice to a mere viral infection. 'I had fucking acute laryngitis,' Keith expostulated. 'Burnt my pharynx drinking spirit – Southern Comfort, whisky and brandy, topped with Coke – all served up by my girlfriend's brother. Viral infection? What a dolt!'

That was how he pulled his women, he told me: through drink and driving. He bagged Nicola the day of the annual Hot Rods meet. And his most recent girlfriend? He first met her at the pub. Almost as soon as she saw him she threw her arms around him and began dancing with him. As for sex, he passed it over just as he had my question about the truncheon. For the life of him he could not remember what had happened with the girl after they danced. 'The next thing I knew,' he insisted, 'I was in a strange bed, with a strange person. Been there ever since.'

Boozing was the making and breaking of him. So too was sex. One time, he bragged, he fucked a girl on the pool table to the applause of all the other men in the bar (suspiciously like the gang bang of film star Jodie Foster in *The Accused*). He told me no more. As with his violence, such sexual exploits were a boast intended to make himself big in his own and other men's eyes, not something he wanted to go into with a woman.

What he did want to let me know was that if he hurt women it was their fault. If only Nicola, the mother of his son, had gone with him to the pub that night he would never have gone with the other girl. If Nicola had been upset – their relationship ended because of the love bites and lipstick with which he was plastered when he returned to her the next day – she had only herself to blame.

He swore he had no idea what happened. It was a repeated story. He liked sex. It proved him a man. But messing with women also threatened to undermine his use of sex as defence against 'female-seeming' emotion. He preferred to blot out his dealings with women, or to talk about them indirectly, for example through an anecdote about a job he did when he was a motor mechanic. He had been fixing a female customer's car:

I had to change the clutch on her Renault 5. It sounds easy. But you have to take the whole front of the car off. It started off bad. First thing that happened was the bonnet cable broke. You had to take the grid off, get in as many extension bars as you could, and unbolt the bonnet. You've got about this much space, and you've got to point your torch in, get your tool in. Arrgh!

It lost him his job. Why? Because he told the foreman point blank he hated getting into and fixing this woman's car. How long, the boss asked, had the job taken? 'Fucking days, you cunt,' Keith swore, his eyes on the lady owner standing right there, at the counter.

He would rather get the sack than fail to stand up for his manhood, even if it was only threatened symbolically by having to get his tool into too tight a space in a woman's car. Nor would he mess with feminine-seeming feeling and chat. It was too unmanning, especially since – despite his fast, hard-hitting, expletive-ridden talk – emotional pain and grief left him at a loss for words. When I gave him space to tell me about his son, from whom he had been so long separated, he protested, 'I thought you were going to ask me questions.' He dreaded the sentimental female quagmire into which he feared my talk might lure him.

Nor did he like it when I invited him to expand on what he called his 'moodiness'. He immediately countered with: 'You can tell you're a psychologist, asking questions like that.' I was worried lest he attack me as he evidently often did others whenever he feared they might puncture his defensive male display. Without thinking, I replied, 'Well, we all have to earn a living. I can't fix cars so I have to make do with trying to fix minds instead.' But my facile attempt at trying to make him feel better failed. He greeted it with the derision it deserved. 'Oh yes. Very clever. I can fix a car. And I can tell one concrete slab from another.' It hardly equalled being a university teacher.

Fearing the emasculation signified by his want of education, but fearing still more the unmanning engagement with women's chatter, he took refuge in threats of action. Like many men who reckon women are likely to get the better of them with words, he preferred deeds. They spoke louder. So too did violence. He had beaten up his son's mother, which was why there was an injunction against him seeing the boy – except occasionally, and even then under supervision.

Indirectly he warned me he might blitz me as he had her.

Equating me, unwittingly perhaps, with a schoolmistress who taught him when he was a child, he recounted how once, when she came into the classroom, he tried to save himself from being punished for smoking by shoving the cigarette into his desk. Its contents went up in flames. It seemed he had been no different from Melanie Klein's patient, with whom I began this chapter and who fended off women symbolically with burning phallic attacks on their insides.

Seeking to protect myself from Keith's implied assault on my sex, without thinking, and in the manner of other cowed women, I found myself seeking to boost his male morale by flirtation. Appeasing smiles won him over: he was more than happy, he said, to see me again the next week.

When I arrived Keith welcomed me with open arms. He called over from where he was sitting, or rather lying, sprawled in the middle of the floor, surrounded by children and adults. Again his adoptive father, Mr Wood, had let me in. Again, unlike his son, Mr Wood felt uneasy. 'Oh dear, oh dear,' he wittered as he opened the front door, 'Keith has only just got back from work, and I haven't dared remind him you were coming this evening.' It was more than his life was worth, he indicated, to ask Keith to see me – now he was busy with family and friends who had just called round. I would have to arrange another time.

I did. But before I could return, Mr Wood phoned to say Keith could not see me. Was it because Mr Wood did not have the courage to remind his son of our appointment? Or because Keith could not bear to see me again in case my woman's talk would bring him down? Perhaps he refused another meeting because it would mean going back to his father's flat, from which he had just moved out to live with his latest girlfriend. It would mean getting back together, even if only briefly, with the man from whom he had so long sought to distance himself. Whatever the reason, Keith was not the first, nor the last, to defend against unhappiness by acting out an inflated, tough stereotype of masculinity.

9

Tomboy

The analysis showed, further, that the girl had brought along with her from her childhood a strongly marked 'masculinity complex'. A spirited girl, always ready for romping and fighting, she was not at all prepared to be second to her slightly older brother... She was in fact a feminist; she felt it to be unjust that girls should not enjoy the same freedom as boys, and rebelled against the lot of woman in general.

Sigmund Freud, 1920[1]

In this quote Freud is describing an eighteen-year-old brought by her father for treatment of her 'lesbian rebellion' against him. We would call her a tomboy; and perhaps see nothing wrong with her rebellion. But it is important to recognise that the bravado described in the previous chapter is not confined to men. It is also a defence adopted by many women, often as a counter to sex discrimination. The problem is, however, that acting out male-dominated society's exalted images of manhood does women little long-term good as means of securing their liberation.

George Eliot observed as much many decades before Freud commented, as he did in his early work, on the social causes of women's ills.[2] True, Eliot adopted a man's name to get her books published. But she also showed that to adopt men's attributes wholesale, as the child Maggie Tulliver wants to do in *The Mill on the Floss*, to combat her mother's preference for her older brother Tom, only exacerbates the oppression such rebellion seeks to cure.

Many feminist theorists would argue the opposite. Decon-structing the various ways by which we are produced as women and men through prevailing 'discursive practices', some argue that

114

we should go beyond language and actively rebel against its gendered images through cross-dressing and other types of 'performative' transgression.[3] But, whatever the promise of such action as means of demonstrating gender's fictive character, acting out its categories only serves to reinforce them and the discrimination practised in their name, as the following case all too painfully demonstrates.

Toni was twenty-one. Jim, her burly probation officer, complained that she had just given him the slip. Then, defiantly, she arrived. Big-busted but petite (she was scarcely five feet tall), Toni contrived to make herself look Jim's equal, ready to take him on any day, calling him 'a black git' to his face and later to me. With her cropped hair, shoulders squared up, encased in an army greatcoat (a present from her stepfather), drawing on a dog-end, she looked with every muscle of her being the hardened prison lag. Jim countered her challenge with the threat of jail. He read her the riot act. He told her, if she went on spending money on drugs rather than paying off her fines, she would be sent down.

It did not bother Toni. She let us both know she was a match for any adversary – big or small. With her fists she could take us all on. It was the same when I saw her alone. She swaggered down the hall, swinging the probation hostel keys, letting me into its official interviewing room. Collar turned down, sleeves rolled up, she proudly displayed fearsome love bites on her neck. Her masculinised name 'Toni' (short for Antonia) was tattooed into her arm. No need for me to sympathise or worry for her. She was no softie. She could look after herself. Her every movement shouted, 'Don't mess with me. I give as good as I get. I'd lay you out rather than argue with you.'

The previous day she had had a 'mega run-in' with Joan, one of the hostel staff. Joan, she said, had unfairly blamed her – just as her mother always did – for things that were actually the boys' fault. Enraged, Toni had threatened to break the hostel windows. She had almost hit Joan too. Her punch, she went on, was no joke. She meant business. The week before she had smashed her brother Konrad's girlfriend in the face; with just one blow she had broken the girl's jaw. Lucky Toni had not killed her, given the way she had gone on about how Toni's mother hated and rejected her.

Toni then regaled me with stories of how she had her mother's current husband, Paul, duffed up. She told me how, like her mother, who often beat her, she too had an evil temper. She fought anyone who crossed her – 'man, woman, beast'. It was the cause of her current brush with the law. A man had called her a 'slag'. He cast aspersions on her sexuality, and Toni replied by toughing it out. She shattered his windows – great big ones like those in the room where we were sitting. 'You'd better call the Old Bill,' she taunted him. 'I'm a girl, you're a bloke. Come and stop me.' But he was too scared – like a girl. He took her to court instead. Toni would have none of that. She did a 'runner'. It took over a year for the authorities to catch her up.

She had always been someone to reckon with. Even as a toddler she used to get into fights. Later she kicked the other girls in school, pulled their hair, brawled in the dinner queue, and challenged them to battle after lessons. When she worked in a factory she was sacked for fighting and laying into a workmate. The woman had goaded her, called her a 'tramp' because of her second-hand sweater and jeans. Toni reacted with the same violence when a passer-by called her a lesbian: 'I fucking hit her.' Then, Toni added as though to warn me, she shouted at the woman, 'Don't fucking criticise people you don't know. Just 'cos I look like a boy, it doesn't mean I'm a dyke.' People had better not call her that to her face. She was on a short fuse and had a ferocious punch. As a mark of her strength, Toni bragged about how she had recently fractured her hand by hitting it against a wall.

The first time she was arrested, she said, it took six policewomen to hold her down and handcuff her. Three of them then assaulted her. They put a mattress on the cell floor and hurled Toni on to it, then, while one woman pinned her down and another held the mattress, a third punched and kicked her. They didn't muck about. But Toni was more than ready for anything they could lash out: she got her own back. She bumped into one of the women on her day off, cornered her in a garage, tapped her on the shoulder, and slugged her in the belly. She 'decked' her, all the time jeering, 'No mattress for you.'

Toni was every bit a man. People even told her she talked like a bloke. 'I've been nicked, in a cell, questioned, beaten up – everything. I'm hard.' If she couldn't have a fight she'd pick one to get the scars. She wanted to go to prison, to see if it was true that you get beaten up there; it would sort her out, fortify her, make others frightened of her. Again she said, 'I'll fight anyone. I'm big built. More like a bloke. I want to go to nick. I'm hard.'

She started our next meeting in similar vein, making a big show of letting me, and a male hostel worker, know who was boss. As we went upstairs she cadged a cigarette off him ('I must be a sucker,' he griped). Soon, however, a quite different picture of Toni emerged, of the loss and wrongs she had suffered by virtue of her sex, against which her tough-guy acting out caused her more trouble than it cured.

Perhaps it was our being exiled from the smoke-filled, womb-like fug of the hostel office that exposed her benighted femininity. We had been relegated to her freezing bedsit, its coldness empha-sised by a prominent non-functioning radiator, its desolation pre-figured by the dregs of half-empty milk bottles and broken glass strewn on the stairs leading up to her room.

Toni had waited in all day to see me. Now I was there, frozen and huddled on her bed, my weakness elicited hers. Restlessly, like a caged animal, she roamed the room as if she could thereby escape my trapping her into feeling sorry for herself – a little girl, dwarfed by the cold winter light. Fretfully she kept on the move. She fidgeted, turned the bedside lamp on and off, paced the floor. Once she left and went downstairs, hoping the doorbell that had just rung was for her, that it would release her from me. She returned still agitated, nerves jangling. Her jitteriness made me aware, for the first time, of her smoking and of the cough that racked and interrupted her halting story.

It began when her mother Sonia, aged three, came to England with her family from Poland. Toni was born eighteen years later, when Sonia was twenty-one, the same age Toni now was. Too bad Toni had not been a boy – her mother much preferred men. Perhaps, Toni reasoned, that was why her mum always treated her as 'the black sheep of the family'. She even implied that Toni's birth was a disaster. Her father never saw her. He was killed going into the back of a lorry on his motorbike on the way to the maternity hospital.

Without him, and in her grief, Sonia abandoned Toni, even leaving the choice of her name to her mother. It was Toni's Nan, not Sonia, who decided to call her Antonia. Meanwhile Sonia was off courting. Within weeks she got pregnant by Dave, a Securicor officer whom Toni, for a long time, believed was her father. At this point, seeking any excuse to act rather than talk, Toni broke off to tip out the contents of a battered bag. It contained all her worldly goods. She rummaged through the pile.

From the middle she retrieved a photo, taken when she was ten months old, of her mother's wedding. Centre stage was Sonia, dark-haired like Toni but, unlike her, very feminine with a shocking pink mini-skirted outfit topped with bouffant hair. There she stood flanked by parents and heavily side-burned groom. She had her man, and soon also had a son. Unlike Toni, Sonia honoured him with a name from the country of her birth: Konrad.

Although, or perhaps because, Sonia favoured him, Toni idolised Konrad, just as George Eliot's Maggie Tulliver idolises her brother Tom in similar circumstances. Toni and Konrad grew up in their grandparents' house. Soon Toni suffered the first of many losses: when she was two the household was turned upside down by the sudden death of her uncle, her mother's older brother. Then Toni lost her home itself. When she was three her mother and Dave took her and Konrad away to a house of their own.

Perhaps these losses first launched Toni on her career of macho defensiveness. Certainly it was then she won her first scar. It was still visible on her face – the result of an accident she had banging a hammer when she was a toddler. When she grew up, however, she told others the gash was caused by someone smashing a bottle in her face. It marked her out as a seasoned fighter. She learnt to be such a character early, as a result of being knocked about by her mother's younger brother, Emil.

She became even more of a tough after her grandmother died when she was six. Hardening herself against any distress she might have felt about her Nan's death, she described it starkly:

Mum was making breakfast. I said, 'I'll take it up.' Well, I did. And there was Nan sitting up. Her eyes were open. I said, 'Here's your breakfast Nan.' And she didn't move. So I went downstairs. Grandad was back from his night work then. I said, 'Nan's mucking about. She's not eating her breakfast. She's awake. But she ain't moving.'

That was the plain unembellished truth – for Toni, not for the others. Her grandfather rushed upstairs, as did her mother Sonia, only to return in floods of tears. It was not until days later that Sonia emerged enough from her misery to remember Toni and explain to her what had happened. Even then she implied that Toni's Nan was still alive – in Heaven. Perhaps that was why Toni treated her as still living. She told me she could still sometimes hear her Nan, with her stick, 'thud, thud, thudding' around her room, keeping an eye on her while she slept, and calming her when she was angry and awake.

Sonia, whose experience of her mother had been as antagonistic as Toni's was to be with her, found no such comfort. Instead she sought it in a succession of lovers, throwing out Toni's stepfather Dave to make room for them. Dave's absence devastated Toni. He had been a real father to her, and although she was his stepdaughter, he was just as attached to her as he was to his son, Konrad. As proof Toni told me that he had given the twins he had by his next wife the same names, Toni and Konrad. But Dave might as well have been dead for all the notice he seemed to take of her over the succeeding years.

Toni reacted to the loss of Dave by becoming even tougher. She began shoplifting. When she was only six, she bragged, she was caught stealing. 'Rubbers. Ninety-nine of them,' she said, fudging whether it was a cache of condoms or erasers she had taken. The police stopped her and took her home. It was then that her mother really started beating her. Toni responded by being equally vicious both in and outside home. By the time she was seven she was renowned as the school bully.

But her hardness could not prevent further upset. When she was nine she was banished from the small space she had earned in her grandfather's and mother's affections when they both remarried. Toni's new stepfather, Paul, was quite different from Dave;

he was a great fat hulk of a stevedore. Worse still, within a few months of his appearance, Toni's mother bore him her second son, Kevin. 'Everything changed from that day.' If only she had been a boy, Toni mused wistfully, as she had at the beginning of her tale, perhaps Sonia might have treated her better.

But she didn't. Again Toni responded by siding with the favoured sex. Her mother was now more lost to her than ever. She had started drinking when she first took up with Paul, and by the time Kevin was born she was often completely befuddled. In her absence Toni took her place: she gave Kevin his bottles, changed his nappies, brought him to school with her, and, when he proved too disruptive, stayed at home with him. Her mother's only thanks was to take him back as soon as he became less of a handful, leaving Toni, by the time I saw her, with only the dream of being with him again. She was desperate for him to grow up and come to live with her. Meanwhile, without him, all she could console herself with were two tiny school photos of him stuck on her wall, and the boast that he looked just like her.

When she was a child she reasoned, as she still did, that she could only improve her lot by becoming a boy. Already tough compared to other kids in the country town where she and her family lived – 'I was hard – a Londoner' – now she made herself even more masculine by cutting her hair short. Shearing it had the same effect as it has on Maggie Tulliver in *The Mill on the Floss*. Just as persuading her brother Tom to cut off her locks only exacerbates Maggie's mother's dislike of her, Toni's cropped hair intensified her mother's discrimination. So she tried to mollify Sonia by growing her hair long again. It seemed to have the desired effect and her mother warmed to her (perhaps because Paul was away in prison). At last Sonia put Toni first, along with her brothers. Even after Paul's release she went on looking after Toni. She took her side against Paul, and stopped him hitting her, telling him, 'She's my child, not yours.'

But it did not last. Soon Sonia was again giving all her time to Paul and to Toni's brothers. 'They were real mother's boys,' Toni said, despairingly. It left her feeling, as a girl, that she was nothing, especially when, a year after Paul's return, her mother miscarried their second child – a baby daughter. Toni reacted as though Sonia had deliberately killed the girl. Sonia would never have miscarried, Toni maintained, had she not drunkenly fallen downstairs. 'She knew what she was doing.' How different things might have been had the baby lived. It might have helped her, Toni speculated, to accept being a girl herself. She might then have kept her hair long.

Instead, her parents' assaults on her femininity continued. No sooner was her sister killed, as Toni experienced it, than she too was attacked. She was thirteen. Her burgeoning womanhood excited her stepfather, Paul, who touched her up. He would have gone further, but Toni's brother Konrad came in. He must have been eleven. Magnifying him in retrospect, Toni told me Konrad retaliated by throwing Paul downstairs, threatening to kill him if he ever caught him doing it again.

Paul replaced sexual with physical abuse. Provoked by Toni's increasingly big-breasted sexuality, he took to hitting her. The more he provoked her hatred, the more fondly she remembered her first dad, Dave. Cruelly Sonia chose this moment to tell Toni she had no father, and told her how her real dad was killed just after she was born.

Stripped of the man she had assumed was her father, Toni looked elsewhere for support. When her mother refused to buy her new shoes, she got her grandad to buy them instead. Perhaps that was why, Toni reckoned, her mother now stopped her seeing him. As a substitute Toni sought comfort from his younger daughter, her Aunt Gizela, who had just returned to England from Poland.

Toni rummaged through her things and produced another photo, of Gizela, Toni's younger brother Kevin, and herself, sitting cosily side by side on a sofa. But where Toni had been in the picture there was a gaping hole. She had torn herself out of the photo because she so hated herself with long hair. She had grown it for a friend's wedding. The next day she shaved it off.

Making herself look like a boy did not endear her to her mother, so Toni tried other ways of winning her love. She began drinking like her and tried to win Sonia's affection by confiding in her, by telling her for instance about Paul's affairs with other women. But Sonia would have none of Toni's confidences, and discounted Toni's stories of being abused by Paul as invented to drive a wedge between her and him.

The struggle between mother and daughter came to a head when Toni got her boyfriend Sean to hit Paul. Toni had been in the kitchen washing up with Konrad when Paul came in and asked, 'Where's your mother?' He then laid into Toni, telling her she wasn't drying the dishes properly. Next he pushed her against the back door and punched her in the face, choking her. Later, when Sean asked Toni about her swollen lip, she told him it was Paul's doing, and invited Sean to beat him up. Sean, she added proudly, was even more of a bruiser than herself. He did her bidding, and Sonia became furious. She forced Toni on to the sitting-room table, put a knife at her throat, grabbed her by the hair, flung her on the sofa, and then threw her out of the house.

Toni was seventeen. Her life now became one of desperate penury and destitution. The little money she managed to scrounge she spent on drink and drugs. She lived on the street. There she met another girl, Susan, and moved in to her place. Soon, however, she was homeless again. While Susan was out at work Toni stole her cheque book and forged her signature to get money to pay the rent she still owed her mother from the time she was living at home. She had hoped to repair things between them, just as she tried to mollify Susan by handing herself over to the police immediately Susan found out.

Nevertheless, Susan beat her up. They became friends again, but Susan would no longer let Toni live with her, so she lived rough – stealing, scavenging, and sleeping in makeshift shelters on the streets or beaches of a nearby seaside town. Spending her days with down-and-outs toughened her, she claimed. She armed herself with a big kitchen knife to defend herself against a thug who was hassling her. The police respected her for it, she said; they recognised she needed the weapon to stick up for herself.

Men in authority, she claimed, had always granted her more esteem and help than women. The police asked her mother to take her back home, and when Sonia refused, despite the cold of winter, the police fed and sheltered her. They let her stay in the cells, and gave her money for cigarettes.

Dave also turned up trumps. Toni had managed to renew contact with him some months before and when she had phoned and told him about Paul hitting her, he had come over and thumped Paul;

he told him he mustn't beat Toni, that she was his daughter not Paul's. He also bought her new clothes. It was then that Toni discovered he had never forgotten her: that he had sent Christmas and birthday cards, but Sonia had intercepted them.

Finding him again cheered Toni, but her nomadic life continued. It made her feel (as her brief experience of gypsy life reveals to Maggie Tulliver) that, inside her tough shell, she was nothing but a pitiful little girl. Twice Toni's tramping ended in her being hospitalised: once because she was starving and dehydrated: another time because she collapsed after overdosing on aspirin and vodka. She hated herself for being 'so cowardly' in giving way to feminine weakness.

Sometimes, like many other ill-used girls and women, she turned her aggression against herself, cutting into her flesh with a knife.[4] This, not tomboy fighting, I learnt, was the cause of the scars on her arm. Physical pain seemed more bearable than emotional suffering.

The night before my last visit she again attacked herself. Why? Because her mother refused to talk to her when Toni rang to wish her 'Happy birthday'. A year earlier, Toni's brother Konrad had got the two women together, but within a couple of months they came to blows, and Sonia again banished Toni from home – this time for promising and then failing to take her favourite child Kevin to the circus. Sonia now planned to cut Toni off altogether: she greeted Toni's birthday greetings by saying she was having her phone number changed so Toni could no longer contact her.

This triggered Toni's latest violent episode. She smashed up the phone booth, then turned her rage against herself. She tore up her food vouchers, and cut her hair shorter than ever despite having resolved to keep herself warm by having it long through December. Unable to put the torn vouchers together, she stole some biscuits, only to court death by running across the road away from the shopkeeper.

She had nothing left. The best she could hope for was that Joan, the hostel worker, would feed her at Christmas. Her own family were lost to her, and anyway her mother was going away with Paul and her brothers over the holiday. Toni could not bear to know, or have anyone else know, how bereft she felt. It would be too awful if Joan saw how much she wanted her to mother her; she was sure Joan would only laugh. She decided to mask her dependency and signal her toughness by giving Joan a cigarette lighter.

Toni hated talking to me about this side of herself, even though she had waited in all day for my visit. It made her feel too vulnerable. She felt it was my doing, cloistering and hemming her in. She tried to escape by shouting at a woman on the pavement outside, calling her a 'nosy cunt' for staring in the window. If I hadn't looked in on her story, like the woman through the window, Toni implied, she wouldn't be feeling so sorry for herself: I had wheedled her into confiding and exposing her miseries, just as the hostel's female residents cloyingly sidled up to her with talk about their boyfriends and their 'monthlies'.

She felt much better being one with the lads: 'They just say what they think. They don't give a shit. That's what I'm like.' So saying, she told me she had just taken up with a strong-arm man employed as a bouncer at the local club. She longed for him or her older brother Konrad to phone and release her from being with me. She was on tenterhooks throughout our last meeting lest they call and she miss them.

Immensely relieved when I brought our conversation to an end, she manfully sought to recoup her equanimity. Stolidly, jauntily, she sauntered beside me as we walked back to the main hostel. She told me how, if she ever got hold of her stepfather Paul, she would kill him, and then, as though counting off the cherry stones, she reeled off the jobs she planned to take up – bricklayer, builder's mate, car mechanic, navvy. She would not leave it to chance – she was already training, doing weight-lifting.

But neither this nor the hefty male pin-ups above her bed nor the vast transistor radio in her room, heavily scored with a boy's name, filled the emptiness. They bleakened her lot by alienating her mother and others, and did nothing to remedy the comfortless maternal rejection she felt she suffered on account of not being a boy. Nor would her aggression and violence end the discrimination that would probably prevent her getting the men's jobs she craved.

For all her rough, tough fight and talk Toni was left with nothing but pipe dreams, passively waiting for something or someone to show up – a welfare cheque, her brother, even me. It was a far cry from the blood and guts panache with which she had begun. Tomboy acting-out is no more a solution to sexism than, as we shall see, conmanship to is racism.

10

Conman

A handsome Negro is introduced to a group of white Frenchmen. If it is a group of intellectuals, we can be sure that the Negro will try to assert himself. He will insist that attention be paid not to the color of his skin but to the force of his intellect. There are many people in Martinique who at the age of twenty or thirty begin to steep themselves in Montesquieu or Claudel for the sole purpose of being able to quote them. That is because, through their knowledge of these writers, they expect their color to be forgotten.

Frantz Fanon, 1952[1]

This is how Frantz Fanon, the Freudian psychiatrist, describes one tactic deployed by his fellow-blacks as defence against the discrimination they suffered under French colonialism. Diverting attention from not being the white man valorised by racist society, blacks and members of other similar groups may rebel by getting others to credit them with being a different kind of 'super male' figure, in this example the intellectual.

Discrimination exacerbates a process Lacan describes as universal: the formation of identity through identifying with our reflection as the phallus which 'the other' desires. Or, rather, we 'misrecognise' ourselves since we are not in fact at all the same as this imposing reflected image.[2] In his account of 'phallic identification', Lacan spelt out the implications of Freud's later theories of the ego and depression: namely of the child first falling in love with himself as whole and undivided; and of the idealised version of the self formed through identification with others, in the first place the father, as a defence against disillusion and loss (beginning with the 'loss' signified by the mother not having a penis).[3] Melanie Klein in turn argued that our minds are entirely constituted by identification with others.[4]

But she and her followers ignored the specifically patriarchal factors involved. In contrast, her contemporary, Freud's analysand and disciple Helene Deutsch, stressed this aspect of 'misrecognising ourselves' in others' regard, when she gave an account of a patient, Jimmy.[5] As a child, Deutsch reports, Jimmy initially founded his self-esteem on identifying with an idealised image of his businessman father. But, when Jimmy was seven, his father became a chronic invalid. Jimmy's belief in himself, based on idealising his father, would have been in danger of collapsing if Jimmy had not defended himself by conning others into crediting him in a succession of impressive male guises – as gentleman farmer, great writer, movie producer and inventor.

In this, Deutsch said, Jimmy was like the hero of Thomas Mann's novel, *Felix Krull*, whose exaggerated image of his father is toppled by the failure of the father's champagne business, followed by his bankruptcy, and suicide. In reaction, Felix makes charlatanism his *raison d'être*,[6] culminating in his passing himself off as a viscount, as the most eligible of bachelors, and in his winning the desire of a wealthy heiress and her mother.

Today the paternal and male aspects of such duplicity, of wittingly or unwittingly acting as though we were the reflection of what others want us to be, is often forgotten by therapists and caseworkers. Instead, they attribute 'false self' behaviour to the mother not being 'good enough' in meeting the needs of her baby's 'true self'.[7] The infant then has no other recourse, if he is to survive, but falsely to comply with what she wants. Within these terms the mountebank is understood as trying to dupe and then disillusion others just as he felt his mother duped and disillusioned him as a baby.[8]

This may be part of the dissembler's trick. But it overlooks the way conmanship often involves defensively adopting male stereotypes. Nowhere, perhaps, is this more apparent than among victims of racial discrimination. Indeed it has been argued that it was precisely Freud's assimilationist response to the anti-Semitism of turn-of-the-century Vienna that inspired his theory of the duplicity involved in unconscious self-deception.[9]

The following case, involving racism, is a clear example of charlatanism as an acted-out defence. It concerns a man, Steve Kumar, who was quite the most charming character I encountered while researching this book. Charm was the way he diverted my attention from his not being white. Instead he sought to pass himself off with being whatever I might most want him to be. Like Mann's Felix Krull, he was 'meltingly attentive'.[10]

Half-Indian, he was born in Glasgow and brought up in a children's home. By the time I met him he was in his mid-forties, and had been separated for some years from his wife and their now grown-up children. He now lived with a young couple and their children, who had taken him in as a lodger when they were living in Hebden Bridge (near Leeds) where his roamings had landed him several years before. The couple did everything for him (everyone always did) and when they moved to Bradford they took him along too. At first he had been reluctant. Compared to chic Hebden Bridge Bradford was too downmarket – too full of Asians like himself – but he did not want to disappoint his friends.

It was in their house in Bradford that I visited him. Exuding confidence (it takes it to win it) Steve unhesitatingly invited me in when I rang the doorbell, though he had no idea who I was, having completely forgotten the appointment. He warned me I would find his tale utterly boring, before launching into the most riveting yarns. It was as if he chain-smoked them – barely finishing one before he was on to the next. He created a veritable 'You want a thief, I'm your man' smokescreen with his stories – the very picture of the black man as described by Frantz Fanon, devoted to diverting me from the colour of his skin.

Steve did it with words. He could talk himself into and out of any and every situation, or so he said. His worst nightmare was to be struck dumb, as in one of his dreams:

> These guys were coming to get me. They came into the room, and I tried to say, 'I know you're there', and I couldn't talk. I was just literally paralysed. I couldn't make any sound at all.

With me, however, words never failed him. Like a well-rehearsed actor, he successfully made it his job, *pace* Oscar Wilde,[11] never to reveal himself, only his art.

A well-versed trickster, Steve began by volunteering testimonials to his sincerity. I should ask the Yorkshire CID about him, he said. They would certainly vouch for his being the great thief he said he was. If I needed further proof, I should consult those in charge of the county's largest clothing chain. He was such a good shoplifter that its detectives had asked his advice when they wanted to improve their stores' security.

Steve revelled in his reputation. Contrary to his initial disclaimer, he proceeded to prove he was no dreary nonentity. He stood out. He was one of the best. He got himself noticed. If anyone wanted anything, they came to him: clothing, guns from museums, crucifixes from cathedrals – you name it, he got it. His business enterprise had become so vast that he had to keep an order book, and this led to one of his most spectacular run-ins with the police. They found his ledger. It took them three days to haul in his loot. They piled it high, but there was so much it would not fit into one room. It overflowed into the corridor and into other rooms as well. 'What an ego trip. I was Top of the Pops.' Lord of Misrule.

It was magic. He could get anything for nothing. But he never let his manic excitement run away with him. He had a job to do, a role to excel in. He kept a cool head. Methodically he plotted his finances and operations on spreadsheets and maps of England, from east to west. He made himself special tools, almost theatrical props: a swag bag, nicknamed 'Eve', with wheels which he always kept well oiled; a 'grab' stick, the kind made for the disabled, with claws especially softened with cotton buds so as not to damage delicate articles such as glass and china; and, last but not least, a fishing reel, the line fitted with clips.

'The trouble with the average person,' he said, explaining this gadget, 'is that if they go to steal something they draw attention to themselves. What you need is front.' The dodge is to get people to look the other way. Any conjuror, or card sharper, could tell you that. Their hoax depends on deflecting attention from what they are doing. As for shoplifting, Steve obviously could not get what he wanted while everyone was looking. So he distracted them. He would clip the fishing line to a shelf, then wheel his trolley into the next aisle. When the tightened thread brought everything crashing down, he cut it; while everyone was looking at the crash he filled his bag, away from their prying eyes.

At other times he acted the DIY man about the house. 'Can I see the manager?' he would ask at the electrical goods counter, having just taken a brand new dimmer switch out of its packaging. When the boss arrived Steve, as polite as could be, would cough, 'Excuse me sir, but look. I can turn this on. And I can turn it off. But I can't actually wire it into our house because we don't have the wattage, the supply to dim the lights. We didn't know that when we bought it. No, we don't have our receipt.' At this the manager would apologise, 'I'm very sorry, sir. There's nothing we can do.' Well perhaps he could. Perhaps he could save face; he would offer Steve a refund.

Yet again, Steve went on,

> I'd phone first – the hardware store, say. I'd tell the shopkeeper I'd bought this mixer shower tap but that I couldn't fit it because we'd got a cast-iron bath at home, where the taps come out of the side, whereas the mixer tap had to be fixed above the bath. I would ask the bloke if he could sort out the right attachments for me.

Again there would be an apology. The storeman was very sorry but he did not have what Steve wanted. At this, having swotted up a legal rights manual (just as Thomas Mann's Felix Krull swots up medical texts to feign illness and get off military service), Steve would put on an act of righteous indignation: 'Pshaw. That's nice. I bought this tap thinking I could use it and I can't. No. I haven't got the chit.' 'Tell you what,' the manager would capitulate, 'you bring it in and I'll see what I can do.'

Steve became so well versed in his artistry he could have anything he wanted. It gave him a real buzz getting away with it. He would even go into shops just for the fun of inviting pursuit and fooling those who wanted to catch him, but like all play-acting, it had its down side – fear of the butterflies – 'praying I wouldn't set off some alarm'.

His whole act depended on distracting others by getting them to credit him in some other role. He became so proficient at it – even at forgery – that he got himself talked about on TV. A friend stole some Matisse etchings, and showed them to Steve. Steve was unimpressed. 'Why,' he said, 'they're rubbish. You're telling me they're worth £1,500, £2,000? I could do those easy.' He did. He would be Matisse. He would use the same materials. He got endpapers from books printed at the time Matisse was doing his work, and used the same charcoal. The resulting pictures were so like the master's, he said, that he had no trouble getting them authenticated and securing buyers. Everyone wanted them. He sold hundreds, and flooded the market.

What bothered him most was whether I liked his own drawings. 'A lot of them are copies,' he admitted as he riffled through his papers. Sure enough. There was a facsimile of Leonardo's hands, but it was not this that Steve wanted me to admire. It was his own handiwork – a pastel of Princess Di. Very kitsch. He went on talking. Then, as I left, he returned to his sketches. 'Do you like them?' he asked. 'Yes,' I lied, 'very impressive.' 'That's the main thing,' he chortled as he saw me out, warning me, the all too readily beguiled punter, to take care on the road – so many sharks around.

It was with the 'sharks' that he began my next visit, by deploring corruption in the arts. Like Herman Melville in *The Confidence Man*, who represents society in microcosm through a group of mountebanks aboard a Mississippi steamboat, ironically called *Fidèle*, Steve saw his own knavery all around.

He worried that solitude might make me feel empty, as he did. Before, he had emphasised to me that he was a shoplifter, not a house burglar. He would never want anyone taking anything from him. He had so little; he gave away or sold everything he took; he had nothing to spare; all he possessed could be fitted into a carrier bag. Mindful that, left alone, I might feel similarly voided of myself, he invited me to join him while he made tea: 'Better than being on your own in another room.'

He explained how he came to feel himself to be such an empty 'nothing'. He began life not knowing either of his parents. His earliest memory, from the age of five, was of arriving in the children's home and being immediately punished: the staff told him he could not have tea until he threaded the strap of his sandals properly. They let him know right away that he knew nothing, that thanks to his Asian background, he didn't even know how to do up his shoes. Had our drinking tea reminded him? Did it worry him, as at that long-ago teatime, that I too might fault him for not being white?

Despite his anxiety that his colour made him culpably different from others, he also feared the reverse – that he might be the same as them. He remembered the rows of identical beds in the children's home where, irrespective of individual difference, the children were regimented into taking a nap at the same regulation hour every afternoon. On Sundays they went to church, every child – regardless of differences of age – dressed in the same uniform short trousers.

Worse still, when he went to school, Steve had no father to call his own. Nor a car. He never even went in one till he was sixteen. As for his want of a dad, he did away with it by inventing one. He gave himself a magnificent father. In hindsight it was a bit embarrassing the tall stories he used to tell about him. But he was only a child. He had no idea then, as he did later, how to varnish his fibs with the truth. He told the other children his dad was a colonel:

> it was the macho thing, the only thing then. In those days an actor or a singer just wasn't important. He had to be some sort of action man. So I said he was in the army – high up – fighting, always in Germany or Russia. Whatever he did it was always the best, the best ever.

Then he told a real whopper. He bragged that his father owned a stately home. Well, Steve did live in one – but he did not tell his fellow-pupils it had been converted into a children's home. He invited them all to a party there, and told them his father would organise cars to collect them. His story was so far-fetched that he promptly forgot it. His audience, however, took him at his word. The next Saturday afternoon, as he was blithely watching TV, one of the nuns who ran the home came in to tell him a whole crowd of children had come for the bonanza he had promised.

Unmasked, he took care not to make the same mistake again. He polished up his act to fit better with the facts – that he was black and his father was never around. He told the others that, during the war, his dad had been in England – in the army – but that he had since settled in Trinidad from where he visited Steve, or where more often Steve went to stay with him, in his mansion overseas.

Within bounds Steve sought to fit not only his father but himself to others' ideals of his sex. The other boys wanted him to be a thief. OK, that's what he would be. He stole food for them from the larder in exchange for cigarettes. It was the same with his first girlfriend, the headmaster's daughter. She wanted him to be the seducer – to touch her up, or so Steve said. Right, he would do it, again for cigarettes.

The authorities punished him. But although they gave him the strap, it did not deter him. He so wanted to escape himself. No wonder. When he was eight, one of the institution's attendants got him to go into the toilets to masturbate him: 'It was unbelievable, horrible.' Steve's only consolation was that the man never buggered him. But he still felt shitty. Most of all because he was black. It was double jeopardy: 'You were looked down on for being from a children's home. Even worse if you were coloured. If I could have scrubbed myself white I would have done so.'

In psychoanalytic terms, he projectively identified the hated aspects of himself with his skin. Like many other blacks he learnt to do so through the way others expel into them their own dis-owned aspects in making themselves 'bleached white'.[12] It made him feel dirty and unclean. If only he could flee himself. The yearning grew particularly intense after he eventually met his father. His mother, a white woman born and bred in England, had occasionally visited him as a child, but he did not meet his father until he was seventeen. It was a bitter blow. He felt ashamed, not so much of his father but of his house: gutted by a recent fire, it was covered in grime. Worse still was the adult recognition that his mother was a foul-mouthed, scruffy, pornography-reading tart.

Steve did not blame his father, and regretted not having got to know him better before he died, ten years before we met. But he could not bring himself to go to his house again, so he never discovered anything about his father's life beyond the fact that, during the war, he had been a boxer in the Indian Army, and afterwards had emigrated to England where he helped set up his family's restaurant business.

Whatever self-respecting image of his father these details fostered was banished by Steve's memory of the dilapidated home. Perhaps, he felt, that was why he was first taken into care: because he was at risk of suffering the same neglect. By contrast the orphanage seemed to Steve, in retrospect, 'absolutely wonderful – brilliant'. He felt 'crap' by comparison, and told me he had always believed, as a child, that only boys like himself did 'pooh'. He was amazed to discover girls did it too.

Nevertheless, he still felt shitty. He recalled the first time he had sex. He was only a lad. A woman picked him up in the cinema where, as though he knew what was in store, he was watching the Beatles film, *Help!* Ever ready to escape himself by enacting others' stereotypes, he went along with the woman's invitation to screw her on the grass behind the bus shelter. He mouthed all the platitudes she wanted to hear, told her 'I love you,' and 'This is great.' In fact, however, he felt humiliated, that he 'just flapped about like a stranded fish'. He put his arm around her, then felt something cold and clammy on his hand – a dog turd. He could not bring himself to tell her. God knows, he wondered, what happened when she got home with his 'filth' still on her.

The racial discrimination he suffered was enough to make anyone feel noxious and unclean. He was picked up as a teenager for wandering the streets late at night. His being out was no reason for him to be arrested; it must have been his colour that made the police throw him into jail. There had been no way out: 'You couldn't say you weren't going to smash that window, or rob that car. You were a suspected person, and that was it.' It happened again, just before we met. He had been dragged off to Wales on suspicion of murder. Somebody put his name to it – because he was black.

He might be a cheat, but he would never kill. Yet he did not feel innocent – neither when I saw him nor as a youth when he settled in a hostel after fleeing his parents' home – and he continued to flee himself by adopting other men's roles.

Just as Melanie Klein describes the hero of Julien Green's novel *If I Were You* fending off other men's envy by, as it were, stepping

134

into their shoes,[13] Steve sought escape from disappointment in his father and himself by trying to become the same as two grown men he knew, whom he looked up to on moving out of the hostel. They were a couple of crooks, Ted and Alan:

> They were sheer class – with their brief cases, all suited up. They drove nice cars. I was really impressed. They were everything I wanted to be, and to be associated with. They were good looking, and so smart. They had the things I wanted. Always had girlfriends. I'd even have them bring them back to my room – just to be there.

Having Ted in his flat – better still, donning Ted's character as shoplifter – Steve no longer had any reason to feel envious of him. As an accomplished thief he could also outwit bad fortune by supplying himself with whatever he wanted.

As long as he could be Ted – or some other 'superior' white man – he was fine. It was only when this stance was questioned that he became embittered. Once, when he was in prison, a white prisoner asked him who he thought he was, joining in their conversation. They had been talking about Muhammad Ali and a fight in which the boxer's glove split. 'Oh,' Steve informed the assembled crew, 'that's what they call a professional foul.' 'Who's asking you?' the man retorted.

He challenged Steve to a fight. At first Steve backed off: 'Nah. Don't take no notice of me.' During the night, however, the man's put-down rankled, and by morning Steve was desperate to have it out with him. But the man wasn't at breakfast, and by dinner Steve was seething. When he finally caught up with the fellow he whacked him so hard that he lost half a year's remission.

That was all in the past. With me Steve felt full of *bonhomie*, sure that I believed he was indeed a superman swindler. 'It's really excellent talking to you,' he said as I left, the accent on me as he asked my name again. 'Give us a bell,' he shouted as I moved off, 'when you're next coming.'

Perhaps he wanted warning to prepare his act. Certainly he had an agenda when I next arrived: he wanted to talk about drugs. He launched straight into them. They were the reason he conned others into seeing him as the one who would make their dreams come true. Conning people was the only way he could get the money to buy the amphetamine sulphate he needed to realise his own dreams.

He first got into speed, he told me, as he had into shoplifting, through Ted and Alan. Until then he had felt cripplingly shy, especially with women, but with this 'confidence drug' he found he could escape himself, become the same as his two heroes, a man who could make any woman he wanted, even his best friend's moll, Nancy.

It was no coincidence that he took another man's place, with a white woman. This scenario became the motive of his drug taking: liberated by speed he would persuade Nancy, whom he soon married, to have sex with other men and then tell him what had happened. His friend Martin, for instance, fancied her. The feeling was mutual, so Steve got Nancy to spend the night with Martin, then recount their lovemaking. It provided the script he needed to 'become' Martin in bed with her. Or he would get another man to watch him and Nancy making love, so that he could enjoy it from the other guy's perspective.

He thereby acted out the three-cornered Oedipal scenario which Freud said is universal, but usually repressed. Steve played the part of both white observer and black stud (alias his father) fornicating with Nancy, the white whore he had made her into (modelled on his prostitute mother). He only did it on sulphate, he assured me. It made him sink to the depths – become his real dirty self – 'the color of evil', an epithet with which Fanon says the black man all too readily identifies.

It gave him a vacation from himself. Drugged up, he became all man, '100 per cent'. Turned on with cannabis, then speed, his erection lasted hours. Nothing brought it down. Sex went on for ages – from dusk to dawn. The fix itself was also a turn-on. Steve kept a special tool for the purpose – not a disposable needle, but his own syringe. He loved the weight of it on his arm.

All this phallic talk was reminiscent of Melville's comparison of the conman to a 'caterpillar', and of Thomas Mann's metaphor of the actor turning from a 'repulsive worm' into a 'glorious butterfly in which... deluded spectators believed they were beholding their own secret dreams of beauty, grace, and perfection'.[14] Like an actor, Steve took on the part that I, his Freudian audience, seemed to want him to play – as phallus. Perhaps he was driven by the impulse Fanon describes:

> Out of the blackest part of my soul, across the zebra striping of my mind, surges this desire to be suddenly white. I want to be acknowledged not as black but as white . . . who but a white woman can do this for me? By loving me she proves that I am worthy of white love. I am loved like a white man. I am a white man.[15]

Steve had made himself the white woman's stereotype of the black man. Sex incarnate. Had I enticed him into it? Was I no better than his 'white whore' of a mother, or the woman at the cinema who seduced him thirty years before? Was my next question unconsciously motivated by guilty retaliation?

He had been trying to establish himself in my clinical psychologist's eyes as a magnificently deluded man. He told me he often heard voices of security guards talking about him, catching up with him. At this I interjected, 'Why was it you got caught so often?' This deflated him, but he tried to restore himself. 'Because I was at it so often. It was a thousand to one I would be found out. When I got nabbed it was because I had already got away with it so many times before.' But he knew his game was up; and implicitly admitted it by going on to recount an incident when he got caught because he had not adequately checked out and disabled an alarm.

Perhaps he felt he had not sufficiently 'disarmed' me. Whatever the cause, he had lost his grip on being 'my' man, and ended instead with another act: that of the religious convert. He had been introduced to the part by Owen, who had also once been into drugs, like Steve, and had been to bed with Steve's wife Nancy. But that was years ago. Since then Owen had struck it rich. He had become a businessman – on a large scale – and religious. Well, Steve thought, if it was good enough for this white man that was how he too would get big.

First though, rendered wary of others' double-dealing by his own, Steve checked out Owen's sect: 'If I'm going to get knowledge from the Bible I've got to satisfy myself that it's real, that it's true.' Paradoxically, given his history of metamorphosing himself into others, Steve went on, 'I satisfied myself that, as this tract said, we didn't come from monkeys, that everything was created according to his own kind, that nothing is one thing and then goes into something else.'

Darwin be damned. If he, Steve, could be one with this white man – with Owen and his religion – then he was not, and never would be the primitive nobody that racism, and his own particular history of it, made him out to be. Certainly, he indicated, now distrustful of me, Owen's breed of Christianity was much better than my trade. Psychologists had never accorded him any dignity.

True to Oscar Wilde's quip, 'A little sincerity is a dangerous thing, and a great deal of it is absolutely fatal',[16] truth proved my undoing: my reminding Steve that, far from getting away with things, he had been caught so often he had spent almost his entire life in jail. It was the same with Helene Deutsch's impostor patient, Jimmy. After many years of analysis he asked her, 'Are you a Freudian? The old man isn't even a doctor.' As soon as Deutsch pointed out that Freud was medically qualified, as soon as she indicated she did not see Jimmy as the know-all he wanted her to believe he was, he quit therapy.

As soon as Steve felt I no longer swallowed his performance as invincible scoundrel, the curtain came down on his act. I had failed him, the man for whom, following Lacan, Fanon asserted, 'The Other alone can give him worth.'[17] I became the nonentity he feared becoming himself, and he hardly summoned a wave as I left for the last time. How different from the enthusiasm with which he had originally greeted me. Now he was on to his next performance: my place as audience already taken by others, by Owen and the watchful God of his new-found religion.

Whatever the promise of this and Steve's other roles – as Malcolm X pointed out, when describing the allure of white man's religion to his fellow black prisoners – they only provide illusory escape from the racial discrimination that made Steve feel so disappointed in himself. Despite the energy put into getting others to credit one with being the incarnation of manhood, the 'conman' defence simply exacerbates the harm this stereotype does us all – whites as well as blacks, women as well as men.

III

Inward Defences

11

Repressed Abuse

At the bottom of every case of hysteria there are one or more occurrences of premature sexual experience . . . a psychological precondition enters in as well. The scenes must be present as unconscious memories; only so long as, and in so far as, they are unconscious are they able to create and maintain hysterical symptoms.

Sigmund Freud, 1896[1]

Even after abandoning his early theory that hysteria is due to childhood sexual seduction or abuse, Freud always insisted that neurosis is caused by repressing the past, often in patriarchal form. Memory can then only be expressed, as in dreams, not consciously but through symbolic and bodily condensation and displacement.

Repression of exaggerated parental figures as a cause of neurotic symptoms is now virtually forgotten. Instead therapists often attend exclusively to other defences – to the introjection and projection of fantasy into people available to us in the present.[2]

Nevertheless repression persists, and with it the patriarchal, as well as maternal, fantasies it forces back into the unconscious. Just as Freud's Dora was troubled by tickling in her throat (a symptom said to result from repressing and displacing from genitals to mouth the past image of the erect penis of her father's friend – see Introduction) so hallucinated oral representations of the father and others, as phallus, doubtless contribute to current symptoms of nervous throat clearing and stammering (for an example see Chapter 14), now more often explained in mother-centred terms.[3] They may also be a contributory factor in eating disorders; in the bulimia, for instance, that afflicted one of my patients who, like Dora, was also sexually abused by a friend of her father and who,

141

in his absence, arguably kept him symbolically present in her body by stuffing herself with food and then vomiting it out as though it were him.[4]

The continuing operation of this defence in preserving a gross figure of a man in his absence is even more dramatically illustrated by the case of thirty-six-year-old Sara, who might almost have modelled herself on psychoanalysis's first patient, Anna O.[5] Like Anna, Sara's symptoms included seeing hallucinated snakes in place of the man who was once the pivot of her life.

I met her through her social worker. Unlike those who energetically act out the fantasy of themselves or others as incarnating inflated ideas of masculinity, Sara was immobilised by the neurotic and bodily ills expressed in repressing a similar idea. Repression made time stand still, collapsing the present into the past. Despite the loud ticking of a clock in her sitting room the pictures in Sara's mind were static, as though set in amber. Each scene condensed and overlaid the next, beginning with the one that had led to her being referred for psychiatric help a couple of years earlier.

She described the occasion as though she had copied it from a Gothic novel. Working late at night, she told me, she had suddenly felt a snake coil round her waist. 'It can't last,' she reassured herself, looking at the clock. But it did. One snake replaced another. One wormed its way round a vase on the table where she sat. Two more emerged from a couple of Toby jugs on the hearth. They were still there the next day – sliding over her boss at work. Later, back home that night, their place was taken by an image of her long-gone stepfather, Colin, standing on the landing outside her bedroom as he had done each time he was about to sexually abuse her in her early teens. This image then gave way to a drawing she had once made of Colin sprawling – enormous – in an easy chair, a big grin on his face; across from him, her mother, as tiny as Sara; the whole covered in snakes, filling and coming out of every crack and hole.

Were they modelled on Anna O.'s serpent? Was Sara, steeped as I learnt she was, in nineteenth-century literature, familiar with Freud's case? Whatever their cause, it was not the first time Sara had been afflicted with such ideas. Ten years before she was convinced her insides were infected, as though by Colin's abusive penis inside her. 'Yuk,' she shuddered, as disgust again invaded her. At the time her pain had been so bad she persuaded her GP there must be something physically wrong. Investigation revealed a possibly spastic colon. Sara, however, was convinced otherwise. Nothing short of a hysterectomy, she believed, would cure her. Just as Karen Horney traced her women patients' gynaecological complaints to bodily repetition of an image of the father sexually penetrating and damaging their insides,[6] so Sara attributed her aches and pains to her stepfather's abuse.

Medically her doctors could find nothing wrong. But their examination cured her by repeating, punishing and thereby enabling her to expiate the guilt her stepfather's abuse caused her. She still regarded treatment, including counselling, as punishment. She wished her stepfather could be subjected to it too.

It was the same when, aged eighteen, she had been given electric shock for depression and physical collapse. These symptoms began, just like Anna O.'s did, when Sara was looking after an older man, Sam, who was like a father to her. He was rich, asthmatic, and nine years her senior. She had eloped with him to get away from Colin.

Punishment of her debility with electric shock proved a relief. Sara quite understood the similar response to ECT described in Sylvia Plath's autobiographical novel *The Bell Jar.*[7] Like Plath, Sara yearned to have doctors or someone else take control of her life.

Ultimately it was only by taking charge herself, not through physical treatment but through psychotherapy, Sara averred, that, as it were, she got back on her feet. It was the beginning of the end of her story of repression, which began with her retelling it as though peeling off successive layers of a palimpsest, each leading further back in time. Nostalgia mitigated the horror, just as the opening line of Daphne du Maurier's *Rebecca*, 'Last night I dreamt I went to Manderley again', serves as palliative to the murder she goes on to relate. Like du Maurier's heroine, Sara was still in thrall to a bygone house and its master. She too began with remembrance of things past.

Going into her home was like entering a time warp. Sepia-tinted photographs lined the hall and lounge; a pair of Regency figurines and a vase of everlasting flowers adorned the mantelpiece, and an old-fashioned coal fire burned in the grate. Along the wall a glass-fronted cabinet was filled with classic novels, and beside the bookcase was an ottoman – a veritable Freudian couch. Surrounded by these things I felt I had donned 'a comfortable old overcoat', as Sara more than once described her propensity for wrapping herself in the past.

In the middle of it all, she sat at my feet, watching me drink the tea that, as though she were a maid, she made for me but not for herself. As in an infinitely mirrored regress, she revived all the previous occasions she had knelt submissive yet defiant, silenced yet overflowing with words, at the mercy of doctors, therapists, and above all her stepfather.

Sara was very welcoming. When I phoned to ask the way to her house, she told me, 'Ignore the "No Entry" sign. Drive straight in.' Obstruction and intrusion mixed. It was the same when I left. The door-handle fell off as I went to go. 'Oh,' she gasped, giggling. 'I loosened it to stop my son coming in.' But then she left the front door wide open – inviting whoever fancied in.

By our first leave-taking she had let me in on many details of her life. She had prefaced their quasi-archaeological retelling (to which Freud likened the excavation of the ever-present relics of the repressed past),[8] with a sigh: 'It's such a long story. It'll take all night.' Yet, she began as if her tale could be telescoped into a single image that in being retold contained and thereby soothed – like the living room in which she felt so safe – the frayed nerves and jagged agitation of her initial greeting.

'I was sexually abused by my stepfather,' she said, as though it had happened only the day before. Her ex-husband Sam's love letters to their thirteen-year-old daughter, Susan, had reminded her. Breaking through her repression, they revived the memory of her own abuse as if it were still going on. Facing Sam in court felt no different from confronting her own abuser when she was a child. In her mind Sam and Colin were condensed into one larger-than-life Perry Mason figure, just as my name reminded her of Lord Peter Wimsey in Dorothy L. Sayers's whodunnits. Such characters, and the snakes that replaced them, mesmerised her. They stopped her in her tracks. So much so they prevented her proceeding with her legal case against Sam. The snakes even threatened to stop her working as a teacher, which led to her being hospitalised again.

Yet they were only ideas. In their effect, however, they were real enough. More real, it seemed, than the people with whom she lived: her mother downstairs; her postman lover Neil; and her children (Sam's daughter Susan, and her five-year-old son Joe, fathered by a drunken layabout Sara met after leaving Sam). They all lived with her, but they seemed little more than shadows.

It was the same with the snakes. Living ones hardly seemed real: they posed no threat. It was not actual snakes but their imagined replicas that paralysed her: serpents seen at one remove, through a glass darkly, as though 'through a photo lens', superimposed on reality. It would have been better, she said, had they been real; or had she been actually crippled and forced to use crutches. Then her colleagues might have made allowances for her.

Just as her illness involved neither live snakes nor physical crippling, nor did what she remembered of her stepfather's repeated sexual abuse involve tangible penetration. The day he came near to penetrating her, symbolically, by pushing his penis back and forth between her cupped fingers, the immediacy of tactile contact proved so cathartic – indeed they both burst into tears – that he never abused her again.

The outrage from which she still suffered, the scene she mentally relived time and again, happened before that. It related to the times when he had slithered his hand towards her under the bedclothes. At first she repressed the memory. She shut the door on it just as she there and then closed the door of the room in which we were sitting lest her mother overhear us. When she was in her early teens, she went on, she pretended her stepfather's sexual advances were not happening. She would drift off instead into a 'dreamlike state', just as years later when her ex-husband sexually propositioned their daughter she 'suspended reality' by retreating into waking dreams.

It was the same when her doctor, despairing of finding any organic cause of her ills, sent her to a psychoanalyst. No sooner did she start talking to him about her stepfather's abuse than she abandoned words for visual imagery. Absurdly she found herself waking each morning with black clouds swimming before her eyes.

She was not alone in thus defending against reality. Repression is a collective as well as an individual process. Nor, contrary to the static illusions fostered by repression, do the factors causing it stand still. Society changes, and by the early 1990s Sara was a beneficiary of the increasing recognition (largely brought about by feminist campaigning) of the hitherto generally repressed awareness of child sexual abuse and its widespread occurrence.

Before that, in keeping with late 1970s disbelief in such outrages, except by strangers,[9] Sara's doctors met her disclosure of her step-father's molestation of her when she was a teenager with 'stunned silence'. She had already told her mother who, like her doctors, told Sara in effect to shut up. If Colin was interfering with her, Sara's mother said, Sara only had herself to blame – she was too sexually provocative. She even asked the vicar round, to tell Sara off. When he came nobody said anything, least of all Colin: he sat in stony silence, terrified of what she might blurt out.

Given her mother's initial response, and despite changing social attitudes, there had seemed little point to Sara in trying to talk to her mother again when the memory of her childhood abuse was triggered by her ex-husband pestering their daughter, Susan. Her mother, she claimed, would always prove deaf to her words.

Hence the snakes. Paradoxically, her mother could not remain impervious to them – even if they were only phantoms. 'They were my way of speaking,' Sara said. Seeing was believing. 'They forced the family to talk.' Sara's mother urged her to 'put them all back in the cupboard'.

Yet it was her mother who first gave her the idea of the snakes – many years before – when Sara was the same age as her daughter was now. Colin had tried to force pills on her, as Nabokov's Humbert Humbert forces capsules on Lolita and as Sara's doctors pushed medicine on to her. She had gone out to be interviewed for a babysitting job, and when she returned later that evening she had terrible neuralgia. Her jaws ached dreadfully. Colin gave her a couple of tablets. 'Take these,' he ordered, telling her he found the pills helpful for backache. At first Sara resisted; then she gave in and took them.

The next thing she knew, she was screaming in the middle of his bed with her mother on one side, Colin the other. Then she was sitting bolt upright, muscles locked. 'Don't do it,' she kept telling herself. Her mother got very annoyed, but her stepfather encouraged her. 'You're floating now, aren't you? Isn't it a lovely feeling?' It wasn't. It was a nightmare – horrible. And the muscle spasms kept returning.

She then found herself on her own at the bottom of the house, in the practice room of the dance school her parents ran, consigned to a camp-bed far away from them because they could not bear her noise. It made her hate her stepfather more than ever. He was so evil. The thought became a picture; she saw him in the glass – as a devil, a face with phallic horns, like the death's head that plagued Anna O.

The idea of reflection was repeated, prettified, in the room where we sat. A reproduction of Degas's picture of a mirrored dance studio, with half-clad female forms, was framed on the wall. It was a scene Sara also kept alive by regaling me with an incident from Charlotte Brontë's *Jane Eyre*, her favourite novel, in which nine-year-old Jane is punished for defying the young master of the house by being sent to the 'red room' where his father died several years before and where Jane feels his ghost return to haunt her.

Sara too was haunted, by the idea that the tablets her stepfather gave her that night were LSD and that he had used the trance they induced to molest her. But she could not bring back any recollection of the abuse itself. It was her mother who filled the gap, who provided as it were the necessary Freudian dreamwork 'secondary revision'; she told Sara that she had screamed because she was seeing snakes. Hence Sara's reversion to this – her mother's – idea when, twenty years later, she wanted her to take on board the reality not so much of her daughter's abuse but of her own abuse as a teenager.

Memory of the 'LSD incident' triggered a yet earlier reminiscence: her first meeting with Colin when she was eleven. Sara was then living in her grandmother's house with her mother and younger sister Julia. The first thing Colin said to her, on coming into this female enclave, was, 'Your vest isn't tucked into your knickers.' So saying he tucked it in, much to her embarrassment.

Remembering her discomfiture then reminded Sara of something still further back – the unhappiness of her mother, which drove her into marrying Colin after being abandoned by Sara's father for another woman. This coincided with the death of Sara's maternal grandfather. The loss of the two men was more than Sara's mother could bear. In their absence she clung to Sara, keeping her home with her, away from school, with all manner of alleged illnesses. Perhaps that was when Sara first learnt to use physical ailments as cover for psychological woes – a strategy to which, Freud wrote, when recounting Dora's treatment,[10] girls often resort for want of more effective means of getting their unhappiness heard.

Recounting her mother's upset brought Sara's real father into her tale for the first time. Until then he had been as absent from her story as the letter 'h' from Sara's name. She lost it with him. Her mother took the offending letter away because the woman he left her for was also called Sarah with an 'h'. Perhaps it made Sara feel guilty at his going, as though her mother changed her name because she felt Sara was otherwise no different from her father's new lover in inciting his desire.

Sara could not remember feeling distressed herself when her father left. She recalled herself at that period of her life, when she was six, blissfully playing in the woods around her grandmother's house. It seemed light years away from another much earlier, desperately unhappy image of herself as a baby 'screaming and screaming for a pink teddy bear, trying to reach it and not being able to', as Orson Welles cries out in memory of his dead brother at the end of *Citizen Kane*, for his childhood sledge 'Rosebud'.

No such anguish accompanied Sara's teddy-bear memory. Instead it was fixed like a photo, severed from any despair at loss of the man the image of her toy perhaps symbolically replaced. Others had told her how attached she had been, as a baby, to her father. She must, she reasoned, have been 'devastated' by his departure. But she said it theatrically – as though in a drama recounted in the third person – as rehearsed and impersonal as her recollection of another picture of her father coming back some months later, bringing a bottle of medicine for Sara when she was sick. Perhaps this also contributed to the way Sara, as a grown-up, converted emotional upset into bodily disorder.

She could not directly recall feeling pain at her father's absence. Instead she plastered it over with another memory. So far she had reiterated, over and over, an image of her stepfather as an enormous overbearing tyrant. Just as Charlotte Brontë conjures up nightmare canine and equine figures to accompany the first appearance of Mr Rochester in *Jane Eyre*,[11] so Sara magnified her stepfather Colin's cruelty. Not only did he subjugate her, she said, he also beat his dog, shut it in the garden shed, and threw it downstairs. Now that she had come to the time in her life when she first lost her father, a completely different picture of Colin emerged – as a man who evoked all her childhood desire.

Sara had found it much easier to recollect her mother's craving for him. Slowly, however, it recalled her own. Perhaps it was her longing to use him to fill the emptiness left by her absent father (just as she remembered longing to recover her teddy bear as a baby) that Colin had exploited in making her victim of his sexual advances. Why else had she given in to them? Why else had she acceded to his wish to dress herself up so he could photograph her, as she put it, 'in adult poses'? Why else did she let him come into the bathroom and take pictures of her having a shower? Was this why she had also been so ready to invite me in with her 'Ignore the "No Entry" sign' overture?

Not that she allowed anybody else to put her otherwise repressed wish into words. Perhaps guessing what I was beginning to surmise she suddenly exploded against me as though I were one of the doctors who had implied she wanted or liked her stepfather. 'I've got to question these words "like" and "enjoy",' she stormed. 'Yes. Your body does respond. But it's a very *isolated*, and very *lonely*, and very *humiliating* experience,' she spat. 'It's nothing to do with love.'

She wanted me to know she hated her stepfather, that there was absolutely no question of love. Yet it now transpired that it was her very love that had provoked her hate. It was his proving as unfaithful to her as her father, and as the doctors who had taken his place, that most aroused her ire. It was bad enough that her stepfather kissed her mother, 'hands all over her, deliberately sexual', but it was the last straw when Colin started pawing Sara's younger sister Julia. Exposed as having betrayed her just as her father had, Sara took to calling him Dad too. She threatened to kill him. She barricaded the door to keep him away from Julia, just as years later she sought to prevent her ex-husband having access to their daughter Susan.

Sara now raged against Susan and the other girls and women in her life. How Susan annoyed her, staying out all hours with her boyfriend. How Julia infuriated her, the way she still kept in touch with Colin, even sending him Father's Day cards. Before, Sara had criticised her sister to me because her mother ran errands for her but never for Sara. Now, after acknowledging her childhood longing for Colin, Sara's complaints against her sister turned to outright loathing. She dreamt of hitting her so hard and dangerously that she decided to get medicine to calm her.

Earlier I had been puzzled why Sara repeatedly emphasised the courage of her social worker, Louise, in working with her murderous hatred of her stepfather. After all, Louise was not the target of Sara's hate. Now it transpired that she might well have been, that unconsciously Sara hated Louise, equating her with all the other detested women in her life, just as she now started hating me.

It began to appear that it was jealousy – 'Hell hath no fury like a woman scorned' – that first drove Sara to leave home just as it caused Freud's patient Dora to quit analysis on identifying Freud with the faithlessness of her father's friend Herr K.[12] When, as a sixteen-year-old, Sara discovered her stepfather propositioning her sister Julia she took her revenge by moving out. It was then, it now transpired, that she decided to marry Sam. It was then, I now learnt, that she suffered the nervous debility that first landed her in hospital. Being hospitalised brought her father back. He visited her just as, after leaving her mother, he returned to visit her when she was sick as a child.

When she was discharged he kept in touch. He phoned every week. Then, suddenly, he announced he was moving house and severed all contact. Try as she might, Sara could not find him.

She tried various numbers. Nobody answered. She wrote letters. Nobody replied. Evidently he did not want to see her – ever again.

At that time she was still living with Sam, but he was not sufficient to replace her father. Again, as when she was eleven, she repressed anger and sadness at his being gone by looking to her stepfather Colin instead. She left Sam and returned to live with him and her mother, then moved into a house facing theirs. From there, after Sam went overseas, she returned to his house and, in Colin's absence, retained him in the form of her snakes. Lovingly they would wrap themselves around her, just as her social worker Louise later enfolded her in her arms when showing her how to hold her children close.

How, though, did Sara rid herself of her snakes' contrary uncuddly, fearful aspect? Behaviour therapy helped. Louise encouraged her symbolically to take on the authority represented by sitting in her professional social worker's chair. She also encouraged Sara to shout out her assertiveness and defiance. She got Sara to imagine her stepfather about to abuse her, then to round on him and berate him with 'Don't you dare go near that child. No.' It was saying 'No', claimed Sara, that finally stopped her snakes.

Hence her anxiety to speak out her rage to me. In the past her doctors had silenced her: they deprived her of her voice. They patronised her. She was furious with herself for having so long mutely acquiesced in their prescriptions, even to the extent of getting pregnant when her GP suggested this as remedy for her various disorders.

Now, having expressed her wrath verbally, she wrote it down. She put all her anger into a letter to her psychiatrist. It had been the same with her father. Cut off from phoning him, she had written to him instead. She wanted me to tell her story too, or so she said. 'There are so many, many out there who have been abused, who yearn to say it all,' she concluded. 'How do they feel? Ask them.'

Freud's Anna O. likewise freed herself from her paralysing symptoms by putting into words the repressed and stagnating phallic figures – a dream of a snake and her hysterically stiffened arm – that substituted for her father when he was dead. She went on to become a leading women's rights campaigner, championing abandoned pregnant women and child victims of male-organised prostitution, and writing about one of her notable ancestors, a woman who also rescued others.[13]

Sara's therapy had a similarly liberating effect. It enabled her to put into speech the immobilising, exaggerated snake images of her abusive stepfather so that she could move on.[14] Having verbalised her previously somatically symbolised story, she was determined to go forward and speak out on both her own and others' behalf against men's abuse.

Meanwhile others continue to suffer, not recognising men for what they are, whether by repressing them as gross figures in the unconscious, or, as I shall now explain, by defending with depression against the recognition that their menfolk are not the ideal figures they want.

12

Depression

The woman who loudly pities her husband for being tied to such an incapable wife as herself is really accusing her husband of being incapable, in whatever sense she may mean this.

Sigmund Freud, 1917[1]

Freud's housewife defends against disappointment in her husband by holding on to, introjecting and identifying with him as a paragon of his sex. She then castigates herself, not him, for being no such marvel. Her self-complaints on this score constitute her depression.

Despair afflicts many more women than men.[2] But men too are vulnerable, as Joseph Conrad demonstrates in *Lord Jim*, his novel about a sailor who abandons his passengers and jumps ship when it is likely to capsize, following which he is driven by a remorseless superego figure inside himself to quit one port after another whenever his spoilt heroic image risks being exposed. Finally he courts certain death rather than be thought to have betrayed an Asian people with whom he settles, who have made him their god.

Today analysis of depressive self-destruction as a defence against disillusion in oneself or in others as magnificent heroes[3] has been largely replaced by the theory that dejection is due to thwarted maternal attachment.[4] Alternatively, Kleinians attribute this mood not, as Freud did, to identification with others as ideal figures, but to the *failure* of this process, in the first place the failure to internalise the mother as a loving figure giving us confidence that we can repair the damage done by hate, such that we then defensively experience her as attacking us.[5]

Paranoia, failed reparation and thwarted maternal attachment are indeed often involved in depression. They were all apparent

153

in forty-five-year-old Ann, as I shall indicate, before describing the Freudian aspects of her story which demonstrate that her depression was mainly a defence against recognising that men were not the ideal figures she wanted them to be.

Ann's house hardly seemed the harbinger of despondency and gloom. It was tiny and packed with cosy clutter. Every spare wall was stacked with romantic novels, children's encyclopaedias and books. In the garden her youngest child, plump six-year-old Katy, basked idyllically in the sun, under a straw hat, listening to taped stories reminiscent of those Ann's sisters used to read her when she was a child. Meanwhile Ann fixed Katy orange squash, and an enormous buttered hunk of bread.

Life had not always been so snug. Nor did Ann feel at ease inside. Instead she felt full of foreboding. Perhaps that was why she never answered my letters. She assumed they would contain bad news. I took my chance going to see her on the date I had suggested. She didn't answer the door when I arrived, although I knocked repeatedly. I peered over the fence and spied her at the end of the garden – bulky, huddled over, weeding, apparently deaf to my shouts.

She must have heard me. Eventually she came over, but without acknowledging my presence she went indoors. She emerged at the front door looking bewildered – blinking as though she had been in the dark. Slowly it dawned on her who I was. She took me in, shooing the cat – 'the only male in the house,' she told me – out of the kitchen door ahead of us. Then she told me the council were harassing her: they were threatening her with eviction. It had almost driven her to another nervous breakdown; the stress had exacerbated her gall bladder trouble and her daughter Katy's asthma.

Having banished the source of her troubles into her cat and the council, Ann relaxed. She bade me do the same, to make myself comfy in her cushion-stuffed rocking chair, while she made tea, a ramshackle procedure involving boiling water in a battered saucepan. Without more ado, she launched into the story of her life.

It was depressing stuff. From the very beginning she had been a 'mistake'. Her parents had both lost their fathers in the First World War and had been brought up by violent stepfathers. They

154

met, when they grew up, in the Far East, where they married and had two daughters, Carol and Betty. They then separated for several years. Ann was the result of one last reunion, which proved so disastrous, Ann's sister said, that her mother immediately exiled Ann's father into the back bedroom.

Ann divided the couple in her mind just as they became divided in fact. Her father again went overseas. Meanwhile her mother, long since driven to drink by his many infidelities, mistook her pregnancy with Ann for the bowel cancer that had killed her own mother ten years before.

It was hardly an auspicious start. Ann's mother was forty-one and did not want Ann. Nor did her father provide for her. He had become an officer, but, far from increasing the allowance he sent home, he halved it. With little support from him, and none from her mother, Ann was cared for by her sister Betty.

Their father was gone. So too was their mother. Retreated into a schizophrenic world of her own, she left Ann to her own devices and its attendant risks. Ann remembered, she said, rocking so vigorously in her high-up baby carriage that she almost brought it crashing down on top of her. Other memories were more benign – of Betty taking her to a sweet shop run by two very old women, and of her fascination with two brightly coloured parrots there. A replica dangled in the window of the kitchen where we sat.

Ann also recalled herself, aged three, careering around on a tricycle, running wild, especially after her sisters left home to work as secretaries. Every weekend they would return loaded with goodies and would fall to and scrub the week's dirt off the neglected Ann, and try to disentangle her matted hair. By the middle of the week, however, chaos reigned again. Grime and desolation returned to do away with whatever good her sisters' care had done.

Their mother never cleaned or cooked. Nor would she accept money from her older daughter, Carol. She threw it in Carol's face. Later, when Carol married, she accused her respectable businessman husband of replacing her good potatoes with shrivelled old ones. Ann shared her mother's suspiciousness. She complained that the mouth-watering chocolate Betty brought her each

Saturday gave her 'collywobbles', she was so ravenous and ate it so fast.

But even the mixed blessing of sweets and her sisters' visits came to an end. By the time Ann was ten both women had married. After that they seldom visited, although they must have known that Ann was in danger of being battered by their mother. After all, she used to beat Betty. But neither Betty nor Carol seemed to care. Nor did anyone else – not even the neighbours.

No one intervened to save Ann from her mother and from damning identification with her. Ann took on her mother's voice and her Welsh accent. Indeed, she still spoke like her whenever she was nervous. She also took on her mother's paranoia. It made going to kindergarten a nightmare: being cooped up with strangers, surrounded by nauseating smells, and noisy screeching slates. Later, in primary school, she was bullied. She was laughed at for her Welsh lilt, ridiculed for being so big, and blamed for anything her fellow-pupils did wrong. She tried to escape by writing make-believe stories at the back of the class, or stayed away altogether pretending to be ill, which suited her mother, since she then did not have to get up to take Ann to school. Or Ann hid in the bushes on nearby waste ground, reading or watching the insects.

It was no surprise when she failed the secondary school entrance exam, but her failure imprisoned her still more in her mother's crazy world. Previously her mother had castigated Ann as a mistake. Now that Ann had failed the eleven-plus she derided her as a fool. Seeing in Ann the folly to which madness had reduced her, and not wanting the shame of Ann attending the school for grammar school rejects, she kept Ann at home instead, never letting her out of the house on her own.

Staying home might not have been so bad, Ann went on, had her mother still been the cuddly, warm, gently singing person she had been when Ann was younger. But now that Ann was verging on adolescence her mother became a different, terrifying figure.

Ann remembered days spent sitting upstairs, rocking herself on her bed, her ears pricked up for the slightest sound from below. There her mother sat in the lounge, hour after hour, silently staring into space. She would start talking – softly at first – on and on. Hearing her, Ann immediately mounted guard at the bend of the stairs. Gradually her mother's voice got louder and angrier as she berated 'them' – her invisible detractors. As their imagined taunts grew, Ann's mother became more agitated. She paced around the sitting room. Then she would be in the hall, clutching a brass poker, restlessly going into the kitchen, to the dining room, to the lounge, and back. Meanwhile Ann crouched, holding her breath, listening and watching between the banisters.

When her mother was at the foot of the stairs, Ann would flee into the front bedroom. Locking the door behind her, she would climb into the massive, old-fashioned wardrobe and sit uncomfortably on a pile of stiletto-heeled shoes, behind her mother's enormous mothball-reeking fur coat. Only when she had it pulled around her did she feel safe. Meanwhile she could hear her mother coming after her – pounding up the stairs, hammering on the door, shouting that if she could only lay hands on Ann she would flay her alive.

After what seemed hours, the noise abated. Her mother went downstairs. Hush descended. Only then did Ann dare creep out. Sometimes it was quite dark when she emerged to find her mother once more ensconced in the sitting room, seemingly oblivious of the ordeal she had just put them both through.

At some level, however, she must have known. Why else did she leave a key in the bedroom door so that Ann could protect herself? Why else did she eventually write to the School Board alerting them that, if they did not stop persecuting her, she would kill both herself and Ann?

It led, Ann maintained, still not distinguishing clearly between herself and her mother, to their both being arrested. They were taken away in a Black Maria, and locked in a police cell. From there Ann was sent to a nearby children's home, but soon her mother abducted her. Pressurised by her two older daughters, she now let Ann go to school, but when Ann failed grammar school entrance again the whole cycle started once more, and Ann was eventually sent away to a residential institution at the other end of the country.

At half-term her mother visited. Afterwards the headmistress told Ann she would never return to her mother again; instead she would be sent to live with her father. At that, Ann's mother died for her. Ann became numb with grief – with guilt and depressive anxiety that it was her fault she had lost her mother, through bad-mouthing her to others.

Ann became mute. People talked to her, and tried to explain, but she could only nod in reply. Along with her voice, she lost all feeling. Life became mere drudgery, a mechanical business of getting through each day. Desolate, she sought comfort in cuddling herself. She felt all the more driven to this lonesome recourse when her father, in effect, annihilated her mother, denouncing her to Ann as evil, as a murderess who wanted to kill Ann. This drove Ann to cut herself off from her mother altogether. She even stopped writing to her.

Moving into her father's house and comparing it with that of her mother she also learnt, as though for the first time, of the deprivation she had suffered at her mother's hands – no regular meals, no gas for cooking, no coal or electricity. Only candles for light, and bed for warmth.

Now that she was better looked after by her father's second wife, Ann's schoolwork improved. Her concentration still wandered, but at last she managed to win herself the grammar school place her mother had so long coveted for her. After finishing secondary school, Ann went on to study shorthand and typing, but she found the work insufferably boring, and decided to become a nurse instead. Perhaps, in Kleinian terms, she thereby wanted to repair the damage she had done her mother by cutting herself off from her as though she were dead. Through nursing Ann first learnt about schizophrenia, and this restored her mother to her – as ill, not bad.

Try as she might, however, Ann could not cure the patients who replaced her mother. Her failure was underlined one dreadful evening when, feeling abandoned by her senior nursing officers to everlasting night duty (as she felt her sisters had long ago abandoned her to her mother as a child), Ann arrived on the ward to find herself in sole charge.

Nothing went right. The qualified nurse who should have been there was off sick, and the only other nurse was a new recruit. Within minutes Ann found herself cradling a terminally ill woman who was terrified of dying. Ann was very fond of her, but all her efforts proved futile. The woman died. No time for grief – Ann immediately had to help a new houseman fix up an intravenous drip for an emergency admission. Briefly her spirits rose when a trained nurse appeared, but it turned out it was this nurse's very first night back on duty after eleven years away.

Ann could not concentrate on laying the dead woman out. The drip had to be attended to. It was not working properly, and the newly returned nurse was too frightened to help. Meanwhile another patient had gone into cardiac arrest. The other staff panicked. Ann was the only one who knew the emergency resuscitation procedure, but this patient too died. Just as Ann was laying out the second dead woman of the night, the drip on the other patient stopped working. It was soon fixed. Another patient called out, and one look at her swollen, inflamed limb was enough to show Ann that this patient's life was also in danger – from deep vein thrombosis. Hating herself for being unable to cope on her own, Ann called out the junior doctor to help.

When it was all over the student nurse congratulated Ann for being so calm. It only compounded Ann's misery. Neither the student nor anyone else knew the turmoil she was in. It left her feeling embittered at everyone – the women who had left her on night duty; the qualified nurses who had either not shown up or been too frightened to help; and the other students, whose seemingly normal home lives Ann so envied. To cap it all she had been unable to allay or make good these hostile feelings by nursing her patients back to health. Two had died. Others had become dangerously ill.

Faced with her failed attempts at reparation, as Klein might have put it, Ann went to pieces. She had to be hospitalised herself. No sooner did she begin to recover than she was recruited to look after the other patients, only to succumb again to despair – like Lady Macbeth – of ever washing away the badness of it all, the suicides and horrible smell of the hospital ward.

At last she recovered and continued nursing. She was still a nurse when I met her, looking after old ladies. It remained one of her main consolations, just as it had been twenty years before.

Through nursing Ann met her first husband, Ray, when he was hospitalised with appendicitis, his stay made longer by his diabetes.

His family in turn nursed Ann through her subsequent nervous breakdown, from which she finally recovered by replacing her lost mother, as it were: following her doctors' advice, she got pregnant and became a mother herself. Soon she and Ray had two daughters, Ellen and Clare.

Within months of Clare's birth, Ann heard that her mother had had a heart attack. She decided to return with Ray and her daughters to live with her mother – even though it meant being disowned by her respectable and recently knighted father. Ann never saw him again; nor did anyone think to tell her when he died.

By then Ann had learnt that her mother had three times nearly starved herself to death out of grief when Ann was first taken from her. Reconciliation, however, came too late. She no longer recognised Ann: she dismissed her as an impostor, just as she had written off Ann's father. Four years later she was dead. Ann felt nothing.

It was not her mother's death, nor her failed attempts to repair the damage she had done her mother by leaving her, nor her persisting experience of her mother as persecutor that caused Ann her worst depression. Certainly these factors did often cause Ann to become depressed, but her deepest despair resulted, as Freud said of melancholia, from defending against loss with idealisation, in Ann's case from fending off disillusion in the men in her life by idealising them as a refuge from her mother.[6]

This returns me to the beginning of her story, this time to its principal male protagonists, starting with Ann's earliest memory of a man walking in through the garden gate to rescue her from upending the pram in which she had been dangerously abandoned by her mother. Then Ann remembered her father's munificence: his playing with her; making her a swing; giving her a doll's pram; building a chicken coop for the hens he left the family to eke out the hardships of rationing when he was posted overseas. She also recalled, after his return, herself aged two sitting on his knee in the garden while he talked with another man, a solicitor, about getting a divorce. Shortly after that he finally left.

Years later, after the grammar school débâcle, when she too wanted to get away from her mother, it was of her father she thought. After all, he had got away. She also remembered, from when she was a toddler, overhearing her sisters talking about him. To this was added a later memory of her teachers at school getting her to recite 'Our Father who art in heaven'. The words conjured up a wonderful patriarch, quite different to the one her mother excoriated as 'the bastard who works for the War Office'. Ann also recalled padding after her brother-in-law, Carol's husband, looking up to him like a faithful puppy following its master. Now, as a teenager, with both her brother-in-law and father gone, she venerated their sex as the Lord's Prayer had taught her to do.

Her mother had said her father worked in London. Like the proverbial Dick Whittington, Ann therefore assumed her fortune also lay there. She determined to go to the capital, even though it meant tramping many miles from the country town where she lived. Her journey, however, was soon cut short. After six or seven hours, just as she was settling down under a hedge for the night, a farmer spotted her. It delayed her finding her father, but Ann did not mind – now she had this other man's attention. The farmer gave her a ride in his tractor, then handed her over to a policeman. The officer let her pat his dog, and gave her a book about alsatians.

He also arranged, through social services, for Ann to meet up with her father. The encounter proved bitterly disappointing. He was just a man, Ann said, no different from the ordinary run of the mill. She felt no sense of belonging. He was an utter stranger who smoked heavily, coughed, and smelt of stale tobacco. He made out he was pleased to see her, but his words were hollow. They felt meaningless.

Ann's experience was analogous to that of Sylvia Plath recounting the disillusion in herself, as though she were her father, that preceded her first suicide attempt:

> I recognized it, the way you recognize some nondescript person that's been hanging around your door for ages and then suddenly comes up and introduces himself as your real father and looks exactly like you, so you know he really is your father, and the person you thought all your life was your father is a sham.[7]

No wonder, faced with a similar disjunction between her idealised image of her father and the sham he seemed to be, that Ann became so dejected when, aged fourteen, she was despatched from boarding-school to live with him. Once arrived at his home, however, she was enchanted. It had all the makings of paradise – it was clean and fresh and had a television, a car, a beautiful garden, a large comfortable bed to sleep in, a cat and dog, regular two-course meals, and, best of all, a six-month-old baby brother.

But heaven proved short-lived. Try as she might she could not please her father. Evidently she was no good. One day, for instance, when she was supposed to be minding her baby brother in the park, she fell asleep. Swinging and dreaming, she did not notice a storm brewing until a thunderclap awoke her. Dreading lest her father learn she had neglected his son, especially since a gardener told her off for having the baby out in the rain, she accepted this man's invitation to shelter in his hut. So she only had herself to blame, she felt, when the man's mate raped her, and the foreman then bawled her out as a 'slut'. She felt sick, dirty, and awful about herself – particularly because she wanted the man and his sex again, she so longed for someone to hold and comfort her.

Without a man to call her own, she tried to stanch her emptiness with food as though the void were physical,[8] but eating only made her hate herself more. It made her feel wicked, especially since her father's slim wife obviously disapproved, and kept putting Ann on diets. Ann's inability to keep to them made her feel guiltier than ever, and shamefully devoid of self-control.

She felt so bad that it came as no surprise when, at the end of the summer, her father told her she could no longer live with them. His new mother-in-law was coming to stay: he had never had the courage to tell her of his first marriage and did not want her to discover Ann's existence. So he told Ann not even to come within sight of his house, adding that when they met she should no longer call him Dad, but Derek.

Ann would have felt totally rejected had she not immediately idealised another man in his place: the foster father to whom she was now sent. Fortuitously he turned out to be called Derek too, and welcomed her warmly into his home. Ann luxuriated in identifying with him and his adored baby daughter. He taught Ann to swim, and to play mah-jong and cards so that she could play them with her father when he visited. He could conjure away the blackest mood, and pick one up out of the most explosive anger. Literally. He would lift his Turkish wife off the floor whenever she was in a rage. It was this admired man Ann kept in mind a year later when she returned to live with her father after his mother-in-law died.

But her sense of not belonging remained, and became overwhelming. Yearning to love and be loved, she drifted into a two-year affair with a boy who was also addicted, not to food but to drink. After leaving school, unable to bear her father's indifference, she moved into the nurses' home. There she had a succession of one-night stands, but her promiscuity made her feel worse.

It was then that she first met Ray. He had grown up in a tiny, one-family fishing village, and was a big, gentle, burly, soft-spoken chap. He seemed the very panacea Ann needed, and remained so after they married. Then, when she was eight months pregnant with their first child Ellen, he became enraged one day when she smiled at his difficulty in putting up a curtain rail. Unable to bear this hint of disillusion, he punched her.

It was the first of many blows. For the next eleven years they rained down on her. His assaults seemed a judgment from God, testimony to Ann of how bad she was. Doubtless, she told herself, she had provoked Ray by being dominating and emasculating, just as his mother, it seemed, had been before her. Ann tried to do away with the badness by being a perfect wife. She cooked, polished and cleaned, driving herself to make their home as spotless as her stepmother kept her father's house. Fearful that her children might aggravate her husband as she did, she bundled them off to bed before he arrived home from work so they would not disturb him.

But it proved useless: Ray beat her even when she was pregnant with their third child. It resulted in her miscarrying the baby – their only son. After that she bore him a third daughter, Lisa. She proved an easy child at first, unlike their second daughter Clare who always seemed to be crying, and for eighteen months all went well. Then the beatings started again. Still Ann stayed, because the rest of the time Ray was always so loving.

One Sunday morning, her already precarious image of him as a loving husband was finally shattered. He woke in a bad temper. Their two older daughters were already out playing, and Ann decided she would take herself and four-year-old Lisa out too. Ray shouted after her to come back and make his bed. 'Make it yourself,' she retorted. She was off, but soon returned to fix his lunch.

It proved the last straw. She discovered the kitchen littered with shards of a china tea-set she treasured so much that she had never even risked using it since receiving it as a wedding present. Ray had already destroyed other things she loved: he had torn up a photograph of their oldest daughter Ellen and thrown the bits into the dustbin; he had shredded her geranium shoots. But smashing her beloved tea service was the end. Worse still, he now came into the kitchen and splintered and crushed the broken pieces with his foot, lambasting her as he did so with blistering verbal abuse.

Suddenly something snapped in Ann. Previously, like many others, she had turned her anger depressively against herself. Now she turned it against him. She wanted to kill him with the carving knife lying on the draining board. Alarmed, she grabbed baby Lisa from the next room and left. She did not return until Ray had left the house for good.

No sooner was he gone than Ann tried – through a dating agency – to find another man. But they all turned out to be 'rotters': only after one thing, sex. All except Jonathan. He was well educated and charming, but he was impotent, little different from his neutered tomcat which he spent hours talking about to Ann over the phone: hardly her male ideal.

Instead she took up with Alan. He was always there for her – thoughtful, supportive, attentive. Mindful of her disappointment in her first husband, Ann would not marry him at first. It took six years before she finally did, only to find even worse disaster.

Alan could not bear to have his new-found status as paterfamilias questioned. Nor could Ann. It was this that caused her deepest depression. It was not due, as it had been before (and as much current therapy and casework would predict), principally to mothering and its vicissitudes. Neither the birth of their daughter Katy nor the miscarriage of their second child two years later caused her anything like the despair she suffered in defending against the disillusion she might otherwise have felt in Alan, who was prone to infantile jealousy, childish tantrums and ridiculous bombast.

It culminated in his taunting of Ann's third daughter, Lisa, whom Ann felt was the most similar of her children to herself. Like Ann, Lisa had grown from a good baby into a naughty truant. Lisa too failed to get into grammar school. She was self-conscious about her looks. She was prone to depression – and even attempted suicide. In jeering at Lisa – calling her stupid, crazy, spotty – Alan was in danger of becoming like Ann's memory of her persecuting mother.

All hope of Alan as a refuge from this black maternal memory ended the day he knocked Lisa about so badly that she was left with two black eyes. Ann's childhood memories of her mother pounding upstairs, banging on the door while she cowered in the cupboard, flooded back, alternating with nightmares of the rape she suffered when she was fourteen (as Lisa now was). Men, she said, only wanted women to be sex objects, machines into which 'you pays your money and you takes what you want'.

Terrified of Alan turning into the despised and feared figure of her dreams, Ann did not dare go to sleep. She was anyway too agitated to rest. Pacing up and down all day and night, she became numb with fatigue. She felt nothing, not even for her youngest daughter, Katy, who was two: the same age as Ann had been when she first lost her father.

She berated herself for feeling so little, for having become an automaton – a zombie – mechanically, lifelessly going through the daily round. Apart from looking after the old lady next door, nothing seemed likely to end the monotonous gloom. The light with which she had endowed the men in her life threatened to go out.[9] Everything became dreary, a living death. Suicide would be better.

Devoid of emotion, Ann fended off disillusion in her men with physical ills. She consulted her doctor, but he was not beguiled. Recognising her organic complaints as essentially psychological, he referred her to a social worker, Marian. Dejectedly Ann told her her story. To Marian, it was as if Ann was emptying a packing case into which she had stuffed her tribulations like so many inanimate objects till the chest got so full that the lid burst open. Slowly Ann began to unburden herself. She signified the change by altering her name – to Pandora. It both contained and went beyond the name her mother had given her.

Pandora was no coincidence. The first feelings to emerge, as for her mythical namesake, were demons. Initially, still unable to let go the men she had so long exalted, she fended off disenchantment by clutching on to, and being clutched by, their idealised replicas, as Klein's analyst and mentor Karl Abraham described depression.[10]

Ann's clutched-onto male-based figures berated her from within. She told herself, as her father used to say of her mother, that she was evil, that she would be the death of her children; or she maligned herself for being the no-good parent she felt her father and her two husbands, Ray and Alan, had been. She vilified and told herself, again as her father had told her *vis-à-vis* her mother, that her daughters would be better off without her. She was no good for them – a guilt-ridden encumbrance imprisoned in a dark cell no different from the one in which the men – the School Board man, the farmer, the policeman – had castigated her mother for incarcerating her as a child.

Recalling her suicidal thoughts – that she should die so Katy could be brought up better by Alan – Ann turned to Katy who was now dreamily reading in the room where we sat. 'Daddy loves you, doesn't he?' Ann murmured to her. At this the well-practised six-year-old awoke, as Ann used to be anxiously roused by her mother's distress. Katy hugged Ann and reassuringly whispered in her ear, 'But I love you too.'

A couple of years before, Katy's older sister Clare had earned the money necessary for Ann to begin buying a house to move into, away from Alan. It was only then that Ann started to be able to acknowledge her disillusionment, rather than depressively defend against it. Only then could she begin to give up her self-punishing identification with men's criticism of her, as though it were she, not they, who had destroyed her belief in their sex.

Anticipating leaving Alan gave her the space, as Kristeva might put it, to speak out her feelings. Just as the Algerian-born writer, Marie Cardinal, describes becoming freed through therapy from 'The Thing' – from being abjectly identified with her mother's obsession with the death of her baby sister and with absenting their father from Marie's childhood home[11] – Ann too now had space to put her feelings into words.

Before, she had been flooded by emotion, drowned by it, just as Beirut hostage Brian Keenan describes sinking into melancholia during solitary confinement:

> I am weeping, not knowing from where the tears come or for what reason, but I am weeping and weeping is all that I am. I cannot think or feel, this thing has possessed me . . . I have tried to scream, but nothing will come out of me. No sound, no noise, nothing.[12]

In a similar state of mind, Ann was so immersed in misery that she did not even know she was so depressed.

As her distress began to have an identifiable separate object – Alan – Ann started telling anyone and everyone about the incipient death of her illusions about the men in her life. She became like children who tell themselves and others stories over and over to give their feelings shape and size, to contain them in words and pictures. In the process, however, Ann told and retold her tale so compulsively that she stripped it of meaning.

Then, just as Kafka, after writing *The Trial* (in which he expresses a similar self-divided excoriation of men) went on to write a never-to-be-posted letter expressing his dissatisfaction with his father, so Ann told her story in a letter written but never sent to the author of a self-help book about overeating – the strategy to which she first resorted as defence against her father's weak-willed rejection of her as a teenager.

For many years Ann had thought the emptiness she had sought to fill with food was caused by the loss of her mother. She had tried to make reparation for this by nursing, but now she told me, she had done with 'wiping old women's bottoms'. She was planning to go to college. Saying goodbye to the school phobia of her childhood (the counterpart of her identification with her mother's paranoia from which she had sought escape through lionising men) she intended to train as a teacher. She was also going to move house again – to get further away from Alan. She dismissed him just as she had previously idealised him – wholesale.

She dismissed me too. It would be no good my trying to contact her. She had no idea when and where she would be going. She split me off. Therapy had been unable to help her, at a deep level, to come to terms with, and put together the bits and pieces of her love and hate. Without this work of grief and disillusion, she remained prey to the fantasy that a perfect man would come along. Indeed, when I last heard of her, I discovered that she never did get to college because she had become infatuated with just such a character. Like Conrad's Lord Jim obsessed with wanting to be the hero of his dreams, Ann remained captivated by the hope that her latest lover would save her from disenchantment with his sex.

13
Death Denied

In what, now, does the work which mourning performs consist? I do not think there is anything far-fetched in presenting it in the following way. Reality-testing has shown that the loved object no longer exists, and it proceeds to demand that all libido shall be withdrawn from its attachments to that object. This demand arouses understandable opposition . . . [Reality's] orders cannot be obeyed at once. They are carried out bit by bit, at great expense of time and cathectic energy, and in the meantime the existence of the lost object is psychically prolonged.

                                                    Sigmund Freud, 1917[1]

The dead live on – their absence for a time denied. Nor is denial confined to bereavement. It can also involve, as Melanie Klein observed when writing about maternal loss, a retreat from depressive concern for those we have lost to hypochondriacal preoccupation with ourselves.[2] Furthermore, psychoanalyst Joyce McDougall observes that when we refuse to take in, or psychologically process, external events there is then nothing to intervene and prevent them impinging directly on our bodies.[3]

This might explain why people bereaved of those they love often become physically sick, or even die, as documented by Bowlby's colleague, Colin Murray Parkes.[4] Few, however, point out that our inflation of men's importance might make their death particularly difficult to deal with without denial and its attendant ailments. We might therefore predict that when disillusion in men – or their loss – is denied any psychological or symbolic representation, their death can result in psychosomatic symptoms.

Such symptoms featured prominently for Sheila, whose father and husband died within days of each other. Rather than know about their death, Sheila – who was in her late fifties – suffered it organically. She still kept going the bodily panic she experienced when they were dying, thereby perpetuating their death unconsummated, unending.

Their passing still hung in the air. When I phoned to ask the way to her house she told me to follow the sign to the cemetery. She lived close by. On her front door a plaque announced, CARL AND SHEILA LIVE HERE. But Carl had died more than three years before. Sheila's sitting room was still full of the heavy scent of funeral flowers, reminiscent of *The Waste Land*:

> April is the cruellest month, breeding
> Lilacs out of the dead land.[5]

There the blooms were, alongside birthday cards. When I commented on them, Sheila told me about cards her neighbour had also recently received. The neighbour was old, Sheila added, she would soon be dead.

She hoped I would not be 'overwhelmed' by the musk of her flowers. Their scent was so oppressive it had given her a migraine the previous day. A sickening pall did indeed weigh over us, and its heaviness did not go away. At the end of our first meeting, Sheila worried that she too had burdened me – worn me out by talking too long.

Outwardly, no such anxieties seemed to bother her. She seemed utterly self-confident, even smug. Solid and roundly built, calm and collected, she organised tea and biscuits for us. I soon learnt, however, of the price she paid for her psychological composure with physical ills. They were as ever present in her mind as those afflicting her and her family just before her husband died. She began by telling me about their ailments: her blocked sinuses; her mother's diabetes and heart operations; her father's crumbling spine. Throughout, she said, Carl had marvellously ferried them all back and forth from hospital.

Then she told me of her father's dying – just after being discharged – suddenly, from a heart attack, when Carl and Sheila were out buying trousers for him. Since Sheila's mother could not contact them when she discovered him collapsed in the chair she phoned Sheila's son-in-law Colin to drive over instead.

170

Within a week Carl was also dead. The day before he died Sheila had invited a friend of her mother's, Mary, over to see what a grand job Carl had made of their garden. Carl would fetch her. But then Mary fell sick with diarrhoea and vomiting. Did she infect Carl? Was that why, Sheila asked herself, he suddenly keeled over that night in the bathroom, knocking his head on the basin as he fell. Now what Sheila most remembered was the pain in her ribs as she heaved him up. She must have pulled a muscle.

She went on to tell me of her frantic carrying-on as Carl lay on the floor. She had phoned her son-in-law Colin, urging him, 'Come quick. I can't move him. Shall I get an ambulance? They'll grumble at it only being sickness.' He told her to get one and within a couple of minutes he was there, clearing her out of the way as he rushed upstairs to give Carl the kiss of life. But it was no good.

All Sheila could remember was her agitation, how she had thrown some clothes on and run to the end of the lane – in the dark, wind and rain. Finding no ambulance there, she rushed back home and phoned again. The receptionist assured her the ambulance was on its way. Sheila was beside herself with rage at it not arriving, and (when it finally came), with irritation at the men taking such an age backing, shunting, and parking, with her all the while screaming, 'Get in here! Get in here!'

At last they were in. They got Carl on to the landing and fixed a monitor to his chest. 'Beep, beep, beep,' it went. He must have been alive. Methodically they worked on him. Sheila still could not keep calm. As if ingesting the frozen grip of death that was clutching her husband's heart, she drank one glass of iced water after another – frenetically going from the tumbler to the toilet and back.

She looked at the clock. It was well over an hour since it had all begun, since she saw the lurid colour mounting in Carl's face, since she first heard his death rattle. The ambulance men went on trying to pummel him back to life. Then they came over and said, 'There's nothing more we can do.' They were off, leaving her more upset than ever. The doctor came. He gave her some pills. Then he too was gone.

After him came the undertakers. 'Quick Sheila,' shouted Colin, 'they need an old sheet to wrap him in.' But she was too fearful to get one. It would mean stepping over Carl. She could not do that – see him stretched out, dead. She grabbed a blanket out of a chest by her side instead. 'No,' Colin insisted. 'They want a sheet.' So she went over to the airing cupboard and reached up for one. As she did so her father's trousers, the ones she and Carl had bought for him, fell on top of her. 'Dad's clothes are in there! My dad's clothes are in there!' she shrieked, over and over.

It brought me to the edge of my chair: the vivid effigy of the two men, father and husband, merged into one tumbling dying mass. Mixed in with it were other, equally persistent but contrary images: the figure of her father, 'sat bolt upright in the chair, his mouth dropped'; and Carl, 'purple with white rising like a line up his face'.

Having finished their work, the undertakers invited Sheila to go and see Carl laid out, still and peaceful, on the bed. But the memory of his death throe churning frightened her away. It was never replaced by the quieter image of him dead and gone; instead the nightmare of his dying remained. It continued to haunt her – just as unconsciously she sought to haunt me in retelling it – the image quite different from the friendly figures of Carl and her father that her seven-year-old grandson Robin imagined listening in, when she read him their favourite bedtime story.

Sheila compared the repeated cycle of Carl's dying to a looped video in her mind that she could not bear to watch. But one can at least switch a tape off, she complained. One can't turn off one's mind. She wished she could draw the curtains on her husband being gone – like those drawn on death at the crematorium. Perhaps she could only end his endless dying by dying herself. Fearing that she would indeed commit suicide, her son Nigel took all her pills away from her the day Carl died.

His younger sister, Penny, also knew how little their mother could bear to know about loss. She left it to the last moment to tell Sheila, after Carl's death, that she too would be going. She and her husband Colin who lived round the corner, were about to move to another, nearby town. Soon I found myself also soft-pedalling anything resembling death lest talk of it upset Sheila too much.

172

By then, as if to warn me to protect her, she had made much of both her own and her family's need to deny what was gone. Her maternal grandfather, she told me, found her grandmother's leaving him so unbearable that he acted as though she had never been. So did Sheila's mother. She had almost wiped from her mind the memory of a woman – who she thought might have been her mother – who once stopped her in the street when she was a child to give her sweets. If she was her mother, nobody ever said. All she knew was that without a mother at home, she had to bring up herself, her two younger brothers, and several children her father then had with her stepmother.

Absence also marked Sheila's childhood. When she was four her father went away to the war. On his return her older brother Tom, then aged sixteen, left home. Two years later, Sheila's younger brother Gordon also left. They went as far away as possible: Tom to Canada, Gordon to New Zealand. Sheila, by contrast, always stayed with her parents, even after marrying Carl.

She met Carl when he was lodging with her aunt, but it was chance, Sheila insisted, that brought them together in the foursome the first night they went out. He was six years older than her, the same age as her brother Tom. Having Carl to replace Tom meant she did not have to acknowledge his absence.

Otherwise Carl had nothing to recommend him. Sheila remembered him in those days as plump and short, a fuddy-duddy, pipe-smoking, tweed-suited clerk. Not her type at all. Even so, and despite being only sixteen, she immediately planned on their staying together for ever. Nor would her 'living a bit' before marrying lose Carl to her. He encouraged her to go out on dates in nearby Manchester and always met her train home to Bolton.

They might as well have been married, and within a couple of years they were. Sheila, however, could not bear to be away from her parents. She and Carl moved to live with his family in Liverpool, but returned every weekend to be with Sheila's family. Within a year they moved back to Bolton, where they rented a flat. Then, upset by the dog upstairs howling all day while its owners were out, they moved in with her parents until at last they acquired a house of their own in the same neighbourhood.

By this time they had two children, Nigel and Penny. Nigel

could no more tolerate absence than she could, or so Sheila said. Attributing his asthma – 'wheezing like a dead thing' – to the fact that she left him to go out to work, she gave up her job and stayed home.

Nigel and Penny grew up to go to grammar school and university. By the time I met Sheila, who was now living in Southend, both were married with children of their own, but Penny still lived close by, and so did Sheila's mother. They had all moved to Southend many years before when Carl's job took him there. He had gone on ahead, but wrote to Sheila every day, and returned to her in Bolton every weekend. Apart from that one time, she had never been apart from either him or her parents.

No wonder his death, following so quickly on that of her father, was such a shock. Nor was she the only one unable to take it in. Her brother Tom could not bring himself to return from Canada for either man's funeral: he said it was because of visa difficulties, but that never stopped him coming home at Christmas. As for Sheila, she could not tell me about Carl being dead. Instead she told me about her physical ills – her blinding migraine – when he was being cremated.

Her seven-year-old grandson Robin was the same; or so Sheila claimed. He had not only lost Carl and Sheila's father, but his other grandfather had also died. Robin could not bear to lose anyone else. The very thought of his own father, Colin, going away even for a day – to take part in a local boat race – threw Robin into terrified anxiety. He woke in the night screaming, 'No, Daddy, no! He won't come back. He won't come back!' The next day Penny, his mother, sat him down, drew him a map of the race, took him along its route, and marked with arrows each of the different places his father would be going. 'And when we get to the last arrow,' she announced, 'Daddy will be back.' And he was.

Nevertheless, forgetting that Robin could handle his grandfathers' absence by retaining a friendly image of them in his mind while she read to him, Sheila assumed that their deaths exacted the same physical toll on him as they did on her, and that this was why Robin started to suffer from asthma.

Perhaps she was thinking of her own chest pains following her men's deaths (like those suffered by the spouses studied by Colin

Murray Parkes in his classic study of bereavement).[6] Sheila said her thoracic agony cut her in two. After Carl's death she also suffered a host of minor anxiety-related symptoms: loss of appetite, insomnia, shakiness. These gave way to more protracted stress-related ills, including migraine and arthritis.

The symptoms crowded out the fact of her father's and husband's death. So too did the physical remedies she took. She fed herself comfort food – sugar and chocolate – to numb the pain. She likewise plied her nephew with milk shakes to stop him feeling any upset at being separated from his mother (who lived abroad) when he visited Sheila in England. Meanwhile she dosed herself with anti-depressants to escape into their narcotic haze.

Drugs were not the only means she used to help her deny their death. She also avoided anything that might remind her of Carl, particularly his car, big and solid like him. She could not bear to see it outside their house – beautiful, spotless, hardly ever driven.

The night before he died she had told him how much she wanted to drive as she once used to do. Paternally he had patted her on the knee, told her his car was too heavy for her, that he had it in hand to trade it in for something lighter – especially for her. The next day he was dead. After that getting into his car made her tremble and shake. Eventually, as though he were still there telling her to do so, she did trade it in for a smaller car. But she couldn't drive that either. Driving without him reminded her too much of his absence – he had always been with her before when she drove.

Other indications of his death caused her more short-lived pangs of grief. Once, after her daughter encouraged her to give a dinner party, she found herself laying a place for Carl only to have to painfully return the cutlery to the drawer on discovering her mistake. Another time, when she went into hospital to have an operation for arthritis, she had to write down her next of kin on the consent form. She had always put Carl's name there, and seeing the space where it should have gone made her scream inside at the thought that nobody, least of all Carl, was there to know or understand.

She was so unable to tolerate the idea that Carl was gone that she blinded herself even to trivial reminders. It was hard to keep to her motto: what the eye doesn't see the heart doesn't grieve over. There was no hour – day or night – when Carl had not been there. For the six years after he had retired, he was with her round the clock.

Some reminders, however, she could avoid. She no longer read books or watched television in bed as they used to do. Instead she read satirical comics and women's weeklies – 'magazines', she squealed, thinking I might disapprove. She would not look at his photo, nor that of her father, both alike, large and balding, in the pictures on the mantelpiece. Anyway, she said, the one of Carl was not like him at all. 'He is much younger,' she said as though he were still present, 'and he is much nicer looking.' She had pulled a shutter down on the picture, she said, yet paradoxically it kept her with the dead; 'stalemated' her, as she put it, stopped her getting on with life.

Denying the two men's deaths, she could not bring herself to collect their ashes. Eventually the local vicar offered to fetch and inter them for her. Sheila chose a spot in a disused part of the graveyard – near the river, under a tree where Carl used to take the children – but she told the vicar she could not bear to be there when he did the job. She was, however, outraged, some weeks later when, taking a friend to show her the plot she had chosen, she discovered the earth newly dug. Her men's remains were evidently already there – the vicar should have warned her.

Some time later she returned. She got as far as the lych gate, but could go no further because, just at that moment, she met a funeral going in. Nor could she brave returning on the anniversary of Carl's death. She kept putting off going. By the time she got to see the church's Book of Remembrance Carl and her father had been dead so long she had to go back through pages and pages to find their names. It was awful seeing them there, she said, the cold print testifying to their demise.

Sheila began to worry that if she had not been such a past-mistress at denial Carl might have been still with her. If only she had seen, taken in and done something about the severity of the symptoms of the illness that killed him, she speculated, he might not have died. The signs were obvious: the pains in his neck some weeks before; his aching teeth; his not feeling up to writing Christmas cards as he always had previously; his talk, after her father's death, of what he wanted done with his own ashes when he died; his making a point of telling her where he kept his will. Then there had been the night itself, when she trivialised the cause of his collapse, attributing it to a mere stomach upset. She also blamed the dentist and doctor for overlooking the gravity of his symptoms.

Others she hated for reminding her of his death – particularly her women friends and acquaintances. Her next-door neighbour was so tactless, she complained; she underlined Carl's absence by inviting Sheila round only when her brother Gordon was staying, because otherwise Sheila's lack of a man left an unsightly gap at her dinner table.

Worst of all, Sheila told me on my second visit, was a woman she met at Cruse, an organisation set up to help the bereaved. It was a wet, miserable, stormy evening the night she went there. Immediately Sheila arrived this woman collared her and in 'a penetrating voice' recounted every detail of her husband's hour-long dying, death rattle included. It 'petrified' Sheila. 'Don't tell me all that,' she thought, 'I'm trying to forget it. I see it a hundred times a day already, the noise and everything.' Now I understood why, at our first meeting, she had feared overwhelming me. With her excruciating story of her husband's dying had she not unconsciously sought to subject me to the same agony the Cruse woman visited on her?

If only, Sheila grumbled, she could see some other image of Carl – not still dying. Her friends told her they saw him alive in their dreams. Not her. Once, it was true, she dreamt he was there, beside her, saving their grandsons from drowning. She had been so comforted by his presence. But she could not see him.

She saved trinkets instead, keepsakes of his maleness. His shaving things were on the shelf; his dressing-gown hung on the back of the bedroom door; his toothbrush was still in the bathroom rack. 'I suppose at the back of my mind it feels like perhaps he's just gone away and he's coming back' – a thought on which Saki makes ingenious play in his short story, 'The Open Window,' which also links denial of men's death with illness.[7]

After all, Sheila argued, hadn't her long-lost grandmother suddenly appeared on the street to her mother when she was a little girl? Hadn't her own father likewise miraculously materialised, when he was supposedly away in the war, at King's Cross station, just when Sheila, her brothers, and mother were queuing there to go on holiday without him? Sheila yearned to be reunited with Carl as she had been then with her father. It almost made her believe in an afterlife.

But she was no believer. She had no religion, no God, no Carl. After staying with her younger brother Gordon overseas, it had been dreadful to return without Carl to England. She had never travelled alone before. It was the same each night, returning late in the dark to an empty house. Without Carl's reassuring presence she peopled the void with threatening male spectres. She imagined a stranger might break in. Hearing sounds, which turned out to be birds in the roof, she became convinced a burglar was lurking behind the curtain.

She asked family and friends to stay, hoping their presence would dispel her fears. Ironically, however, she thereby risked her anxieties coming true. She was nearly raped. Not by her brother, she added revealingly, but by her uncle, her mother's brother. Twice, when he was staying at her house, she had woken to find him in her bed, forcing himself upon her.

Apart from having people to stay, she fended off the terrors of the night by keeping herself busy. She dreaded being awake between dark and dawn – the time when Carl lay dying – a period peculiarly prey to the faceless figures of the dead. To avoid being conscious in that betwixt and between time, Sheila would do the accounts, clean the house, and have a bath at midnight, in the hope of exhausting herself so she could sleep through till morning.

She also filled the daylight hours. All the fetching and carrying she once wished on Carl, the ferrying and family entertaining that perhaps contributed to his final collapse, she now took on herself. She packed her days with errands: collecting and looking after her grandchildren; helping an old lady move house; taking her mother to Age Concern, shopping, or out to lunch. Her busy schedule jostled with our appointments. 'Suggest a time,' Sheila would say at the end of each of my visits. 'I'll see if it fits in.' Even if it did she often found later that it clashed with something else. She was always over-booked.

Above all, she filled her days by trying to tidy up and get rid of her mother's disarray. It reminded her too painfully of the psychological turmoil into which she feared her men's absence would throw her. Refusing to recognise that her mother's confusion might also be due to emotional upset at their loss, Sheila explained it as an after-effect of a recent heart operation. Even so it made her furious. She could not abide her mother's absentmindedness – her going on and on about the central heating not working only to discover she had forgotten to switch it on. 'Go and check it. Go and check it,' Sheila would shout at her over the phone. Or, still trusting more in men, she would get the chap next door to fix it.

She hated her mother's mess. Each time she visited she cleaned it up – all the while criticising her mother's charlady for leaving her flat in such a state. She could not bear the way her mother overstuffed her fridge, as though to fill the gap left by Carl's and her own husband's deaths, and tried to stop it by taking her mother shopping, to limit the food she bought. When I last visited, Sheila's blocking of her own loss through such control (something Melanie Klein points out regularly accompanies denial),[8] had reached such a pitch that her mother told her to stay away.

When Carl was alive, already prone to denying loss and disillusion, Sheila tried to stamp out any depression that disappointment aroused in him. His dejected moods made her really angry. They were, she admitted, a cause – the only cause, she hastened to add – of friction between them. Yet his depression had been so serious he had had to retire twelve years early because of it.

I kept forgetting this aspect of his life, so much did Sheila idealise him as an 'exceptional' tower of strength, as a real 'pillar to lean on'. It was this that made it so hard. Nobody, she felt, could ever replace him – not even her younger brother Gordon (whom she evidently liked her workmates to mistake for her boyfriend).

She regarded Gordon as a paragon of his sex. He might seem feckless, constantly flitting from one job, woman and country to another, but he was a genius. Even when he was a schoolboy he was known as 'the professor'. As for her son Nigel; he might be nothing but a charity worker and his wife a useless alcoholic, but he was brilliant. He even outshone his father. Hadn't he won himself both a grammar school place and a scholarship to Cambridge? The younger males in her family promised to be just as clever: Gordon's son was top of the class, and her grandsons were already outstanding.

She desperately needed to have faith in all the men and boys in her life. Without them who would keep her in order? But for her father shouting at a boy who propositioned her in the street when she was a teenager, she told me, she would doubtless have abandoned herself to his advances.

It was the same with her garden. Only by keeping Carl alive in her mind could she stop it, like her, going to rack and ruin; only through remaining mindful of his gardening rules could she keep the flowers and vegetables neatly arrayed, the lawn trim, and the paths as free of weeds as Carl had kept them. Without him she looked to other men to rescue her from chaos: her son, her brother, even her seven-year-old grandson, who reminded her, for instance, to put tea in the pot when she forgot. Another time his three-year-old brother Martin transformed an ugly teacup stain she had left on the table into a beautiful face, with arms and legs, and a 'scrum' bit for her hair. 'Ever so clever.'

Without these idealised male figures Sheila dreaded going haywire, even becoming murderous. As we spoke she swatted a fly dead; that morning, she went on, she had subjected herself and the cat to 'a lethal dose' of insect spray. Just before I arrived she had broken a vinegar bottle; she drew my attention to its pungent smell. Years before, Carl moved ahead of her to Southend and she then suffered 'all sorts of calamities': the television broke; their son had to go into hospital; and so on, and so on. Now, since Carl's death she had lost almost all the money they had saved. It had just drained away.

No wonder she psychosomatically kept going through his dying, and denied the death of her idealising illusions about him – as perfect support and provider, as archetypal male breadwinner. She needed him to be this man as a counterbalance to her sense of herself as a wreck. Hence her assumption, the night he lay dying, that she was the one who was most debilitated, with her cracked and bleeding lips, and pus in her mouth from her recent sinus operation. She never dreamt his sickness could be fatal – that he was mortal.

Without him she felt crippled – like her cat who, she pointed out, had only one ear, and her daughter-in-law who had no tail-bone (she had lost her coccyx, Sheila said, as a result of her first husband battering her). Sheila felt that all women were deficient; that without a man they were nothing. She derided her 'spinster' relatives. She could not bear to be called a widow.

That was another reason she hated Cruse. All widows. A widower no sooner loses his wife, she explained, than he acquires another. The speaker at Cruse had told them all how to shop for one. She referred to her husband every other word. 'You stupid woman,' Sheila thought. 'You don't mention your husband to us. We haven't got one.' It was so galling that Sheila crawled away never to return.

A neighbour had tried to condole with Sheila, telling her, 'I know exactly how you feel.' She too had lost her husband, but to another woman. 'Ridiculous woman,' Sheila simmered. 'She had no idea. Anyway, he came back. At least she could see him.'

Again and again Sheila enviously scorned the women who had men. Some she dismissed as feeble-minded, others as wicked. She told me, for instance, how her mother cruelly blamed Sheila's brother Tom for her pregnancy with him driving her into unhappy marriage with their father. It was her cruelty to Tom that forced him to leave home when he was scarcely more than a boy. Their mother was still utterly selfish. When their father was ill in hospital she refused to visit because she wanted all the attention for herself. Self-servingly, Sheila went on, her mother would doubtless outlive them all – like the proverbial 'creaking gate'.

Every villain, every lame duck in her story was a woman. By splitting off and evacuating all badness, incompetence and lack into her own sex she sustained the illusion that boys and men – above all, her husband Carl – lacked nothing. Denying Carl's psychological and physical ills, she idealised both him and their life together as perfect. Her mother had adored Carl; according to Sheila she grieved his loss much more than that of her own husband. Others too envied Sheila her marriage. 'At least Carl died loving you,' her jilted neighbour complained. 'My husband won't love me when he dies.' Sheila's tale of married bliss was enough to make anyone feel wanting.

Stirring others' envy, triumphing over them, as Klein observed, is one means of denying death,' But this does away with them then being the comforting figures we need to recognise and work through grief. Klein, however, never addressed the socially exaggerated image of men that makes this triumphant defence against recognising their demise so widespread. Without therapy to confront this issue, victory over others remained the order of the day when I last visited Sheila.

Previously she had kept me close. Her voice had sometimes dropped to an almost inaudible confidential whisper so that I had to move near to hear what she was saying. Now she indicated she was happy to see me go. She announced she had just acquired a boyfriend – younger and better looking than Carl, a lovable rogue. Then she added that a well-known psychologist had also taken a shine to her. Who was he? She left me guessing – me not her the one bereaved – triumph verging on mania.

14
Mania

A very schizoid patient dreamed that he was balancing a long pole on his nose; it reached right to the sky and had a baby balanced on the end. As he awoke he said to himself, 'This fucking penis is good for nothing, it is so big that it is useless.' The patient . . . had identified his whole body with a phallus and he felt himself enlarge physically and became invaded by delusions of grandeur. In the manic state there is a pseudo penis which repairs nothing; it serves to deny the reality of destroyed objects and presents itself as the universal substitute.

Henri Rey, 1977[1]

Mania, wrote Freud,[2] is fired by the energy let loose when the work of grief is done. His followers, however, pointed out that it is not exactly due to grief, but is a defence against it. Karl Abraham characterised mania as 'gargantuan gobbling', so much does it involve the fantasy of incorporating and fusing with another, in the first place with a superego version of the father.[3]

Melanie Klein,[4] as I mentioned at the beginning of this book, attributed mania's origin to the time when the infant first learns to fend off guilt and despair lest his hatred lose him his loved mother, by declaring himself so self-sufficiently omnipotent he can get on perfectly well without her. As so often, in attending to mothering, Klein lost sight of mania's patriarchal aspects.

So does her follower, Henri Rey, quoted above. He suggests that, in manic states of mind, women and men alike imagine themselves incarnated as a magnificent phallic figure. They thereby illusorily bring together and unify the shattered fragments resulting from the wreckage done, at least in fantasy, out of envious hatred of what they most love, in the first place in the mother.

183

The penis lends itself to this magic, says Rey, because of its biological properties: its turgidity, erectile defiance of gravity, penetrative character, function in excretion and making babies, and the fact that it has a life of its own yet is part of something greater – man. More likely, I would suggest, the penis serves the purposes of mania because, as phallus, it is a prime symbol of the grandiosity that mania involves.

Rey is, however, right in pointing out that manic identification with the phallus is not confined to men. *In extremis* the illusion of becoming an 'all male' mind, the cleverest of the clever, of outwitting bodily need to become the thinnest of the thin, straight-up-and-down phallus incarnate, is arguably a central factor in many women's anorexia.[5]

It is however, obviously less contentious to demonstrate the phallic aspect of mania with the example of a man, especially with someone whose delusions of grandeur were so extreme he was often hospitalised on account of them. Peter Butcher was just such a man. He was in his late fifties when I met him, and was outwardly utterly normal and ordinary. His surroundings were no different from the general run: his house was mundane, even drab, with dark furniture, old-fashioned cabinet wireless, and glass-fronted dresser replete with a standard assortment of china and wooden ornaments. In the centre of the living room was a coffee table. On top of it sat a bowl of fruit, a stoppered jar of biscuits, and a vase of faded artificial flowers. On the walls hung photos of his male relatives: grandfather, father, brothers, nephews and great-nephews. These had been collected over the years by Peter's mother, with whom he had lived since his second wife died eleven years before.

In the bookshelves were the usual whodunnits and do-it-your-self manuals. Only a few titles – *World Mythology, The Diamond Throne, Mysteries of the Unexplained* – hinted at something grander. It was the same with Peter. He was balding, good-looking, neatly dressed, almost punctilious. Nothing flash – except for his sorcerer-like ring, with bright blue stone, glinting on his shaking hand.

Almost as soon as he started talking he transformed the room, lit it up, dispelled dullness with his infectious glee. Charmingly, amusingly he chuckled on. Like Alice rushing after the White Rabbit in Lewis Carroll's *Alice's Adventures in Wonderland*, I found myself speeding helter-skelter – now following, now ahead – after his bubbling stream of consciousness.

It evaporated any unhappiness. His story was a riot of colour, a hubbub of fact and fiction, a welter of poetry and prose. It was a veritable ferment of words – one suggesting another, concrete and abstract combined, tumbling over each other, a catch-me-if-you-can race against time. Peter worried I might be watching the clock. He was so set on dashing against the seconds dribbling away, against emptiness and death. His dictum 'However fast you go you can never live long enough' chased at his heels.

I had explained that I would be changing all identifying details. 'So many, so many,' he declared. He was his father's oldest son, the middle child of five. There had been another baby. A girl. But she was born dead. 'I would have loved to see her – especially now,' he mused. Her loss preyed on his mind. All the verses he wrote were about daughters, but he did not connect them with his own loss. He viewed his lyrics more as a hymn to creation in which he was progenitor of all, like the God Wotan in Wagner's four-opera epic, *The Ring*, which Peter so admired.[6]

Peter was born in Cockermouth in Cumbria, like William Wordsworth. The nation's famous poet put him in mind of his own writing, of his diary – full of glorious schemes. He started it when he was doing a particularly boring job: 'It was deadly. Fourteen hours with the workers every day. Plus three hours getting there and back.' It had been so tedious, so dreary – or it would have been but for his mania.

He scurried on. He could not abide nothingness. Like the garrulous Mad Hatter quizzing Alice, he posed me the following conundrum. 'Consider,' he said as if logic could defeat disillusion in himself having made virtually nothing of his life, 'when someone says, "There's nothing in the cupboard." Well, OK, it's clear. But there is something in the cupboard. There is never nothing.' ' "Nothing",' he continued, 'is an aborted word of "something". It comes back on itself.' He had even written a poem about it:

To dwell upon one's thoughts too
Long, brings about a mournful song
So, if you think of Nothing long,
The words of Wisdom come along

Writing in turn triggered off thoughts of books, of one about Zarathustra. 'According to him,' Peter told me, 'man may surpass God. One day we will become great – a beautiful race. I'd love to be here then.' From nothing to superman, Nietzsche and *Ecce Homo*. Words sped their way into an endlessly expanding glorious male future.

I returned him to his beginning. Why had he been christened Peter Grieg Butcher? It set him spinning again. 'Such a noble name – Peter – if you're on the religious side. And then you've only got to think of Peter the Great – founder of St Petersburg. All the famous Peters.' And Grieg? That was his father's idea. He had been a band-leader. Peter's grandfather had been one too. A picture of the old man, bugle in hand, adorned the wall above me. 'My father thought if ever I became a good musician,' Peter went on, 'I could drop "Butcher", and call myself "Grieg".'

The composer's name reminded Peter of a dream he once had in which he landed on a planet and entered a concert hall. There he found an organ, and played it – for hours. Choral music. It led him on to the magnificence of Beethoven's 'Ode to Joy', from there to Wagner, to God and the Valkyries. It was all so inspiring – *Tannhäuser* and the Holy Grail.

We all search for something. And *The Rhinegold*. This elusive bloody metal that they made so prominent in their lives. I hate it. And the Niebelung, the serfs – hog-whipped, hog-tied – and the people above abusing their station. The gold. It was in the river, wasn't it? Brutal. Some of Wagner's slow melodies just knock you out.

Peter's own musical career began inauspiciously. His father started teaching him the piano when he was five. He was a perfectionist. Peter would play something, then he would make a mistake at which his father would shout, 'That's awful.' Peter would start playing again. Again he got it wrong. His father's angry voice grew louder and higher until eventually he hit him.

It happened with Peter's school music teacher, too. Peter would start a piece and the master would tell him off, saying 'That's no good.' Peter knew he was bound to strike the wrong note. Something in him – anger or fear – drove him to mess it up. The teacher became as furious as his father. Then he would quieten down and leave Peter on his own until he gave up on him altogether.

It was then that Peter began stammering. His speech impediment lasted all through primary school. He found himself about to falter with me. 'You get yourself in such a turmoil,' he said. 'It nearly came out then. I was going to say "tiswas" and then changed it to "turmoil".' Was it the effect of fear, anger, or simply the result of the torrent of ideas, words and questions with which he sought to magic himself into being the man – the great musician, the *maestro* – his father had so wanted him to be? In the flood of ideas one inevitably tripped over the next in their rush to get out. They made him great. 'Like the Emperor Claudius. He too used to stammer,' Peter informed me. 'He too was a writer, and so intelligent.'

It was with thoughts of male magnificence that Peter finally cured himself – specifically with that of Faust and his quest for omniscience. 'I wanted to know everything, find out everything.' Discovering he could not learn everything from books he tried, like Kipling's Elephant's Child, to quench his insatiable curiosity by asking questions of everyone he met. 'And from there, progress.' He conquered his stammer all on his own, through sheer willpower.

Whenever there was a halt in our conversation he questioned me too, hectoringly almost, urging me to fill the gaps. How did I think it all started? Life? Manic depression? Then he was off again. He compared himself to Churchill: 'He too was manic depressive – like many of the composers.' Did I think it was hereditary? Without pausing to consider my reply, he rushed on. Daringly, he announced, he would go out on a limb. He often did. He recounted his own theory of mania and its superlative origins: 'Over thousands of years,' he told me, 'the brain has grown.

Massively.' His illness, he said, came from using a new part of the ever-enlarging cortex that others had never used before.

Like a businessman intoxicated with his own self-aggrandising momentum, Peter saw nothing but expansion ahead. Unlike the hysteric fixed in the repressed past, he lived in the future. His mania carried him ever forward, feet barely touching the ground. Free-floating, untethered, his roots became lost to view. He rendered himself a veritable *tabula rasa*. All he could recall of his childhood was a mere scattering of isolated incidents, beginning with a pun on his name, 'buying sausages at the butcher's'. Then he recalled other fragments: music lessons, a visit to the psychologist about his stammer, going into a bomb shelter – and a murdered woman.

He must have been seven or eight when he came across her body. He and his sister found it behind a hedge. He couldn't remember it himself, he had 'no inward sight of her'. Nor did they ever find the murderer. It reminded him of a gruesome killing reported in the press the day we met involving a woman stabbed over fifty times by her lover's wife.

It was the last I heard of these women, or of Peter's early youth. Like the director of a blockbuster movie, he cut and leapt over the years to when he was fifteen. He had wanted to become a carpenter, like Jesus, but his father insisted he go away and join a Marine band, like the one he himself led. Going away did not upset Peter in the least, or so he claimed. Getting into the band proved he did have some musical talent. It was a great opportunity, he insisted, he wouldn't have missed it for the world.

For five years, from his mid-teens, he travelled about from one posting to the next. His parents were hardly ever there; they were mostly abroad. Then his father started to suffer the first symptoms of the cancer that was to kill him.

Peter, however, was more mindful of himself as hero, remembering an incident that occurred when he was twenty and flying to see his father. In the aeroplane he was reading books about the devil and about the composer Brahms. Suddenly he heard a middle-aged woman's voice telling him, 'The plane isn't going to crash.' It was reassuring – 'securing' – countering the fear of his manic excitement going out of control.

Grandly believing himself to be in charge, Peter took himself off to the cockpit, tapped the pilot on the shoulder and gave him the woman's message. Far from soothing the pilot, Peter's words made him desperate. He changed course immediately, landed the plane, and had Peter shipped off to a mental hospital. But Peter escaped.

Like a self-important customer angered by the service he went in search of the superintendent of the hospital and tore him off a strip. 'I was like a volcano erupting,' he said. 'The stuff had to come out, be exposed, so fertile land could grow again.' Just as doctors answer the 'omnipotence' of the anorexic by controlling and force-feeding her,[7] Peter's doctors answered his omnipotence with their own. They knocked him out with ECT and insulin.

Afterwards they discharged him. So too did the Navy. Nevertheless he retained his manly fight to do away with regret at being dismissed. He was no coward, he insisted. He would never pull any punches. His dying father asked him how he was. 'Fine,' Peter replied, 'but you look bloody awful.' That was the exact phrase. It was still imprinted on his mind. He didn't mince words. He could call a spade a spade – as good as the next man. Better.

He also found work. He had wanted to be a glassblower. He had seen a wonderful film about it – expanding bubbles of silica – but he had to make do with office jobs, first in England, and then in Zambia. It was there he met his first wife. Like his other girlfriends, however, she remained a blur, not half so distinct or vivid as the male figures with which he peopled his mind.

His marriage only lasted a couple of years. There had been a daughter, but Peter never told me her name. He had long ago lost touch with her. Well, he added, he once held her physically but emotionally it was as if she had never been. As for his first wife, he had no idea why she left. 'Buckshee,' he concluded, making a bonus of her disappearance.

He conjured away his failure as husband and father with another waking fantasy – an extravaganza involving a motor-cycle crash, a surgeon knocking him down, a gun he was wearing ripping open his thigh as he fell, and the surgeon fixing it. Then, as though this incident too was part of a fast-moving dream, Peter found himself on a train. It arrived at a station in the middle of nowhere. Peter got off and walked, then ran across the tracks on to empty land. Perhaps it was mined, he speculated, as in the thrillers he read. Eventually he arrived at a huge factory, then everything went blank until he woke to find himself in hospital again – this time in Lusaka.

Another time, he was on holiday with his sister. He was getting his swimming trunks from the washing line, when, returning past the servants' quarters, he suddenly saw a warrior behind him with a sword above his head and bamboo clothing. Peter turned and struck the figure on the neck with his fist. This made him disappear, at which Peter congratulated himself: 'God you were quick. Didn't know you could act so fast.' He kept thinking about the point of the fighter's sword. Was it curved? or straight? Either way, Peter praised himself for standing up to the challenge.

He was so much grander, he went on, than his younger brother Richard whom others stupidly celebrated. Richard had been a paratrooper, and had then gone into business before returning to work in the forces. One day the usual officer was off sick. Like a fool, said Peter, Richard agreed to fly in his place. He got into the plane and started the ascent, when suddenly the instrument panel failed. He was 3,000 feet up and didn't know whether he was coming or going. He switched to the reserve panel, but it too stopped functioning, so he and his co-pilot ejected. All at once, the cover came down on Richard's head – 'Bonk. Dead.'

In the same breath Peter both puffed up and reduced his brother's demise to comic-strip proportions. He described the death of his second wife, Joyce, in similar terms. The cancer that killed her was caused, he said, by the stress and distress of his losing his job as a hospital porter. His downfall affected her, not him. 'I was a happy-go-lucky fellow. I couldn't give a damn about the world cracking up. I was still riding my little rocket.' He reacted to the first diagnosis of her fatal illness just as nonchalantly as he had to his brother's end – 'I lost fuel – poof.'

He could not imagine losing something he owned. Then the enormity of possessing another person struck him. 'It sounds wrong,' he said. Undismayed, he reiterated his feeling that he owned and controlled his wife Joyce. Her death would have destroyed this illusion had he not replaced it with another, a dream of himself, along with his former mate Jock from the Navy, in a sports car, Joyce beside them – alive – her cancer a baby. But the trick did not work; it had no substance. The car crashed. The baby was gone. Joyce disappeared. In vain Peter searched and searched. He could not find her.

Jock also featured in later adventures. In one Peter was on another car journey. Whatever unhappiness fired it was concealed by the voyaging excitement that took its place. Calling himself 'a busy bee', as in the brain teaser with which Alice taxes the caterpillar in Lewis Carroll's *Through the Looking Glass*, Peter had revved himself up. He got into such a state he could have burnt himself out, he was going so fast.

He could not sleep, so he got up and went out in the middle of the night. He found himself going across the park – as though it were a flight deck – taking cover here, falling flat there, dodging imaginary missiles. It reminded him of the war; not winning, just enjoying it. Then he arrived at his brother Adrian's house. What a stand-offish, down-to-earth bloke, he complained. And an atheist too. He didn't even believe in God. As for Adrian's wife, Peter dismissed her as a bossy, judgmental fusspot. She thought him mad to call on her and Adrian at such an early hour. It was her doing that the police arrived to take him off to mental hospital.

The next morning Peter discharged himself. He drove away, his car a fabulous phallic extension of himself (like Pinocchio's elongated nose implied by Henri Rey's patient with whom this chapter began). Suddenly, out of nowhere, Peter imagined his pal Jock bobbing up on the road ahead. Peter stopped, loaded this apparition of his chum with cigarettes, abandoned the car, and went off again – from Exeter to Bristol – this time on foot. There he found the flat where he had lived when Joyce was alive. Climbing in through a window, he tore his finger, down to the bone. But it didn't bother him. He stuck the pieces in his pocket and went on walking. Again the police caught up with him. This time they put him in jail.

'Now here's the nice part,' Peter went on, drawing his story out. From thin air, as though he were Macbeth in Kurosawa's film *Throne of Blood*, swords came through the walls at him, followed by a samurai master standing before him, a red band about his head. Peter was just practising his karate chops – perfecting his performance, flicking his head like the tongue of a snake, from side to side – when the police returned and carted him off to hospital again. Yet his travels that day, he insisted, were no crazy fantasy. He had blisters on his feet to prove how far and fast he had gone. He did not need medicine, he needed a rest – he was so exhausted, never still, always on the go.

More recently he had had another manic outburst involving mirrors and broken glass, astronomical plans and calculations, culminating in his erection of a telescope in the garden. Since then he had been 'in limbo'. Or so he said, as much to reassure himself as me.

Hardly had I returned for our last meeting, after holidaying in Spain, than his mind sped off again: from Spain to the Olympics; to multi-millionaire sportsmen; to digging for gold. He hated it. But he was also into it – into money and collecting 'stamps, royalty, penny blacks'. He blamed society: 'It conditions us all, makes us all into workers.' He could no more bear to be made the same as others than Ibsen's plutocrat, Peer Gynt, can bear the idea of the Button Moulder he meets allegorically melting him down with the common herd in his casting ladle.

Fleeing the nonentity of humdrum unemployment, Peter took me, as Peer Gynt takes his mother Aase, on one last flight of male fancy. 'I think quite a bit about how we all started,' he began,

I'd love to think that we're sort of let loose from somewhere and travel our own sort of way, that you formulate yourself into the sperm, fight the fight, get through the egg, and build yourself, starting up the brain – the mind.

Having illusorily created himself, he recounted a dream in which he was going through space: 'On my left was a powerful man. Very tall. Massive compared to me. Four or five times as big. God.' He giggled as his imagination cosmically leapt ahead. Then:

I came to this sort of void in space. No stars. Nothing. It had a sort of floor to it. Riveted. I was placed there. And something said to me, 'Now Peter. You have the power of God. Whether you have to wait here one, two, millions of years, you can live through it. You can cause a big bang and create a solar system. And start all over again. Then you'll have to pick the type of planet you want.

That did it: just as he thought he had got light years away, emptiness stared him in the face. He could never fill it with anything good:

Say I did get a planet going. Think of the traumatic effect it would have. What foliage would you use? What trees? Would you have poison plants? Aggressive animals? Monsters? Gorgons? Good God. It would take thousands of years to sort all that out before you dared put man and woman there.

It reminded me of another fantasy he had described when we first met:

I was meditating on the word 'infinity'. Then, in a flash, I moved my mind's eye into space. I was going through galaxy after galaxy. It went on so long I had to stop and pull myself out because I realised I would never find infinity. I was looking for the ultimate. But it's just a word.

He felt he had been led astray by print – beyond reality and reason. It could never fulfil its promise, or repair his damaged world.

Faced with the task of confronting the fact that he was neither God nor Superman, that he could not people his own world, let alone a planet, without going through the wearisome business of putting the bits and pieces of his life together – Peter gave up. His gargantuan dreams, as he put it, making play on his name, 'petered out'.

This also happened when I read through the transcripts of our conversations. Without the pyrotechnics of his spellbinding voice and charm, the Promethean vision with which he had intoxicated us both collapsed, like the pile of playing cards at the end of *Alice's Adventures in Wonderland*.

Away from Peter's ebullient fizz, distracting and keeping me scurrying and glossing over the tatters, the aggressive shards showed through – broken glass, missiles, savaged dying father, erupting volcano, the devil, war, mines, crashed cars and planes, poison plants, murdered and murdering women, gorgon heads. It was a salutary reminder of the wreckage done by less insane manic excitement – by market hype; by the busy scurrying of the businessman or parent relentlessly driving themselves and their charges inexorably forward, 'hog-whipped' as Peter put it; by the tycoon, Robert Maxwell, say, mesmerising and bending his employees to his will; or by bigoted national leaders ready to go to war and sacrifice others to their convictions.[8]

15

Schizoid

I spoke of Melanie Klein's picture of the paranoid-schizoid position and the important part played in it by the infant's phantasies of sadistic attack on the breast. Identical attacks are directed against the apparatus of perception from the beginning of life. This part of his personality is cut up, split into minute fragments, and then, using the projective identification, expelled from the personality. Having thus rid himself of the apparatus of conscious awareness of internal and external reality, the patient achieves a state which is felt to be neither alive nor dead.

Wilfred Bion, 1956[1]

In later life Freud drew attention to a defence, first used, he said, in earliest infancy, whereby something no sooner upsets us than we project and push it out, declaring 'it shall be outside me'.[2] Klein and her followers likewise described projection and splitting, as well as fragmenting and dispersing oneself as defence against perceiving what we do not want to know.[3] The process suggests the rubric, 'What I don't see, other people don't, and indeed it doesn't exist.'[4]

It is to this defence that Klein's follower, Wilfred Bion, referred in describing what he called the 'attacks on linking' he believed to be characteristic of schizophrenia.[5] Like Klein, Bion characterised this defence in maternal terms, but he attributed it less to the death instinct than to the mother not having the capacity for 'reverie', for taking in, digesting and thinking about her baby's sense impressions, and his disowned and projected feelings, so as to take them back into himself in thinkable form and integrate them, not least to form the furniture of his dreams.[6]

Other Kleinians mention in passing the role of the father in schizophrenia. Herbert Rosenfeld records a patient blaming his illness on his father not telling him the facts of life.[7] But neither Rosenfeld, nor his fellow-Kleinians, pay much attention to paternal aspects of schizoid splitting and fragmentation.

Freud, by contrast, regarded fathers – and men generally – as central to the genesis of schizophrenia. He first developed his account of this illness through analysing the autobiographical report by a judge, Daniel Paul Schreber, of a schizophrenic break-down in his late fifties.[8] Freud attributed Schreber's illness to his loss, when he was nineteen, of his father, a man made famous by his inventions of 'therapeutic athletics', a rigid form of treatment for skeletal muscular disease, and by his advocacy of disciplinarian childrearing. More immediately Freud attributed Schreber's psy-chotic illness to his being passed over for promotion, and to his learning he would never become a father. Rather than know about these upsets to his image of himself as a man, Schreber developed the delusion that God and his doctor Flechsig (divided into forty to sixty subdivisions) were impregnating him so that, out of the mass of feminine nerves he believed he had become, he would sire a whole new race of men.

The fragmentation of self and others involved in such delusions is not confined to the mad. Nevertheless, this defence can result, as with Schreber, in insanity. David Small was in his early forties when I met him. He was living in a small seaside town where he spent his days attending the local mental health centre. Located in a converted workhouse built like a church, this was entered through an imposing, heavy wooden door that was opened with an enormous key. Just inside there was a porter's lodge. Hardly had I announced myself than the warden heard David's 'voice from the deep', as she put it.

He lolloped into view, a book under his arm, the centre's resi-dent egghead. Expecting me, he greeted my arrival with easy familiarity, rummaged for a pack of cigarettes in a battered sports bag, and then asked if I would like tea. He fixed it, like the sixth-form prefect he had once been, in the canteen. After that he ushered me along the corridor into the room he had booked for us, took a comfy chair for himself and, mindful of his manners, indicated a seat for me.

His officialdom was utterly childlike. His appearance too, but for a broken tooth, seemed almost untouched by age. He was tall, good-looking, without a trace of grey. His clothes hung about him loosely, as though he were still growing into them. His talk was also boyish. 'Am I doing all right?' he asked at one point. At other times he punctuated what he said with a running commentary on what he was doing. Several times he interrupted himself with, 'Brief pause while I take a drag on my cigarette' – like a schoolboy asking to be excused.

He told his life as though reading it from a copy-book ruled out with lines, margins and headings specifying dates and places, akin to the lists preluding F. Scott Fitzgerald's mental recovery, described in his autobiographical short story, 'The Crack-Up.' David 'agglomorated' the facts, the term Bion used to characterise the unintegrating and fragmenting effect of schizoid attacks on linking, involving severing feelings from thoughts, and each thought from the next.[9]

David's story was more benchmarked with chronological and geographical detail than any other I heard. His 'run-down' of his life began with his father's military rank when he first met David's mother. He then told me the name and location of the hospital where he was born, and the date – 1951. After that he itemised two early memories – a distinct image of his father dangling a poisoned mole by the tail, followed by a recollection of his mother and himself feeding some pigs.

He jumped to 1954. 'We heard that my father had been posted to South America. We followed him out there.' He recalled discrete sense impressions: a hillside home overlooking the jungle, wildlife, trees, beauty, warm weather, winding roads, forest paths, snakes, a waterfall, the smell of ferns and rotting earth, the yellowness of the sun.

By 1957 it was all gone. His father was posted back to England, to Buckinghamshire. Tropical scents were abruptly replaced by the smell of fresh paint. All connection with life abroad was lost. Previously David had spent all day every day with his mother, and since no other form of education was available she taught David herself. Now, on their return to England, David was sent first to prep and then to boarding-school.

He remembered balmy days playing cricket with his father. 'He was the only man who bothered to play with us. Boys from miles around used to come, in the evening, all those long light hours of summer.' When he was eleven, David suffered the first of many failures in his father's eyes. His father had taken him for an interview at a prestigious public school, but he was not accepted, and instead had to go to the local grammar school.

It was his father's idea that he should board there. Only a few boys did, but Mr Small anticipated that his job might take him abroad again. It would be more secure, he supposed, for David to get used to living away. In fact Mr Small did not go overseas until years later, and when he did he went alone, leaving his wife to run their house in England, a couple of miles away from David's school. Nevertheless, despite being so close, David was not allowed home in term-time except for half-day breaks once a fortnight, on Sundays.

He felt dreadfully homesick at losing his parents and his younger brother and sister, who continued to live together – without him. It marked the 'first big split', David told me, made even bigger by the time we met, by the distance he now lived from his childhood home; all the rest of his family were still there. The bell clanging him awake each morning in boarding-school brutally reminded him of this separation. Returning home on Sundays he cried when he had to go back, overcome by 'the gnawing feeling of the lack of my parents, and missing the feel of it all'.

He never told them of his distress. He assumed they knew; he cried so much. Nobody in his family ever talked about such things, least of all his father. Only his sister acknowledged having witnessed his tears, and then not until they were in their thirties. It was on those long-ago Sundays, she told him, she first learnt boys could cry.

By the time of our second meeting he had switched himself off to the unhappiness involved. When I reminded him of the sad tale he had told me on my first visit, about being sent away from home, he could not connect with what I was saying. 'Pardon,' he asked. 'What did you say? Yes it was a bit tragic. Mainly because I didn't realise I could do anything about it.' Then, dismissing all thought of tragedy, even of plain ordinary misery, he told me that the only pupil who managed to leave because of homesickness was made a laughing stock by the other boys.

David himself eventually got over his grief. He learnt the British trick of keeping a 'stiff upper lip'. This, and playing the cricket his father taught him, helped. He cultivated passivity. It earned him a place in the school team – as a 'stonewaller'. He could stay in for hours, scoring a few runs here and there, helping turn defeats into indifferent draws.

Then, in the sixth form, when his father was indeed posted overseas, David's passivity failed to serve even this end. He was dropped from the school's cricket eleven. He himself, however, connected his father's absence with more world-shattering events – the assassination of President Kennedy, and with the earlier Bay of Pigs disaster with its threat of 'nuclear war between the two superpowers, missiles landing all around, holocaust'.

News of this threat interrupted prep. After middling achievement in the lower forms, David was now on the fast track for university entrance. He worked hard. Since 1967, at a friend's suggestion, he had also begun playing bass guitar. (His left-handedness made him fumble too much with the chords to manage any other instrument.) Band playing went fine, with songs like 'When a man loves a woman', but Oxbridge entrance was not such a success. He failed to get in. Again he had disappointed his father; he had to go to a new university instead.

Just before he went to college he had his first major bust-up with Mr Small. After leaving school David worked in an office. All he could remember of the job was the mindless boredom of filing. It was not that, however, but feeling so upset when his girlfriend of two months' standing dropped him, that led to the row with his father. David was so distressed by the girl's rejection that he stopped working, and spent all his time in bed. It drove his father crazy: 'No son of mine,' he roared, 'is going to spend his life lounging around not going to work.'

Nor did he take kindly to David going off to bum round Europe. It was someone else's idea. One of his schoolfriends suggested they hitch-hike, and David passively tagged along. In his memory the trip's high spots were marked out by famous men; a leading dress designer who gave them a lift; a film director who put them up in his Tuscan villa; a star British footballer with whose name crowds of little boys hailed them.

Otherwise David drearily listed the towns of Italy and Greece they passed through, voiding them of the resonance their names usually evoke. He reeled them off so boringly that I began to drift off. He noticed. Perhaps, he asked, he had already gone through this part of his story before? 'No,' I assured him. Remaining detached, he itemised other details: places, lifts, begging, ending with his initiation into drugs. It coincided, he said, with the first landing of men on the moon. 'In those days,' he informed me as though telling me news from another planet, 'the flower power movement was still on and people used to indulge in cannabis and LSD, recreation drugs taken for entertainment.'

It did not sound very entertaining. He told it all so impersonally and prosaically, an extreme version of the way people often go over their holidays and show their holiday snaps in tedious detail, so as to bleach and iron out into flattened patchwork monochrome the colour and ups and downs of experience.

David's defensively fragmented catalogue was not unlike the dutifully recounted life of the butler in Kazuo Ishiguro's novel, *The Remains of the Day*, who sustains a venerated image of his dead master, Lord Darlington, by meticulously itemising the tasks and daily observances by which he, the butler, presents himself as a picture of unruffled 'dignity'. He thereby conceals from himself, and at first from the reader, that, far from being a perfect lord, Darlington was a traitor, collaborated with the Nazis, and after the war left his ancestral estates to fall into ruin. Defending himself against disillusion in his former master, the butler punctiliously details the events occurring off-stage when his own father dies. He also scrupulously logs a subsequent motoring trip to the West Country, from which it emerges that he could also never let himself know about, let alone respond to, the love of the former house-keeper, his colleague.

The finale of David's journey was more dishevelled than that of Ishiguro's butler. He too, however, tried to make himself dignified. He had a quick wash and brush-up, he told me, on his return from Europe, but it did nothing to mollify his father. Mr Small utterly despised him for his jaunt.

200

Denied the patriarchal welcome due to a prodigal son, David went off to university. At first he worked hard, but his efforts still failed to gain him his father's love. So David turned to dreams instead. He began dropping out with 'drugs, sex, and rock'n'roll.' He fantasised that lead pop singers were addressing their songs to him.

Sex also became fantasy. He had drifted – 'gravitated', he told me – into living with a girl because he had nowhere else to stay, and when the relationship ended he made do with memories of its supposed other-worldly ecstasy. Dreams without action however could not sustain him. Imagining the girl was beckoning him to return, through the window, he smashed it to get in. Next thing he knew he was in hospital with his thumb cut in several places. The scars, he added, were still there to prove it.

He was only hospitalised overnight, but it frightened him – not hospital, but his violence, and most of all the injuries his acting on his desire had done his hand. He reacted by switching off all feeling. He became like Dick, a four-year-old autistic patient of Melanie Klein.[10] Having learnt to play and speak, Dick suddenly became so frightened of all emotion, fearing it would cause his destruction, that he became completely withdrawn. He lost all interest, feeling and curiosity about the world around him. He stopped talking and playing. He even stopped eating unless his food was mushed up so he would not have to bite into it.

David did much the same. He would no longer eat meat and he stopped studying; his university tutor, like his father, gave up on him. He told David that if he went on cutting lectures and seminars he would be sent down. Hitherto David had assumed everyone was destined to like and love him, and he would have been completely downcast had he taken in the man's warning. But he ignored it. He continued to take refuge in fantasy. He did no work. So he was finally expelled for 'not applying himself'. At this point in his story, David interrupted himself, and told me he would pause to have a sip of tea.

That done, he told me how, after leaving university, he drifted back home into a gardening job. He became so passive and empty, however, having ejected into the outside world all the bits and pieces into which he had defensively fragmented himself, that he feared they would now come back to plague him from outside. He tried to block them out by wearing a Walkman and concentrating on the music – note by note, second by second. Or he followed the advice of a meditation manual and focused his attention on just one thing at a time. But this defence only exacerbated his problems: yet another man gave up on him, this time his boss, who sacked him for not having his mind on the job.

Soon after that his father completely disowned him. They had already had many rows. One time David had infuriated Mr Small by ridiculing his surname – it was so belittling. Echoes of Lacan, who attributed Schreber's breakdown to his foreclosing 'the-Name-of-the-Father'. In other words he expelled from himself the very idea of the father, the precondition, Lacan thought, of using the chains of signifiers constituting language.[11] Ineptly David told his father, taking up a carving knife as he did so, 'If you're that angry with me why don't you put it in me?'

Another time he told his father he was an automaton, as though he were the same unfeeling clockwork machine David dreaded becoming himself:

> He used to come in every night, about the same time, put his keys on the side, come into the sitting room, and start reading the paper. He'd been doing that – going to the office at nine o'clock in the morning, coming back at five o'clock in the evening – ever since I knew him. The fact he could do that – for forty years – and expect me to do it too: that's what made me call him a robot.

Here David lost his train of thought. Someone had just knocked on the door. 'Where was I?' he resumed after the visitor went. 'Oh yes. My father hit me – on the jaw.' David dared not retaliate: the old man had already had four heart attacks. Fearful of his anger killing him, David retreated to his room. He went to bed and wept. He gave up doing anything, but his inactivity incensed his father more than his anger ever did.

Things came to a head one day when David was watching a yoga programme on TV, at midday, when his father said all self-respecting men should be at work. He exploded and got David's mother to tell David to go. He would not even do David the courtesy of telling him himself.

'He says it's a question of either him or you,' his mother said. 'Well, still being fairly naïve in those days,' David told me, 'I said I'd go. I'd probably say the same now – from a point of view of fairness – because he'd bought the house, kept the family in food and clothing and relatively well off for years and years.' It was just a matter of bleak market rationality. David laughed, drily, without humour. Logic shorn of emotion. In psychoanalytic terms one might say that he did not want to know anything of his father's prior sexual claim on his mother which meant that, when it came to a choice between his father and himself, it was David who had to go.

As for Mr Small, not only did he not speak to David then, but he never willingly spoke to him again.

> Apart from talking to me by mistake if he happens to lift the phone, he would never acknowledge my presence – from that day to this. He was so disappointed in me.

He sounds like the father in Kafka's *Metamorphosis* who, horrified at his commercial traveller son Gregor's internal world of stiff obsessionality becoming visibly hardened in the form of a beetle shell, peremptorily closes the door on him. David's father equally could not bear to see his son's disintegrating inner life materialise. So he cut him dead.

David reacted by cutting himself off. After his father exiled him he moved into a bedsit in Hackney. Within weeks, he was again evicted. 'The landlord asked me to leave because his family was expanding. He had another member of the family on the way, apparently,' David said (doing away with any knowledge of the sexual coupling responsible for the newcomer forcing him out).

He also uncoupled his mental life. He evaded unhappiness at this further household exclusion by attending to details of his bodily functions and diet, just as anorexics fragment their existence by obsessive focus on its minutiae, on the calories and grammes they eat and weigh. As for David, he focused on eating nothing but chocolate and briny brown rice – with lots of salt. It left him

203

feeling dreadfully thirsty. At first, however, failing to put two and two together, he did not realise his dry mouth was an effect of the salt. He went to the market, bought some boxes of apple juice, returned home and drank one after the other – anxious that this might contravene the dictates of his macrobiotic regime against drinking too much.

He had now become so isolated he could only imagine company. He again fantasised an affair – with the girl behind the counter in the health food store. His crush on her reminded me of that of Somerset Maugham for an anonymous waitress, in his autobiographical novel *Of Human Bondage*. Unlike Maugham, however, David's passion remained unconsummated – 'hopeful but impractical,' as he put it.

Again he was kicked out of his lodgings. The building was about to be demolished, so he would be physically removed if he did not leave voluntarily. He left passively, accepting a friend's suggestion that they move into his father's house in Eastbourne. But yet again David was soon out on his ear. From there he landed up in a bedsit in Bexhill, where he had lived ever since.

At this stage in his story I had to go. I fixed another appointment, regretting we could not meet for several weeks, that I had to break off his narration of the chronology of his life which, he said, so helpfully 'sorted out all the influences'.

When we next met he told me of his time in Bexhill – years structured more by internal than external events, the two perilously mixed together. He mistook the fragmentation of his mental world – by which he fended off the emotional impact of not being the man his father wanted – for bodily disintegration: 'My digestion never took to macrobiotics. I felt so weak. My insides were not supported. My muscles and abdomen were collapsing.' He tried yoga, but it was a vicious circle: 'I couldn't do much exercise because I was falling to pieces. And I was falling to pieces because I didn't do much exercise.'

Again the fragments seemed to assail him from without. Bits of himself negated and projected into the external world became menacing 'bizarre objects', as Bion might have termed them,[12] located in tiny specks on the carpet and walls that mesmerised and obsessed him. All feeling about others became deadened, split off and projected into these inanimate bits and pieces – and into words. Words became like talismans, 'hypercathected', as Freud describes this aspect of schizophrenia,[13] as though they could serve instead of people. But words could not do the trick. They remained unassimilated, unintegrated, not joined but "compressed",[14] leaving no space for connecting metaphor.

The Kleinian analyst Hanna Segal illustrates the resulting 'symbolic equations', as she calls them, that occur in schizophrenia. She contrasts a neurotic who dreamt he was playing a violin (with which he associated ideas of fiddling and onanism), and a psychotic for whom the very notion of a musical performance was an outrage. 'What? Me? Masturbate in public?' For Segal's patient the violin did not merely remind him of a penis. It was the thing itself.[15]

Similarly with David. He not only dismantled his thoughts, but became the resulting fragments. 'I was falling to pieces. Well, eating muesli for seven or eight months, there was no real substance in it to bind me together.' He became its grains. He became preoccupied with putting them together, as Holden Caulfield in J. D. Salinger's *Catcher in the Rye* imagines himself bringing together all the bodies of Robert Burns's song, 'Coming through the rye'.[16]

David tried eating bananas to coalesce the particles. He stopped smoking. Like Tessa (in Chapter 1), he hoped he might conserve the energy that otherwise undid him, by lying for hours absolutely still, as though this could make him divine – immortal – and he would 'last for years and years into the future'.

His bid for godlike everlasting life was its own undoing. It deadened him: it lost him all the personal interaction with others that might have enlivened him. He avoided people because he felt so awkward in their company. He was nervous they might notice he was not feeling normal; then he panicked at not being able to relate to them. Again, as at university, he tried to fill the void with fantasised relationships with others. Ironically it is just such attempts at recovery, as Freud observed of Schreber's delusion of peopling the world,[17] that are often mistaken for the first signs of schizophrenic illness.

David gave birth to a host of friendly figures in his mind. Voices inside his head conversationally told him what to do. But this benign confusion of inner and outer became sinister. He became convinced his thoughts were being overheard by others – that his landlady was listening in to them. He started shouting at her, and at her son's girlfriend. David had imagined he was her man, and could not bear seeing her with someone else. He yelled at her from 'a sort of rawness inside', like the sore throat he said he got from talking to me.

His shouting against her puncturing his delusion of himself as her Romeo landed him in hospital again, but he soon ran away – back to his mother. 'It was a long hot summer – in those days – in 1976,' he added, distantly. Again his father ousted him. 'He didn't want anybody unemployed at home,' David said, so he returned to Bexhill and his landlady. Negating and doing away with the emotional furore that had led her to get him hospitalised before, he reasoned she accepted him back because he now agreed to eat meat. He had hoped that, like the 'unified field theory' about which he later told me, vegetarianism would make him whole. That and transcendental meditation. His meditation teacher gave him permission to eat meat. So he did. And he spent his days being his teacher's administrative assistant, posting leaflets for him, preparing his teaching materials and making the tea.

Again, however, Peter's mind broke down; its crack-up more memorable than whatever absence it warded off. And again he cut himself off from others. Again he imagined himself begetting his own company. For hours he would nurse a half-pint of bitter in the pub, daydreaming about the barmaid. But when she too went off with another man, David screamed at her. Hearing his yells her father, the landlord, called the police to throw him out. Another time he hit a girl in his lodgings, after becoming convinced she was leading him on; that it was her fault, not his, that he had become so attracted to her.

Would he become similarly obsessed with me? I took the risk. By contrast David hedged his life about for fear of chance. He voided his existence of all spontaneity. Disowning any agency in himself, unlinking himself from himself, he fell apart. Then, like the hero of Dostoevsky's *Double*, he attacked his stricken self for not being his father's phallic ideal. He recounted a confusing story of 'threatening to punch in the nose of a girl with a broken nose'

– leaving it unclear who broke up whose smashed-up phallic protuberance.

It certainly left me muddled. Was that why I got lost every time I went to see him? I could not follow the map. Had I become projectively identified with his fragmented disoriented state? In his mind, others seemed to be infected with it. He would loudly berate the confusion and stupidity of passers-by on the street, as though they shared the idiocy to which he felt reduced.

He lambasted others just as pedantic teachers and parents glee-fully jump on the follies of their pupils or offspring. David's outbursts were on a continuum with those of the pettifogging bureaucrat or obsessional housewife who attends to the slightest fault in their charges, fearful that they themselves may be reduced to folly by the hair-splitting sophistry or nit-picking cleanliness with which they fend off knowing they are not the ideal figures they want to be.

David was simply much less inhibited in giving vent to this common defence. Sometimes he bawled people out. He atomised their minds as he did his own, tripping himself up like other pedants in spurious quantification. His polemic went off at half-cock. 'Your IQ is only one!' he shouted. 'The general IQ around here is about one.'

It did him no good. His anger threatened to destroy him. He could never express it, nor his inflated delusions of himself as romantic *conquistador*, without being hospitalised. Nothing for it, therefore, but to anaesthetise himself, to avoid anything that might annoy or arouse him. He took to carefully ordering his days. Like someone fearful of being destroyed by a heart attack such as the one which had nearly taken his father's life, and like Eliot's J. Alfred Prufrock David measured out his days, in coffee spoons. He was not altogether different from many others who timetable themselves in the hope of battening down the hatches on an inner inferno.

In Kafka's *Metamorphosis*, Gregor is so fearful of losing his job, through giving vent to his wish to knock his boss off his perch that he circumscribes his existence with the dictates of his alarm clock, railway schedules, mealtimes, cloth samples, orders and invoices. He makes his life as strait-jacketed as the segmented insect into which he turns.

David similarly disciplined himself with the rules of vegetarianism, transcendental meditation and his psychiatric drug regime. He compartmentalised his daytime hours into meetings, doctor's appointments and committees, on which he served as the mental health centre's honorary secretary. Our sessions were fitted in between. He also scheduled his evenings: TV news, followed by a soap opera ('simple, nothing too tragic, everything works out for the best'), and some music. Not opera: too large scale. He preferred something shorter – a piano concerto, 'the best combination of individual instrument and orchestra'. He liked Beethoven because, unlike Mozart, he lived to a good age. Twice a month he attended a local music club, and helped organise its programme.

He also read. Not novels. He used to like Thomas Hardy, but now found his stories too mournful. He opted instead for non-fiction: a social history of England. Facts were less disturbing. And poems – 'not melancholic ones about suffering, death, and lost loves', but verses about nature. Keats's 'Ode to a Nightingale' came to mind. 'You've got to look on the positive side,' he added, of this hardly cheerful poem.

His nights, he claimed, were also fantasy free. Well, he knew that was not strictly true. He regaled me with the latest scientific discoveries about dream and non-dream sleep, then told me how he used to follow the Gestalt therapy prescription of imagining himself as each distinct dream element. But he would rather not think about his dreams at all. Instead, on waking, he filled his mind with reassuringly mundane worries – with ruminating, say, on whether he had booked enough tickets for the centre's next theatre outing. Otherwise every day was the same. 'Nothing to distinguish one from the next. No great upheavals. Nothing like that. Normal, boring routine.' Comfortingly so. The only unusual event recently had been the purchase of a hi-fi.

David's leisure, like his work, was always the same. So were his holidays. Twice a year, regular as clockwork, at Christmas and summer, he stayed with his sister, a fortnight each time, four weeks in all. He told me exactly where she lived relative to his mother's house. When he visited his sister he would see his mother too, an hour each time, five or six occasions each year, provided that his mother could get away. Or David went to her place. If his father happened to see him he quickly made himself scarce. If he bumped into David in the kitchen 'he might venture a grunt and then leave. Not very welcoming. He makes his intolerance of my situation quite plain.'

David laughed, eerily, as he added that he was not the first in the family to be consigned to oblivion for failing to live up to its male ideals. His father had also written off his own brother, Alec. He acted as though Alec had never been. David had not even known of this uncle's existence until a few weeks before I visited:

> He was never mentioned in our childhood. He did something against the law. Or perhaps he dropped out of the army. Something that was not to be looked upon with much happiness. Since then my father never spoke of, or talked to him. It's a family tradition to cut off anybody who does not go along with supporting the system.

It was a tradition with which David's mother did not hold, at least as far as David was concerned. She wrote to him, and in between details of what she was growing in the garden she told him she prayed his father would one day acknowledge him again. The fate of David's Uncle Alec, however, left little room for hope.

It seemed that his father would always disown him for disappointing his ambitions. Peter might have become utterly downcast had it not been that in England, which makes such a virtue of queuing, he staved off knowing emotionally about his father's rejection by lining up his hours, days and nights like pocket money, tuck, lessons, prep, exams. He regulated the unruly human crush by marshalling his experience as though it were so many toy soldiers, or beads from which all meaningful thread has been removed.

It resulted in a dispiriting tale – without life – as if nobody were there, and it made me feel similarly estranged. It was time to leave. I found myself making excuses – pressure of the diary, another appointment. 'Quite so, quite so.' Politely David saw me to the door. Heavily it shut behind me.

Outside I blinked in the sun: surprised by the hubbub of the street; by the shoppers, prams, exuberant sounds of children, motorbikes, cars, and seagulls squalling overhead. It was like emerging from a matinée performance, startled to discover that, all the time one was passively watching a tightly scripted scenario, life was going on outside – unprogrammed, replete with the ebb and flow of its ever-changing, forward-moving hustle and bustle.

Strange that, in the name of postmodern deconstruction, many recommend the fragmentation David suffered, as though it were the only authentic way of being. In fact, it is a defence that, like all the other defences I have described, unnecessarily shackles, hobbles and depletes our existence. What then is to be done?

Conclusion: Therapy and Politics

> I said good-bye
> and saw his old head
> as he turned,
> as he left the room
> leaving me alone
> with his old trophies,
> the marbles, the vases, the stone Sphynx,
> the old, old jars from Egypt;
> he left me alone with these things
> and his old back was bowed.
>
> H. D., 1934–35[1]

We are all at risk of succumbing to imagined images of men – as patriarch or phallus, monster or idol – sustained by the harmful childhood fixations, acted-out rebellion and inward defences my tales describe. Therapy is about undoing these defences so as to become aware of and measure the fantasies they sustain against reality. Treatment involves disenchantment – as in the poem above where the symbolist poet Hilda Doolittle describes the ending of her analysis with Freud, leaving him, the man she called her master, arrayed with his trophies of the past, seeing him as he was – old and bent.

Learning that none of us is, or ever will be, the grand figures we so often imagine men to be is not a recipe for despair. It may be the only way forward. Ibsen depicted as much in *The Doll's House*. It culminates in Nora, having gone through torment trying to maintain her husband's high regard, learning that she cannot depend on him standing up for her. Discovering he is not the man she thought he was launches her on a quest for liberation that

211

rightly remains an inspiration to this day for feminists all over the world.

The trouble is, as my tales make all too plain, we are deeply resistant to becoming conscious of, let alone giving up the defensive fantasies about men that rule our lives. Freud was nevertheless hopeful that by attending to his patients' free associations, and to their transference on to him of their damagingly repressed and internalised fantasies about his sex, it might be possible to undo their resistance.[2]

Therapy has begun to do its job when – as in a play – we realise we were immersed in a drama, whose figures, however real their effects, were mere spirits. Only when we recognise these figures to be the invention of fantasy can we begin to test them against reality. Only then is there any chance of our nightmares dissolving, and of our beginning to bring our dreams to fruition. Only then can we hope to be released from the stranglehold of the past to become makers of our own future – with our eyes open.

Freud himself, however, eventually despaired that psychoanalysis might prove an 'impossible profession' especially, he said, when faced with treating women who are convinced the solution to their ills lies in having or becoming a man, or with men who refuse to submit to the analyst's cure, in the unconscious belief that to do so would be tantamount to inviting castration, to losing them their manhood.[3]

Psychoanalysis will indeed prove impossible as a means of relieving the ills done by such fantasies if it continues to lose sight of them in attending exclusively to mothering. But paying them due attention means also attending to the evacuation and projection into others of the damaging mechanisms holding them in place. This means attending to our male fictions' countertransference effects.

Hence my drawing attention to the reactions elicited in me, as listener and therapist, to my characters' tales: to feeling as 'unwelcome', for example, as all the male figures Tessa phobically avoided and whose importance she magnified in seeking to secure her fantasy of virgin birth. It was for this reason too that I pointed out how I found myself seduced into imagining myself the 'paragon' my Don Juan patient, Chris, wanted to see of himself reflected in me; and to the way I found myself being drawn into smiling with Rachel's envious derision of men, and into being the third person 'Oedipal spectator' to Celia's and Mark's phallic goings-on.

Awareness of the countertransference also led me to make explicit the feelings aroused by my interviewees' acted-out rebellions: my sense that I was the phallic abuser Mr Benn perversely imagined his victims to be; my wanting to baby Barnie, so successfully did he emasculate himself in courting male authority; or worrying about provoking and puncturing the tough guy, tomboy and conman brag of Keith, Toni and Steve.

I was also very conscious of being infected with the nostalgia by which Sara kept going the repressed gross male figure of her abuser: with the cosiness with which Ann cushioned herself against her depressing internal male detractors; with experiencing myself, not Sheila, as bereaved of the ideal man whose death she denied with her psychosomatic ills. I found myself rushing with Peter's mania, and becoming deadened with the fragmentation David used to numb himself against the tragedy of being disowned.

Psychoanalysis can only alleviate the ills done by these defences by attending to their transference into therapy. Therapists, as well as patients, have to resist acting out the psychological mechanisms involved, and attend to the form as well as content of what we think and say, so as to interpret and work our defences through.[4] It is a painstaking and time-consuming process, involving testing and revising each interpretation in relation to the patient's response,[5] often muddled by their here-and-now resistance to the analyst as a patriarchal superego figure from the past.[6]

Even then therapy is not enough to undo the damage done by the defensive personality traits sustaining our unwarranted notions about men and masculinity in so far as these are rooted in the power, privilege and wealth enjoyed by men in the ruling class. Men's social dominance also has to be exposed, challenged and overthrown – a matter not so much of therapy but of politics.

Entrenched interests are at stake. We no more willingly recognise our false ideas about men to be fantasies than believers abandon their faith in God, or scientists their theories, simply because of symptoms of their not working. Men, as Freud observed, did not take kindly to having their 'naïve self-love' disturbed by Copernicus's discovery that their earth is not the centre of the universe, nor to Darwin's evidence that their species was not the first. Nor do men welcome psychoanalysis's revelation 'to the ego that it is not even master in its own house'.[7]

More than therapy is needed to persuade us to the contrary – not least because of the economic and political purposes served by the cock-and-bull stories we tell ourselves about our lives. At present this means we must expose as fantasy the myth exploited by those who, in the interests of destroying state education, health and welfare blame social problems – unemployment, poverty and crime included – on men not being the patriarchs they supposedly once were, in supporting and bringing up their children to become hard-working, law-abiding citizens like themselves.[8]

It also means challenging the idea exploited in Britain, for example, by the recently established child support agencies that the poverty of women-headed households can be relieved by chasing so-called 'runaway fathers' to pay for their children's upkeep irrespective of whether they can do so, or of the risks to which this often exposes the mothers of their children (as it did in Celia's case).

Beyond this, feminist academics must continue to deconstruct the myths of masculinity involved – including Jungian-inspired attempts to revive, and portray as truth, the folktale symbol of the Wild Man, depicted by the Brothers Grimm in their story, 'Iron John'.[9]

Some people think that once this is done we must reconcile ourselves to never being any more than the resulting 'deconstructed' fragments, that it is an illusion to believe they could ever be put together to make us whole. Certainly, in Freudian and Kleinian terms, we have to recognise the psychic splitting of the conscious and unconscious mind, of love and hate, good and bad. We have to go through the emotional pain of recognising that neither we nor anyone else ever was or ever could be the ideal man promulgated by male-dominated society (symbolised in Lacan's view by the phallus). In sum: we have to grieve the man who never was.

But grieving and accepting loss is not the end of the story. It is only the beginning – a necessary precursor to working to realise our ideals actually and in fact so as to build ourselves and our world on a sound basis, so that it better meets the needs of both women and men. This means being mindful of the snares and delusions, revealed by psychoanalysis, by which we imagine that the job is already done.[10]

The task is again analogous to that of the scientist, this time the researcher who, having lost faith in his theories, and wary of reverting to them, then has to go through the laborious process of collecting, experimenting, piecing together and reconstructing the evidence to discover the truth. It is also like the work of artists who, once they have figured out their ideas, then have to sketch and test them out, using the materials to hand, and means that others can understand, to realise what they want to communicate – whether through music, writing, acting, directing, film, painting, sculpture or architecture.

Sublimating desire, putting our ideas into creative effect, beginning to realise our ideals in fact rather than fantasy, is an exciting business. Getting there, however, is often dreary. This is the gist of Sonya's warning, at the end of Chekhov's play *Uncle Vanya*, after Uncle Vanya loses heart in the imagined brilliance of his brother-in-law, the professor:

> We shall go on living, Uncle Vanya. We shall live through a long, long succession of days and tedious evenings. We shall patiently suffer the trials which Fate imposes on us; we shall work for others, now and in our old age, and we shall have no rest. When our time comes we shall die submissively, and over there beyond the grave, we shall say that we've suffered, that we've wept, that we've had a bitter life, and God will take pity on us. And then, Uncle dear, we shall both begin to know a life that is bright and beautiful and lovely.[11]

Sonya's God is now dead. Nevertheless, as I have sought to demonstrate, his destructive legacy lives on. Hence the need to continue the psychoanalytic and feminist task of exposing, as Freud did, the mechanisms sustaining the myths bequeathed to us by nineteenth-century religion. More generally, we have to go on revealing the shortfall between our defensive pleasure-driven dreams and reality.

Recognising the gap – our 'lack-in-being', as Lacan put it – is a necessary prelude not only to repairing our damaged world, but to forging ourselves and the society in which we live, not in some imagined patriarchal heaven above but on a better, more sure, sexually and racially equal basis on earth below. The job still needs doing. Let's wake up and get on with it.

Notes

Abbreviation

SE The Standard Edition of the Complete Psychological Works of Sigmund Freud translated and edited by James Strachey, London, Hogarth Press, 1953–74.

Epigraph

1 S. Freud (1895) *Studies on Hysteria, SE* II, pp. 160–61.

Introduction: Imagined Men

1 Or, according to a limerick invented and told me by the psychoanalyst Charles Rycroft, people are blithely unaware of Freud's phallocentrism: 'Young men who frequent picture palaces/Haven't heard of psychoanalysis./As they've never read Freud/They are still overjoyed/To cling to their long-standing phalluses.'
2 S. Freud and J. Breuer (1893) 'On the psychical mechanism of hysterical phenomena', in *Studies on Hysteria, SE*, II, p. 7.
3 For Freud's reinterpretation of this case in phallic terms see S. Freud (1914) 'On the history of the psychoanalytic movement', *SE*, XIV.
4 Breuer and Freud, *Studies on Hysteria.*
5 S. Freud (1900) *The Interpretation of Dreams, SE*, IV, p. 121, n. 1.
6 S. Freud (1905) 'Fragment of an analysis of a case of hysteria', *SE*, VII.
7 Ibid.
8 S. Freud (1909) 'Notes upon a case of obsessional neurosis', *SE*, X.
9 S. Freud (1909) 'Analysis of a phobia in a five-year-old boy, *SE*, X.
10 S. Freud (1918) 'From the history of an infantile neurosis', *SE*, XVII.
11 S. Freud (1897) 'Letter to Fliess', 15 October, *SE*, I, pp. 263–66.
12 S. Freud (1917) 'Mourning and melancholia', *SE*, XIV.

13 S. Freud (1923) *The Ego and the Id, SE*, XIX.

14 Freud 'Analysis of a phobia in a five-year-old boy', p. 8, n. 2 (added 1923).

15 W. H. Auden (1939) 'In memory of Sigmund Freud', in *Collected Poems*, London, Faber & Faber, 1976, pp. 216–17.

16 Klein makes few concessions to her readers in describing the stark bodily and nightmarish anxieties involved in our love and hate of others. I have sought to make her work more accessible by recounting its development via the story of her own and her child and adult patients' lives. See J. Sayers (1991) *Mothering Psychoanalysis*, London, Penguin Books. For further explanation of the technical terms I use in this book see R. D. Hinshelwood (1989) *A Dictionary of Kleinian Thought*, London, Free Association Books.

17 As a feminist I deplore the generic use of the male pronoun to refer to women and men, girls and boys, regardless of their sex. Nevertheless I shall adopt this convention to distinguish babies from their primary caregivers, who, because of the continuing unequal sexual division of childcare, are almost always women.

18 For an account of the argument Klein thereby provoked within psychoanalysis see J. Rose (1993) *Why War?* Oxford, Blackwell.

19 J. Green (1947) *If I Were You*, London, Eyre & Spottiswoode, 1950; analysed in M. Klein (1955) On identification, in *Envy and Gratitude*, London, Hogarth Press, 1975.

20 See, for example, P. Heiman (1950) 'On counter-transference', *International Journal of Psycho-Analysis*, 31, pp. 81–4; W. R. Bion (1961) *Experience in Groups*, London, Tavistock; B. Joseph (1985) 'Transference: the total situation', *International Journal of Psycho-Analysis*, 66, pp. 447–54; O. Kernberg (1988) 'Projection and projective identification: developmental and clinical aspects', in J. Sandler (ed.) *Projection, Identification, Projective Identification*, London, Karnac.

21 The danger of making seemingly untestable psychoanalytic interpretations based on the assumption that we are subject to, and can know about someone else's experience directly, without verbal mediation, is well brought out by S. Frosh (1994) *Sexual Difference*, London, Routledge.

22 W. R. Bion (1962) 'A theory of thinking', in *Second Thoughts*, London, Karnac, 1984.

23 See, for example, E. Bott Spillius (1983) 'Some developments from the work of Melanie Klein', *International Journal of Psycho-Analysis*, 64, pp. 321–22.

24 See, for example, M. Klein (1959) 'Our adult world and its roots in infancy', in *Envy and Gratitude*.

25 This topic is very accessibly explored from both a personal and a political angle by the psychotherapist S. Orbach (1994) *What's Really Going on Here?*, London, Virago.

26 See, for example, J. Bowlby (1944) 'Forty-four juvenile thieves', *Inter-*

national Journal of Psycho-Analysis, 25, pp. 19–52. The subsequent development of Bowlby's work is detailed by, among others I. Bretherton (1991) 'The roots and growing point of attachment theory', in C. M. Parkes, J. Stevenson-Hinde and P. Marris (eds) *Attachment across the Life Cycle*, London, Routledge; and J. Holmes (1993); *John Bowlby and Attachment Theory*, London, Routledge.

27 For further details of Winnicott's work see the engaging brief biographical introduction by A. Phillips (1988) *Winnicott*, London, Fontana.

28 This is made particularly explicit by M. Mahler, E. Pines and A. Bergman (1975) *The Psychological Birth of the Child*, New York, Basic Books; and is very usefully criticised by J. Doane and D. Hodges (1992) *From Klein to Kristeva: Psychoanalytic Feminism and the Search for the 'Good Enough' Mother*, Ann Arbor, University of Michigan Press.

29 D. W. Winnicott (1953) 'Transitional objects and transitional phenomena', in *Playing and Reality*, London, Penguin Books, 1974.

30 N. Chodorow (1978) *The Reproduction of Mothering*, Berkeley, University of California Press.

31 D. W. Winnicott (1969) 'The use of an object and relating through identifications', in *Playing and Reality*.

32 J. Benjamin (1988) *The Bonds of Love*, London, Virago, 1990. Benjamin's account of dominance and submission has in turn been adopted to explain women's lack of self-esteem by R. Coward (1992) *Our Treacherous Hearts*, London, Faber & Faber.

33 A useful glossary can be found in J. Laplanche and J-B. Pontalis (1973) *The Language of Psycho-Analysis*, London, Hogarth Press, 1980. I have also found helpful the expository overviews provided by B. Benvenuto and R. Kennedy (1986) *The Works of Jacques Lacan*, London, Free Association Books; E. Grosz (1990) *Jacques Lacan: A Feminist Introduction*, London, Routledge; and S. Frosh (1994) *Sexual Difference*, London, Routledge.

34 J. Lacan (1956) 'Le seminaire sur "La lettre volée" ', translated by J. Mehlman (1972) *Yale French Studies*, 48, pp. 38–72.

35 For a helpful and easy introduction to these developments in cultural studies see M. Sarup (1993) *Post-Structuralism and Postmodernism*, London, Harvester Wheatsheaf.

36 L. Segal (1990) *Slow Motion: Changing Masculinities, Changing Men*, London, Virago.

37 K. Silverman (1992) *Male Subjectivity at the Margins*, London, Routledge.

38 J. Kristeva (1974) *Revolution in Poetic Language*, New York, Columbia University Press, 1984.

39 J. Kristeva (1977) 'Stabat mater', in *Tales of Love*, New York, Columbia University Press, 1987. In this Kristeva refers to Freud's theory that, behind the ego ideal, 'lies hidden an individual's first and most

important identification, his identification with the father in his own personal prehistory', S. Freud (1923) *The Ego and the Id*, SE, XIX, p. 31.

40 J. Kristeva (1980) *Powers of Horror*, New York, Columbia University Press, 1982.

41 G. Lorca (1928) 'On lullabies', in *Deep Song and Other Prose*, London, Marion Boyars, 1980, pp. 14–15.

42 S. Plath (1959) 'Poem for a birthday', in *The Colossus*, London, Heinemann, 1960.

43 S. Plath (1958) *The Journals of Sylvia Plath*, New York, Random House, 1982, p. 188.

44 J. Rose (1991) *The Haunting of Sylvia Plath*, London, Virago, p. 234.

45 S. Plath (1962) 'Daddy', in *Ariel*, London, Faber & Faber, 1965.

46 S. Olds (1993) *The Father*, London, Secker & Warburg, p. 71. Earlier US confessional, psychoanalytically based examples include Berryman's reaction to his father's suicide: 'When will indifference come, I moan & rave/I'd like to scrabble till I got right down/away down under the grass/and ax the casket open ha to see/just how he's taking it', J. Berryman (1969) *Dream Songs*, London, Faber & Faber, no. 384, p. 406.

47 See, for example, J. McDougall (1989) 'The dead father', *International Journal of Psycho-Analysis*, 70, pp. 205–19; A. Limentani (1991) 'Neglected fathers in the aetiology and treatment of sexual deviations', *International Journal of Psycho-Analysis*, 72, pp. 573–84; L. A. Kirshner (1992) 'The absence of the father', *Journal of the American Psychoanalytic Association*, 40(4), pp. 1117–38; M. Mancia (1993) 'The absent father; his role in sexual deviations and in transference', *International Journal of Psycho-Analysis*, 74(5), pp. 941–50.

48 I have also described the latter extensively in *Mothering Psychoanalysis*.

Chapter 1: Virgin Birth

1 S. Freud (1928) 'The future of an illusion', *SE*, XXI, p. 24.

2 See, for example, G. McNeil (ed.) (1994) *Soul Providers*, London, Virago; and D. Taylor (1994) *My Children, My Gold*, London, Virago.

3 See, for example, J. Lacan (1955–56) 'On a question preliminary to any possible treatment of psychosis', in *Ecrits*, London, Tavistock, 1977. Others characterise as narcissistic those who 'will not try to triumph over the father (to identify with him in order to surpass him later) but will try to abolish the principle of paternity itself and the whole frame of reference to which it was the organizer': B. Grunberger (1989) *New Essays on Narcissism*, London, Free Association Books, p. 39.

4 M. Milner (1969) *The Hands of the Living God*, London, Virago, 1988, pp. 325, 402, n. 2.

5 See, for example, C. Steedman (1986) *Landscape for a Good Woman*, London, Virago.

6 S. Freud (1930) *Civilization and its Discontents*, SE, XXI.

7 M. Kundera (1973) *Life is Elsewhere*, London, Faber & Faber, 1986, p. 7.

8 See, for example, J. Kristeva (1977) 'Stabat mater', in *Tales of Love*, New York, Columbia University Press, 1987.

9 See, for example, J. Lacan (1953) 'The function and field of speech and language in psychoanalysis', in *Ecrits*.

10 J-P. Sartre (1964) *Words*, London, Penguin Books, 1967.

11 J. Kristeva (1980) *Powers of Horror*, New York, Columbia University Press, 1982.

Chapter 2: Don Juan

1 S. Freud (1923) 'The infantile genital organization', *SE*, XIX, pp. 142–43.

2 R. Edgcumbe and M. Burgner (1975) 'The phallic-narcissistic phase', *Psychoanalytic Study of the Child*, 30, pp. 161–80.

3 J. Temperley (1993) 'Is the Oedipus complex bad news for women?' *Free Associations*, 4(2), pp. 265–75.

4 W. Reich (1949) 'The phallic-narcissistic character', in *Character Analysis*, New York, Farrar, Straus & Giroux, p. 203.

5 H. Deutsch (1944) *Psychology of Women, Vol. I, Girlhood*, New York, Grune & Stratton, p. 246.

6 S. de Beauvoir (1949) *The Second Sex*, London, Penguin Books, 1972, p. 306.

7 See, for example, J. Lacan (1958) 'The meaning of the phallus', in J. Mitchell and J. Rose (eds) *Feminine Sexuality*, London, Macmillan, 1982.

8 For other examples see M. A. Doane (1991) *Femmes Fatales*, London, Routledge.

9 S. Freud (1912) 'On the universal tendency to debasement in the sphere of love', *SE*, XI.

10 S. Kierkegaard (1843) 'The immediate stages of the erotic', in *Either/ Or, Part I*, New Jersey, Princeton University Press, 1971.

11 J. Kristeva (1991) *Strangers to Ourselves*, New York, Columbia University Press.

12 Kierkegaard 'Immediate stages of the erotic', pp. 93, 94, 97.

13 See, for example, J. McDougall (1989) *Theatres of the Body*, London, Free Association Books; N. Coltart (1993) 'Blood, shit, and tears', paper given at the University of Kent, 23 October.

14 In *The Second Sex*, Simone de Beauvoir characterises as general this stage in which the boy 'measures the length of his penis'. The banter and competition to which it gives rise is also a central motif in the

novel by G. Grass (1961) *Cat and Mouse*, London, Penguin Books, 1966.

15 S. Freud (1930) *Civilization and its Discontents*, SE, XXI.

16 K. Horney (1932) 'The dread of women', in *Feminine Psychology*, New York, Norton, 1967.

17 J. Kristeva (1983) *Tales of Love*, New York, Columbia University Press, 1987, p. 202.

18 See Introduction p. 4–5, and, for example, W. R. Bion (1962) 'A theory of thinking', in *Second Thoughts*, London, Karnac, 1984.

19 O. Rank (1924) *The Don Juan Legend*, New Jersey, Princeton University Press, 1975.

Chapter 3: Penis Envy

1 S. Freud (1925) 'Some psychical consequences of the anatomical distinction between the sexes', *SE*, XIX, p. 252.

2 See, for example, K. Horney (1923) 'On the genesis of the castration complex in women', and K. Horney (1926) 'The flight from womanhood', in *Feminine Psychology*, New York, Norton, 1967.

3 K. Abraham (1921) 'Manifestation of the female castration complex', *International Journal of Psycho-Analysis*, 3, pp. 1-29.

4 I review some of feminism's resulting theories in J. Sayers (1982) *Biological Politics*, London, Routledge.

5 For a useful illustrative case history see M. Klein (1924) 'An obsessional neurosis in a six-year-old girl', in *The Psycho-Analysis of Children*, London, Hogarth Press, 1975; and M. Klein (1957) 'Envy and gratitude', in *Envy and Gratitude*, London, Hogarth Press, 1975.

6 K. Abraham (1924) 'A short study of the development of the libido, viewed in the light of mental disorders', in *Selected Papers on Psycho-Analysis*, London, Hogarth Press, 1968, p. 455.

7 A. Freud (1936) 'Identification with the aggressor', in *The Ego and the Mechanisms of Defence*, London, Hogarth Press.

Chapter 4: Oedipus

1 S. Freud (1925) 'Some psychical consequences of the anatomical distinction between the sexes', *SE*, XIX, p. 256.

2 A. Freud (1952) 'Adolescence', *Psychoanalytic Study of the Child*, 13, pp. 255–78.

3 See, for example, J. Benjamin (1988) *The Bonds of Love*, London, Virago; and J. Bowlby (1988) 'Violence in the family', in *A Secure Base*, London, Routledge.

4 J. Johnson (1991) *What Lisa Knew*, London, Bloomsbury.

Chapter 5: My Father Myself

1 S. Freud (1924) 'The dissolution of the Oedipus complex', *SE*, XIX, p. 176.
2 S. Freud (1920) 'The psychogenesis of a case of female homo-sexuality', *SE*, XVIII.
3 See, for example, N. O'Connor and J. Ryan (1993) *Wild Desires and Mistaken Identities*, London, Virago; N. Chodorow (1994) *Femininit-ies, Masculinities, Sexualities*, London, Free Association Books.
4 S. Freud (1928) 'Dostoevsky and parricide', *SE*, XXI, p. 177.
5 For a particularly influential contribution to this about-turn in psychoanalysis see R. Britton (1989) 'The missing link: parental sexu-ality', in *The Oedipus Complex Today*, London, Karnac.
6 See, for example, S. Freud (1923) *The Ego and the Id*, *SE*, XIX, p. 34.
7 S. Freud (1918) 'From the history of an infantile neurosis', *SE*, XVII.
8 Freud 'Dissolution of the Oedipus complex', p. 177.

Chapter 6: Pervert

1 S. Freud (1940) *An Outline of Psychoanalysis*, *SE*, XXIII, p. 202. For further explanation of Freud's concept of 'disavowal' and its relation to Lacan's theory of 'foreclosure', see J. Laplanche and J-B. Pontalis (1967) *The Language of Psycho-Analysis*, London, Hogarth Press, 1973.
2 R. Stoller (1975) *Perversion: The Erotic Form of Hatred*, New York, Delta.
3 E. Weldon (1988) *Mother, Madonna, Whore*, London, Free Associ-ation Books.
4 See, for example, G. Kohon (1987) 'Fetishism revisited', *International Journal of Psycho-Analysis*, 68, pp. 213–28; L. J. Kaplan (1991) *Female Perversions*, New York, Doubleday.
5 See, for example, J. Chasseguet-Smirgel (1984) *Creativity and Perver-sion*, London, Free Association Books, 1985; J. McDougall (1978) *Plea for a Measure of Abnormality*, London, Free Association Books, 1990.
6 See, for example, D. Meltzer (1979) *The Psycho-Analytical Process*, Perthshire, Clunie; Hanna Segal, interviewed by J. Rose (1990) in *Women: A Cultural Review*, 1(2), pp. 207–12; and J. Temperley (1993) 'Is the Oedipus complex bad news for women?' *Free Associations*, 4(2), pp. 265–75.
7 M. Klein (1945) 'The Oedipus complex in the light of early anxieties', in *Love, Guilt and Reparation*, London, Hogarth Press, 1975.
8 See, for example, Chasseguet-Smirgel *Creativity and Perversion* and McDougall, *Plea for a Measure of Abnormality*.
9 See, for example, W. Reich (1933) *The Mass Psychology of Fascism*,

New York, Farrar, Straus & Giroux, 1970, and E. Fromm (1941) *The Fear of Freedom*, New York, Norton.

10 J. Lacan (1951) 'Intervention on transference', in J. Mitchell and J. Rose (eds) *Feminine Sexuality*, London, Macmillan, 1982.

11 For a psychoanalytic account of the psychological impact of regal deaths see W. R. D. Fairbairn (1936) 'The effect of a king's death upon patients undergoing analysis', *International Journal of Psycho-Analysis*, 17, pp. 278–84.

Chapter 7: Wimp

1 J. Lacan (1958) 'The meaning of the phallus', in J. Mitchell and J. Rose (eds) *Feminine Sexuality*, London, Macmillan, 1982, p. 84.

2 J. Rivière (1929) 'Womanliness as a masquerade', *International Journal of Psycho-Analysis*, 10, pp. 303–13.

3 A. Freud (1952) 'Studies in passivity', in *Indications for Child Analysis and Other Essays*, London, Hogarth Press, 1968.

4 S. Freud (1918) 'From the history of an infantile neurosis', *SE*, XVII.

5 A. Aichhorn (1925) *Wayward Youth*, New York, Viking, 1935.

Chapter 8: Tough guy

1 M. Klein (1927) 'Criminal tendencies in normal children', in *Love, Guilt and Reparation*, London, Hogarth Press, p. 182.

2 See, for example, S. Freud (1916) 'Some character-types met with in psycho-analytic work', *SE*, XIV.

3 See, for example, J. Bowlby (1944) 'Forty-four juvenile thieves: their characters and home life', *International Journal of Psycho-Analysis*, 25, pp. 19–52, 107–27; D. W. Winnicott (1965) 'The antisocial tendency', in *Deprivation and Delinquency*, London, Routledge.

4 See M. Rutter, B. Maughan, P. Mortimore and J. Ouston (1979) *Fifteen Thousand Hours*, London, Open Books; and for a more recent example of studies in this vein see D. M. Ferguson, L. J. Horwood and M. T. Lynskey (1992) 'Family change, parental discord and early offending', *Journal of Child Psychology and Psychiatry*, 33(6), pp. 1059–75.

5 R. Lindner (1944) *Rebel Without a Cause*, New York, Grune & Stratton. For further cultural studies discussion of the fantasies involved see, for example, J. L. Neibaur (1989) *Tough Guy: The American Movie Macho*, London, McFarland.

6 See Rutter *et al.*, *Fifteen Thousand Hours*.

7 J. McVicar (1974) *McVicar by Himself*, London, Huchinson; J. McVicar (1992) 'Cheers dad', in J. Hoyland (ed.) *Fathers and Sons*, London, Serpent's Tail.

Chapter 9: Tomboy

1 S. Freud (1920) 'The psychogenesis of a case of female homo-sexuality', *SE*, XVIII, p. 169.
2 See, for example, S. Freud and J. Breuer (1895) *Studies on Hysteria*, *SE*, II; and S. Freud (1908) ' "Civilized" sexual morality and modern nervous illness', *SE*, IX.
3 See, for example, J. Butler (1990) *Gender Trouble*, London, Rout-ledge. For a nice example of this perspective applied to theatre see L. Hart and P. Phelan (1993) *Acting Out: Feminist Performances*, Ann Arbor, University of Michigan Press.
4 For accounts of bodily self-harm in teenage and adult women see, for example, E. Welldon (1988) *Mother, Madonna, Whore*, London, Free Association Books, 1994; L. J. Kaplan (1991) *Female Perversions*, New York, Doubleday; J. Woods (1988) 'Layers of meaning in self-cutting', *Journal of Child Psychotherapy*, 14, pp. 51–60; T. Tantam and J. Whittaker (1992) 'Personality disorder and self-wounding', *British Journal of Psychiatry*, 161, pp. 451–64.

Chapter 10: Conman

1 F. Fanon (1952) *Black Skin, White Masks*, London, MacGibbon & Kee, 1968, p. 193.
2 See, for example, J. Lacan (1949) 'The mirror stage as formative of the function of the I as revealed in psychoanalytic experience', and J. Lacan (1958) 'The signification of the phallus', both in *Ecrits*, London, Tavistock, 1977.
3 See, respectively, S. Freud (1914) 'On narcissism', *SE*, XIV; Freud (1917) 'Mourning and melancholia', ibid. and Freud (1923) *The Ego and the Id*, *SE*, XIX.
4 This aspect of Kleinian theory and its problems are particularly well brought out by C. Fred Alford (1989) *Melanie Klein and Critical Social Theory*, New Haven, Yale University Press.
5 H. Deutsch (1958) 'The impostor', in *Neurosis and Character Types*, New York, International Universities Press, 1965.
6 For a recent account of changes occurring in a son's identifications following his father's suicide see D. Rosenfeld (1992) 'Psychic changes in the paternal image', *International Journal of Psycho-Analysis*, 73, pp. 757–71.
7 D. W. Winnicott (1960) 'Ego distortion in terms of true and false self', in *the Maturational Processes and the Facilitating Environment*, London, Hogarth Press, 1965.
8 C. Bollas (1987) 'The liar', in *The Shadow of the Object*, London, Free Association Books.
9 See, for example, S. L. Gilman (1993) *Freud, Race and Gender*, Prince-ton University Press; R. Meyerowitz (1993) 'The cultural origins and

prospects of psychoanalysis: "Jewish science" and/or "Jouissance" ',
American Imago, 50(2), pp. 131–59.

10 T. Mann (1954) *Confessions of Felix Krull, Confidence Man*, Harmondsworth, Penguin Books, 1958, p. 183.

11 'To reveal art and conceal the artist is art's aim', O. Wilde (1891) *The Picture of Dorian Grey*, London, Penguin Books (1949), p. 5.

12 M. Fakhry Davids (1992) 'Frantz Fanon: the struggle for inner freedom', talk given to the Sixth Conference on Psychoanalysis and the Public Sphere, University of East London, 31 October.

13 M. Klein (1955) 'On identification', in *Envy and Gratitude*, London, Hogarth Press, 1975, also mentioned on p. 4 above.

14 H. Melville (1857) *The Confidence-Man*, London, John Lehman, 1948, p. 155; and Mann, *Felix Krull*, p. 28.

15 Fanon, *Black Skin, White Masks*, p. 63.

16 O. Wilde (1891) *The Critic as Artist*, in R. Ellmann (ed.) *The Artist as Critic*, Chicago, University of Chicago Press, 1982, p. 393.

17 Fanon, *Black Skin, White Masks*, p. 154.

Chapter 11: Repressed abuse

1 S. Freud (1896) 'The aetiology of hysteria', *SE*, III, p. 203, 211.

2 This is well explained by J. Mitchell (1986) in *The Selected Melanie Klein*, London, Penguin Books.

3 See, for example, P.Tyson (1978) 'Transference and developmental issues in the analysis of a prelatency child', *Psychoanalytic Study of the Child*, 33, pp. 213–36.

4 I discuss this further in J. Sayers (1994) 'Consuming male fantasy', in A. Elliott and S. Frosh (eds) *Psychoanalysis in Contexts*, London, Routledge; and J. Sayers (1994) 'Psychoanalysing patriarchy's ills', *European Journal of Women's Studies*, 1, pp. 227–39.

5 S. Freud (1905) 'Fragment of an analysis of a case of hysteria', *SE*, VII; also discussed on p. 141 above.

6 K. Horney (1932) 'Psychogenic factors in functional female disorders', *Feminine Psychology*, New York, Norton, 1967.

7 S. Plath (1963) *The Bell Jar*, London, Faber & Faber. For further discussion of this point see E. Showalter (1987) *The Female Malady*, London, Virago.

8 See, for example, S. Freud (1909) 'Notes upon a case of obsessional neurosis', *SE*, X.

9 For documentation on this point see e.g. L. Gordon (1989) *Heroes of Our Own Lives*, London, Virago.

10 Freud, 'Fragment of an analysis of a case of hysteria'.

11 C. Brontë (1847) *Jane Eyre*, Harmondsworth, Penguin Books, 1966, p. 143.

12 Freud, 'Fragment of an analysis of a case of hysteria'.

13 For further details about the life of Anna O. see L. Freeman (1972)

The Story of Anna O., New York, Walker; and L. Appignanesi and
J. Forrester (1992) *Freud's Women*, London, Virago.

14 For a less extraordinary example of the ill-effects of repressed abuse
that also magnifies men's importance as patriarch, see S. Fraser (1987)
In My Father's House, London, Virago, discussed further in J. Sayers
(1991) 'Blinded by family feeling', in P. Carter, T. Jeffs and M. K.
Smith (eds) *Social Work and Social Welfare 3*, Milton Keynes, Open
University Press.

Chapter 12: Depression

1 S. Freud (1917) 'Mourning and melancholia', *SE*, XIV, p. 248.

2 See, for example, M. Barnes and N. Maple (1992) *Women and Mental
Health*, Birmingham, Venture Press.

3 See, for example, H. Deutsch (1959) '*Lord Jim* and depression', in
Neuroses and Character Types, New York, International Universities
Press, 1965.

4 See, for example, T. Harris and A. Bifulco (1991) 'Loss of parent in
childhood, attachment style, and depression in adulthood', in C. M.
Parkes, J. Stevenson-Hinde and P. Marris (eds) *Attachment across the
Life Cycle*, London, Routledge.

5 See, for example, M. Klein (1935) 'A contribution to the psychogenesis of manic-depressive states', and (1940) 'Mourning and its
relation to manic-depressive states', in *Love, Guilt and Reparation*,
London, Hogarth Press, 1975. For a more detailed overview of Klein's
account of depression see my book, J. Sayers (1991) *Mothering
Psychoanalysis*, Harmondsworth, Penguin Books.

6 For a Kleinian account of defensive flight to the father from the
mother see J. Chasseguet-Smirgel (1964) 'Feminine guilt and the Oedipus complex', in *Female Sexuality*, London, Virago, 1981.

7 S. Plath (1963) *The Bell Jar*, London, Faber & Faber, p. 34.

8 In J. Shute's novel, *Life Size*, the food-obsessed heroine observes,
'Perhaps a similar hunger drives men in search of sex – the difference
being that my frenzy led me to seek something to cram into myself,
while they crave something into which to cram themselves': quoted
by P. Craig, *London Review of Books*, 3 December 1992, p. 28. Also
relevant is the attribution of women's eating disorders to the absence
from their lives of men's emotional attention: M. Maine (1991) *Father
Hunger*, Carlsbad, California, Gurze Books.

9 See the descriptions of depression as 'black dog days' and 'black sun'
in A. Storr (1990) *Churchill's Black Dog*, London, Flamingo, and J.
Kristeva (1987) *Black Sun*, New York, Columbia University Press,
1989.

10 K. Abraham (1924) 'A short study of the development of the libido,
viewed in the light of mental disorders', in *Selected Papers*, London,
Karnac, 1979.

11 M. Cardinal (1975) *The Words to Say It*, London, Women's Press, 1993. For a very useful critique of such mother-blaming accounts of depression see J. Doane and D. Hodges (1992) *From Klein to Kristeva: Psychoanalytic Feminism and the Search for the 'Good Enough' Mother*, Ann Arbor, University of Michigan Press.
12 B. Keenan (1992) *An Evil Cradling*, London, Vintage, p. 67.

Chapter 13: Death denied

1 S. Freud (1917) 'Mourning and melancholia', *SE*, XIV, pp. 244–45.
2 See, for example, M. Klein (1935) 'A contribution to the psychogenesis of manic-depressive states', in *Love, Guilt and Reparation*, London, Hogarth Press, 1975.
3 J. McDougall (1989) *Theatres of the Body: A Psychoanalytic Approach to Psychosomatic Illness*, London, Free Association Books.
4 C. M. Parkes (1972) *Bereavement: Studies of Grief in Adult Life*, New York, International Universities Press.
5 T. S. Eliot (1922) 'The burial of the dead', in *The Waste Land*, London, Faber & Faber, lines 1–2.
6 Parkes, *Bereavement*.
7 In H. H. Munro (1914) *Beasts and Superbeasts*, in *The Penguin Complete Saki*, London, Penguin Books, 1982.
8 See, for example, M. Klein (1955) 'On identification', in *Envy and Gratitude*, London, Hogarth Press, 1975, p. 143.
9 M. Klein (1940) 'Mourning and its relation to manic-depressive states', in *Love, Guilt and Reparation*.

Chapter 14: Mania

1 H. Rey (1977) 'The schizoid mode of being and the space-time continuum (beyond metaphor)', *Journal of the Melanie Klein Society*, 4(2), p. 33. See also, in contrast to the clinging dependence of the 'ocnophile', the phallic symbolism of the manic individualist, the 'philobat', M. Balint (1959) *Thrills and Regressions*, London, Hogarth Press.
2 S. Freud (1917) 'Mourning and melancholia', *SE*, XIV.
3 K. Abraham (1924) 'A short study of the development of the libido, viewed in the light of mental disorders', in *Selected Papers on Psycho-Analysis*, London, Hogarth Press, 1968.
4 See, for example, M. Klein (1952) 'The emotional life of the infant', in *Envy and Gratitude*, London, Hogarth Press, 1975.
5 I develop this point further in, for example, J. Sayers (1988) 'Anorexia, psychoanalysis, and feminism: fantasy and reality', *Journal of Adolescence*, 11, pp. 361–71; and J. Sayers (1994) 'Psychoanalysing patriarchy's ills', *European Journal of Women's Studies*, 1, pp. 227–39.
6 Some argue that Wagner himself was motivated by manic defence in

composing *The Ring* in reaction to the failure of his affair with Mathilde Wesendonck; see R. D. Chessick (1990) 'On falling in love', in S. Fader, R. L. Karmel and G. H. Pollock (eds) *Psychoanalytic Explorations in Music*, New York, International Univerisities Press. Others adopt a Jungian account: see, for example, the feminist analysis by J. S. Bolen (1992) *Ring of Power*, San Francisco, HarperCollins; and, for an account of Jung's patient Sabina Spielrein adopting, rather than undoing as Freud might have done, the heroic motif of Siegfried to transform both her past and future see J. Kerr (1994) *A Most Dangerous Method*, London, Sinclair-Stevenson.

7 See, for example, S. Orbach (1993) *Hunger Strike*, Harmondsworth, Penguin Books.

8 For further examples see R. Money-Kyrle (1951) *Psychoanalysis and Politics*, London, Duckworth; and J. Rose (1993) *Why War?*, Oxford, Blackwell.

Chapter 15: Schizoid

1 W. R. Bion (1956) 'Development of schizophrenic thought', in *Second Thoughts*, London, Karnac, 1984, p. 38. Like Lacan's work, Bion's later work is also notoriously difficult. For a recent overview see L. Grinberg *et al.* (1993) *New Introduction to the Work of Bion*, New York, Jason Aronson.

2 S. Freud (1925) 'On negation', *SE*, XIX, p. 237.

3 M. Klein (1946) 'Notes on some schizoid mechanisms', in *Envy and Gratitude*, London, Hogarth Press, 1975.

4 S. Isaacs (1943) 'The nature and function of phantasy', in J. Riviere (ed.) *Developments in Psycho-Analysis*, London, Hogarth Press, 1952, p. 106.

5 W. R. Bion (1959) 'Attacks on linking', in *Second Thoughts*.

6 W. R. Bion (1962) 'A theory of thinking', ibid.

7 H. Rosenfeld (1952) 'Notes on the psychoanalysis of the superego conflict of an acute schizophrenic patient', in E. Bott Spillius (1988) *Melanie Klein Today, Vol. 1*, London, Routledge. In 1908 Freud likewise observed, regarding his colleague Otto Rank's book *The Myth of the Birth of the Hero*, 'The conflict with the father has its origin not in sexual rivalry for the mother, but in the father's concealment of the facts about the sexual processes connected with birth': see J. Kerr (1994) *A Most Dangerous Method*, London, Sinclair-Stevenson, p. 251.

8 S. Freud (1911) 'Psychoanalytic notes on an autobiographical account of a case of paranoia', *SE*, XII.

9 W. R. Bion (1957) 'Differentiation of the psychotic from the non-psychotic personalities', in *Second Thoughts*.

10 M. Klein (1930) 'The importance of symbol-formation in the early

development of the ego', in *Love, Guilt and Reparation*, London, Hogarth Press, 1975.

11 J. Lacan (1955–56) 'On a question preliminary to any possible treatment of psychosis', in *Ecrits*, London, Tavistock, 1977. 'Foreclosure', a term invented by Lacan, denotes 'primordial expulsion of a fundamental "signifier" (e.g. the phallus as signifier of the castration complex) from the subject's symbolic universe': J. Laplanche and J-B. Pontaliss (1967) *The Language of Psycho-Analysis*, London, Hogarth Press, 1980, p. 166.

12 Bion, 'Development of schizophrenic thought', p. 39.

13 S. Freud (1915) 'The unconscious', *SE*, XIV, p. 202.

14 Bion, 'Development of schizophrenic thought', p. 40.

15 H. Segal (1957) 'Notes on symbol formation', in *The Work of Hanna Segal*, New York, Jason Aronson, 1981.

16 Salinger's book has become something of a cult among would-be heroes. Mark David Chapman carried it the night he murdered John Lennon. So too did John Hinchley when he shot Ronald Reagan. See J. Jones (1993) *Let me take you Down: Inside the Mind of Mark David Chapman – The Man who shot John Lennon*, London, Virgin Books.

17 'The delusional formation, which we take to be the pathological product, is in reality an attempt at recovery, a process of reconstruction': S. Freud (1911) 'Psycho-analytic notes on an autobiographical account of a case of paranoia', *SE*, X, pp. 209–10.

Conclusion: Therapy and politics

1 H. D. (1934–35) 'The master', *Collected Poems, 1912–1944*, Manchester, Carcanet Press 1984 7(3), 1981, p. 459.

2 See, for example, S. Freud (1912) 'The dynamics of transference', *SE*, XII.

3 S. Freud (1937) 'Analyis terminable and interminable', *SE*, XXIII.

4 S. Freud (1914) 'Remembering, repeating and working-through', *SE*, XII.

5 S. Freud (1937) 'Constructions in analysis', *SE*, XXIII.

6 J. Strachey (1934) 'The nature of the therapeutic action of psychoanalysis', *International Journal of Psycho-Analysis*, 15, pp. 127–59. For an update on current psychoanalytic thinking about psychic change see the articles devoted to it in the 1993 issues of the *International Journal of Psycho-Analysis*, 93.

7 S. Freud (1916–17) *Introductory Lectures on Psychoanalysis*, *SE*, XVI, p. 285.

8 For examples of such propaganda from both Left and Right see C. Murray (1990) *The Emerging British Underclass*, A. H. Halsey (1992) Foreword, in H. Dennis and G. Erdos, *Families without Fatherhood*, and J. Davies (1993) *The Family: Is it Just Another Lifestyle Choice?*,

all from London's Institute of Economic Affairs; R. Skynner (1994) 'A time to lay down the law', *Guardian Weekend*, 1 January, p. 27. I discuss such propaganda further in J. Sayers (1994) 'Consuming male fantasy', in A. Elliott and S. Frosh (eds) *Psychoanalysis in Contexts*, London, Routledge.

9 See R. Bly (1990) *Iron John*, New York, Addison Wesley. Similar examples include S. Keen (1991) *Fire in the Belly: On Being a Man*, New York, Bantam; J. Lee (1991) *At My Father's Wedding: Reclaiming Our True Masculinity*, New York, Bantam; G. Corneau (1991) *Absent Fathers, Lost Sons: The Search for Masculine Identity*, Boston, Shambhala.

10 For more on this point see S. Frosh (1991) *Identity Crisis*, London, Macmillan.

11 A. Chekhov (1897) *Uncle Vanya*, in *Plays*, Harmondsworth, Penguin Books, 1959, p. 244-45.

Index

abjection 9, 26, 107, 166
Abraham, Karl 42, 45, 166, 183
acting out 8, 11, 71, 104, 115, 125, 127, 142, 211, 213
addiction 21, 23, 49, 163
adolescence 53, 70, 72, 156
adoption 44, 45, 47, 52, 56, 60, 96–7, 98, 99, 100, 105, 106, 113
agoraphobia 62
Aichorn, August 97
alcoholism 50, 71, 179
Allen, Woody 93, 94
ambivalence 15
anality 28, 67, 81
Anna O. 2, 142, 143, 147, 151
anorexia 2, 46, 184, 189, 203
anxiety 4, 5, 6, 15, 34, 39, 43, 49, 58, 93, 132, 151, 158, 166, 170, 174, 175, 178, 204
attachment 5, 53, 103, 148, 153, 169
Auden, W.H. 3
authoritarianism 86, 96, 100, 109
autism 201

battering 24, 55, 59, 156, 163, 165, 181
Beatles, the 22, 134
Beethoven, Ludwig van 186, 208
Bellini, Gentile 10
Benjamin, Jessica 6
bereavement 169, 175, 177, 213
Bion, Wilfred 4, 39, 195, 204
Bowlby, John 5, 6, 103, 169
Brahms, Johannes 188
Brando, Marlon 104, 105
breast 3, 5, 28, 195
Breuer, Josef 2
Brontë, Charlotte 147, 149
bulimia 141
Burns, Robert 205

Cardinal, Marie 166
Carroll, Lewis 185, 191
casework 5, 6, 15, 53, 81, 127
castration 36, 78, 81, 82, 83, 93, 103, 212
Céline, Louis-Ferdinand 10
Chekhov, Anton 215
Churchill, Winston 187
Chodorow, Nancy 6
Claudel, Paul 126
compulsion 40, 47, 167
condensation 7, 141, 142, 144
Conrad, Joseph 153, 168
control 5, 11, 179, 188, 189
Copernicus 213
countertransference 4, 12, 212, 213
cunnilingus 90

Darwin, Charles 138, 214
Dean, James 104, 106
de Beauvoir, Simone 28
deconstruction 9, 114, 210, 214
defence 1, 3, 5, 11, 12, 18, 19, 29, 42, 44, 54, 66, 67, 81, 88, 103, 104, 111, 112, 114, 118, 126, 127, 138, 141, 142, 146, 152, 153, 154, 167, 183, 195, 196, 200, 202, 207, 210, 211, 212, 213, 215
Degas, Edgar 147
delinquency 97, 103, 107
delusion 8, 74, 136, 137, 183, 184, 196, 205, 206, 207
de Nerval, Gérard 10
denial 11, 18, 68, 169, 173, 176, 177, 179, 180, 182, 213
dependence 5, 30, 31, 40, 41, 47, 48, 49, 124
depression 3, 16, 32, 36, 45, 48, 50, 68, 77, 84, 126, 143, 152, 153, 154, 158,

160, 164, 165, 166, 167, 179, 187, 213

depressive position 5, 67, 82, 169
Deutsch, Helene 28, 127, 138
Dickens, Charles 96
Dietrich, Marlene 29
disavowal 78, 81, 82, 84, 92
discrimination (see also racism, sexism) 114, 115, 120, 124, 126, 127, 134, 138
disillusion 3, 15, 29, 32, 37, 41, 126, 127, 153, 160, 161, 163, 164, 165, 166, 169, 179, 185, 200
displacement 2, 3, 7, 75, 103, 141
Doolittle, Hilda 211
Dora 2, 8, 90, 141, 148, 150
Dostoevsky, Fyodor 10, 66–7, 70, 73, 77, 206
dreams 1, 2, 7, 34, 72, 74, 84, 120, 128, 135–6, 141, 145, 147, 162, 165, 168, 177, 189, 190, 192, 195, 201, 208, 212, 215
du Maurier, Daphne 143
dyslexia 30

ego 28, 35, 37, 126, 129, 214
Eliot, George 114, 118
Eliot, T.S. 170, 207
envy 4, 5, 11, 38, 41, 42, 43, 45, 46, 47, 48, 49, 50, 51, 52, 81, 134, 135, 159, 181, 182, 183, 213
exhibitionism 16, 28, 29

false self 127
Fanon, Frantz 126, 128, 136, 137, 138
fantasy 2, 3, 4, 5, 8, 10, 11, 15, 16, 29, 31, 37, 41, 42, 64, 71, 72, 75, 78, 81, 141, 142, 168, 183, 189, 192, 193, 195, 201, 205, 208, 211, 212, 213, 214, 215
Fassbinder, Rainer Werner 9
fellatio 61, 90
femininity 29, 44, 47, 93, 107, 112, 117, 118, 121, 123, 196
feminism 1, 6, 28, 42, 52, 114, 146, 212, 214, 215
fetishism 81, 82
Fitzgerald, F. Scott 197
fixation 8, 11, 27, 28, 29, 35, 41, 54, 55, 64, 211
foreclosure 202

free association 3, 7, 205, 212
Freud, Anna 47, 53, 93
Freud, Sigmund 1, 2, 3, 4, 6, 7, 8, 11, 12, 28, 29, 41, 42, 47, 52, 66, 78, 81, 95, 103, 104, 114, 126, 127, 136, 137, 141, 142, 144, 148, 150, 151, 153, 154, 169, 183, 195, 196, 205, 211, 212, 213–4, 215
Freudo-Marxism 86

gambling 74
Gestalt therapy 208
Giotto di Bondone 10
God 30, 44, 67, 68, 77, 84, 138, 163, 178, 185, 186, 190, 191, 192, 193, 196, 213, 215
grandiosity 31, 184
Green, Julien 4, 134
Greer, Germaine 11
Grieg, Edvard 186
guilt 39, 63, 90, 92, 103, 137, 148, 158, 162, 166, 183

Hans, Little 3
Hardy, Thomas 208
Harrison, Tony 11
head-banging 55
heterosexuality 9, 66, 89
Holbein, Hans 10
homosexuality 8–9, 66, 75, 81, 93
Horney, Karen 37, 42, 143
hypochondria 169
hysteria 2, 34, 141, 188

Ibsen, Henrik 43, 47, 192, 211
idealisation 3, 5, 15, 31, 66, 67, 68, 70, 126, 127, 160, 161, 162, 166, 167, 179, 180, 181,
identification 3, 6, 11, 24, 28, 35, 47, 59, 66, 97, 105, 126, 136, 153, 156, 162, 166, 167, 183, 184
impotence 43, 67, 90, 164
internalisation 3, 5, 42, 103, 153, 212
interpretation 213
introjection 141, 153
Irma 2
Ishiguro, Kazuo 200

James, Henry 9
jealousy 53, 57, 59, 62, 63, 64, 66, 150, 164

Index

Joyce, James 10
Jung, Carl 214

Kafka, Franz 167, 203, 207
Katharina 2
Keats, John 208
Keenan, Brian 167
Kierkegaard, Sören 30, 31
Kipling, Rudyard 187
Klein, Melanie 2, 4, 5, 6, 12, 28, 39, 42, 43, 67, 81, 82, 93, 103, 113, 126, 134, 153, 158, 159, 166, 169, 179, 182, 183, 195, 196, 201, 205, 214
Kristeva, Julia 2, 7, 9–10, 24, 26, 31, 37, 166
Kundera, Milan 20
Kurosawa, Akira 191

Lacan, Jacques 2, 7, 8, 9, 10, 15, 25, 26, 29, 81, 85, 90, 93, 98, 126, 138, 202, 214, 216
Lawrence, D.H. 15
Lawrence, T.E. 9
Leonardo da Vinci 131
lesbianism 8, 63, 66, 114, 116
libido 53, 169
Lindner, Robert 104
Lorca, Garcia 9

McDougall, Joyce 32, 169
McVicar, John 107
Malcolm X 138
Mallarmé, Stéphane 10
mania 5, 8, 11, 67, 77, 129, 182, 183, 184, 185, 187, 188, 192, 194, 213
Mann, Thomas 127, 128, 130, 136
masculinity 1, 8, 9, 29, 34, 35, 37, 40, 50, 66, 67, 72, 73, 82, 84, 85, 86, 87, 91, 93, 94, 95, 96, 100, 103, 104, 106, 113, 114, 115, 120, 142, 213, 214
masochism 77, 87, 91
masquerade 29, 93
masturbation 42, 91, 93, 133, 205
Maugham, Somerset 204
Melville, Herman 131, 136
metaphor 7, 15, 51, 77, 136, 205
metonomy 7
Milligan, Spike 77
Milner, Marion 16
Mitchell, Juliet 1

Molière, (Jean-Baptiste Poquelin) 31, 33
Montesquieu, Charles-Louis de Secondat 126
Morrison, Blake 11
Mozart, Wolfgang Amadeus 31, 208
Muhammad Ali 135
mysogyny 86, 105

Nabokov, Vladimir 86, 146
narcissism 32, 35, 41, 71
neurosis 8, 141, 142, 205
Nietzsche, Friedrich 186

obsessions 5, 11, 46, 55, 166, 168, 203, 204, 206, 207
Oedipus 3, 11, 28, 42, 52, 53, 54, 62, 64, 66, 67, 71, 75, 77, 78, 136, 213
Olds, Sharon 11
omnipotence 6, 69, 183, 189
orality 10, 19, 67, 90, 141
over-valuation 29, 41, 52

panic 170, 205
paranoia 4, 153, 156, 167
paranoid-schizoid position 4, 67, 195
parapsychology 73
Parkes, Colin Murray 169, 174–5
passivity 28, 63, 66, 124, 199, 201, 204, 210
patriarchy 1, 2, 3, 11, 25, 58, 70, 76, 127, 141, 161, 183, 211, 213, 214, 215
penis 2, 3, 5, 7, 11, 16, 28, 32, 33, 35, 37, 42, 43, 53, 78, 81, 88, 126, 141, 143, 145, 183, 184, 205
perversion 11, 78, 81, 82, 83, 85, 213
phallus 2, 7, 8, 10, 19, 24, 28, 29, 31, 32, 33, 34, 35, 37, 38, 40, 41, 42, 45, 66, 67, 76, 78, 81, 82, 85, 90, 92, 93, 98, 113, 126, 136, 137, 141, 147, 151, 183, 184, 191, 206, 207, 211, 213, 214
phobia (see also agoraphobia) 3, 27, 43, 95, 167, 212
Plath, Sylvia 10–11, 143, 161
Poe, Edgar Allan 7
postmodernism 210
post-structuralism 8
projection 5, 28, 29, 33, 86, 90, 107, 141, 195, 205, 212

235

projective identification 4, 17, 81, 133, 195, 207
Proust, Marcel 9, 10
psychosis 15, 67, 196, 205
psychosomatics 32, 180, 213

racism (see also discrimination) 8, 63, 105, 125, 127, 138
Rank, Otto 39
rape 34, 35, 91, 162, 165, 178
Rat Man 3
regression 16
Reich, Wilhelm 28, 29, 35
reparation 5, 38, 122, 153, 158, 159, 160, 167, 193, 216
repression 2, 11, 136, 141, 142, 143, 144, 145, 146, 149, 151, 152, 188, 212, 213
resistance 212, 213
Rey, Henri 183, 184, 191
Riviere, Joan 93
Rose, Jacqueline 10
Rosenfeld, Herbert 196
Roth, Philip 93, 94

sadism 48, 91, 195
Saki (W.H. Munro) 177
Salinger, J.D. 205
Sartre, Jean-Paul 25, 50
Sayers, Dorothy L. 144
schizoid 4, 5, 11, 15, 16, 183, 196, 197
schizophrenia 4, 155, 158, 195, 196, 205
Schreber, Daniel Paul 196, 202, 205
secondary revision 147
Segal, Hanna 205
Segal, Lynne 8, 9
self-cutting 123
self-esteem 6, 29, 30, 32, 45, 48, 59, 65, 78, 96, 100, 106, 127
semanalysis 9
sexism (see also discrimination) 105, 125
sexual abuse 2, 82, 83, 84, 86, 89, 90,

91, 92, 93, 121, 141, 142, 143, 144, 145, 146, 147, 151, 152, 213
Shaw, Fiona 43
Silverman, Kaja 9
splitting 4, 39, 181, 195, 196, 204–5, 214
stammering 141, 187, 188
Stoller, Robert 81
Strindberg, August 91
sublimation 215
suicide 10, 32, 51, 52, 61, 127, 159, 161, 165, 166, 172
superego 3, 97, 103, 106, 153, 183, 213
symbolism 2, 7, 8, 9, 10, 29, 34, 42, 67, 76, 81, 103, 112, 113, 142, 145, 148, 151, 152, 169, 184, 205, 211, 214

Temperley, Jane 28
teenager 46, 48, 53, 75, 76, 77, 83, 134, 146, 147, 161, 167, 180
therapy 1, 2, 3, 5, 6, 12, 15, 33, 43, 51, 52, 53, 67, 68, 74, 75, 81, 103, 127, 141, 143, 144, 152, 168, 182, 212, 213, 214
Tolstoy, Leo 53, 55, 60, 65
transference 2, 5, 212, 213
transitional objects 6, 26
triumph 51, 57, 64, 182
truancy 62, 165

unconscious 1, 2, 3, 5, 7–8, 55, 75, 91, 103, 110, 127, 137, 141, 150, 152, 172, 177, 212, 214

vagina 81
voyeurism 11

Wagner, Richard 185, 186
Warner, Deborah 43
Welles, Orson 148
Wilde, Oscar 128, 138
Winnicott, Donald 5, 6, 15, 16, 26, 81, 103
Wolf Man 3, 77, 95